A GUIDE TO BUSINESS PERFORMANCE MEASUREMENTS

Also by Edwin Whiting

HOW TO GET YOUR EMPLOYMENT COSTS RIGHT

A GUIDE TO BUSINESS PERFORMANCE MEASUREMENTS

Edwin Whiting
BA (Econ), FCA

MACMILLAN

First published 1986

Published by
THE MACMILLAN PRESS LTD
Houndmills, Basingstoke, Hampshire RG21 2XS
and London
Companies and representatives
throughout the world

Filmsetting by Vantage Photosetting Co. Ltd
Eastleigh and London

Printed in Hong Kong

British Library Cataloguing in Publication Data
Whiting, Edwin
A guide to business performance measurements.
1. Organisational effectiveness
I. Title
338.7′4   HD58.9
ISBN 0–333–37416–9

To Patricia

Contents

PART II   THE MEASURES IN DETAIL

PART IV   PERFORMANCE RATIOS

Preface

At Manchester Business School there was a project for the MBA students called the Corporate Appraisal Project. The teaching of accounting at the school was based mostly on historic cost; case studies and exercises were generally in that vein.

The Corporate Appraisal Project attempted to teach something of alternative methods: current cost, value added and cash flow. At the end of the project I could never say which method of appraisal was best. The only true answer I could give was 'It all depends'. If asked 'It all depends on what?', I could list a few factors, such as type of business, philosophy of the management, entity and equity measure and so on. But I ought to be able to do better than that, I thought, if I had time to study all the issues.

Professor Gerry Lawson, who participated in the project with me, is an expert on cash flow accounting, and hence naturally biased in its favour. Was it not possible, I mused, to produce something which would impartially show all the advantages and disadvantages of each method and in what situations each kind of measurement was most appropriate?

The result of my ruminations is this book. It has been greatly assisted by my research work for the Financial Control Research Institute (FCRI) at the Business School. It was from this that I gained most of the knowledge about what happens in practice and what managers, accountants and financial directors actually think. The research itself was perhaps less valuable than the contacts and conversations with senior financial managers of the member companies and others associated with the FCRI.

I must acknowledge also the knowledge gained from research on a project funded by the Social Science Research Council (as it was then called) on the effect of inflation on planning and control systems during 1979–80. This provided much practical insight, through visits to companies, into their use of current cost accounting, cash flow, funds flow and productivity measures.

The book is not an academic treatise or a scholarly work. Most of it is unoriginal. But there is some new material based on the more recent research and my own opinions. The arrangement, I believe, is completely new. It is intended to make looking-up easy while providing a logical order for all the many issues in performance measurement. It is not likely that many will read the whole book from Chapter 1 to Chapter 25. In a sense it is an encyclopaedia of measurements arranged, not in alphabetical order, but in accounting order, that is, the order in which accounts are usually produced.

References are kept to a minimum, used only to identify a source where a reader wishes to look up the actual words and their context.

The reasoning behind the explanations and descriptions is brief. Rarely does it add up to a fully argued case. But the main points are always listed, and definitions clarified where there could be doubt. History, I believe, is not bunk and the origin of the measurement is an important pointer as to where and how it may be used.

For revising and commenting on the text I acknowledge the great help given to me by David Gilbert and James Carty, who have made many constructive suggestions. On the more routine aspects I must thank my freelance typist, Ann Poole, who has typed all the text, and my wife for carefully checking it.

Manchester
January 1985

EDWIN WHITING

Part I
Objectives and Scope

'I once knew of an old manufacturer who said: "All information is false." And he was right, for almost everything is exaggerated, distorted or suppressed.'—André Maurois

'. . . as if explanation can help anybody. The facts may be right, but the explanations are nearly always wrong, because they have to be in terms of our limited intelligence.'—George Bernard Shaw

1 Introduction

PROBLEMS OF PROFIT

All those in business wish to improve their performance. But many are bewildered by the variety of ways in which performance is measured.

On one measure they have done better, while on another they have done worse. 'What is the true position?', they ask. 'Is there not one simple answer?'

The answer used to be 'profit'. If a business made a bigger profit this year than last year, all would be well.

The word 'profit', however, has no simple meaning. Is it to be adjusted for inflation? If so, how? Is it before tax or after tax? Excluding non-recurring items or not? Should it be 'trading', 'operating', 'gross' or 'net'? What is the real meaning of profit now?

Profit alone is scarcely a sufficient measure anyway. If a business has more capital invested in it, it should make more profit. How can this be taken into account? 'Profitability' may be a more useful measure than profit alone.

PROFITABILITY

Return on capital employed, is a measure of 'profitability'. If profit is related to the amount of capital invested in the business, the profit can be seen in perspective, against some yardstick of what it ought to be. But this measure depends not only on a reliable measure of profit but also on a reliable measure of capital invested. When both are in doubt, the answer is doubly suspect.

The basic ratio of return on capital employed may be broken down into many other ratios using a different profit related to different types of capital invested, for example, whether invested in buildings, machinery, stocks or credit given to customers. These subsidiary ratios may explain the increases or decreases in return on capital employed, but do little to prove that the measure itself is reliable.

As profit alone has become suspect, other measures have come to the fore.

OTHER MEASURES

Cash flow solves some of the difficulties of profits as a measure, but not all, and creates some other problems of its own. Like profit, cash flow comes in various guises with the same difficulty of deciding which 'cash flow' to use.

Funds flow is another variation which depends on a definition of 'working capital', and therefore not so clear and simple as cash flow.

Value added is a further measure to consider. It is nothing revolutionary, being largely a different presentation of the profit and loss account with the same snags carried through to value added. It can be computed in as many ways as profit and even on a cash flow basis. But it has the advantage of the controversial profit figure not being stated at all.

Activity or volume measures may give a good idea of business performance without the problems of matching revenue with costs. Income from sales, turnover, orders, or volumes of production are used by almost all businesses as their first preliminary indicator of performance.

Some measures are more useful to particular businesses than others. In a retail business, for example, with a fairly fixed profit margin, sales are an excellent quick measure. In a business with fluctuating selling prices and costs, the sales figures are a bad measure of the ultimate performance.

Measures of productivity of labour and capital are useful in some businesses. Combined with sales, measures of labour productivity and machine capacity utilisation can say much about the business performance without calculating a profit.

Among the host of methods used for measuring performance, there are no golden rules which will lead to the best measure. It all depends.

EXTERNAL AND INTERNAL

First, one must consider whether the measure is to be published to the outside world or is to be purely internal. If it is external, it comes under the heading of 'financial reporting', which is subject to the rules of the Companies Acts, the standards laid down by the accountancy bodies and unwritten accounting conventions. The final result is audited and published to shareholders and other interested parties in the form of the annual report and accounts.

Internal measurements need not be the same as those used externally. Legal requirements, accounting standards and conventions can be ignored. They therefore tend more and more to reflect the size of the company, the way it is organised, the type of industry, the style of management and the willingness of the internal management accountants to diverge from the rules required for external financial reporting.

SHORT-TERM AND LONG-TERM

Second, there may be a difference between short-term and long-term measures. Internally, performance measurements tend to be required, and examined, monthly. Externally less frequent information is needed.

Shareholders and potential investors are generally interested in performance over a long period. Similarly managers and directors within the business are interested in capital investment and the returns gained from it from the long-term point of view. But for them, with many other needs as well, a measure of performance produced only once a year or less is much too infrequent.

TAILORING TO THE USER

Third, then, are the requirements of the users of the measures produced. Different businesses need different information in different circumstances. A measure that suits one may not suit another. However, there is evidence that many businesses adopt the performance measures which are conventional and universal without considering other measures that may be more appropriate.

Yet managements are generally very concerned about the performance of their business. Employees, lenders, creditors and shareholders may also be concerned. The measures of performance used must be the right ones for the business and its objectives. The wrong ones may seriously mislead.

Wrong measures for the circumstances may cause jubilation among managers instead of apprehension, may lead to decisions to expand sections of the business which should be contracted, may mean that selling prices are increased instead of lowered, and vice versa. The right measures should mean that progress towards business objectives is reasonably controlled, that capital investment is decided and located with better information and that strategic decisions on sections of the business or products are supported by the best information on past performance.

One standard measure is rarely enough. To measure the distance from the earth to a star requires a radio-telescope with a scale in light-years. To measure the distance from London to Southampton needs a different technique with the answer in miles or kilometres, depending on the user. Measures of performance, similarly, should be appropriate, useful and understandable to those concerned.

In business performance there are a host of measurements available. But only a few can be fully used by most businesses. This book is neither a story nor a textbook. It is a book to guide managers and directors through the labyrinth, stopping only where the measurement is likely to be essential or useful in their business.

2 Purposes and problems of measurement

EXTERNAL USERS

In choosing a measure of performance one has to be clear about the main purpose of the measure. The purposes are rather different for external and internal users and for different levels of management within a business or groups of businesses.

Those outside the business, such as shareholders, potential investors, lenders and creditors, may need a different measure of performance from those inside.

Ordinary shareholders have to be content with the annual report and accounts, plus, if they are shareholders of a quoted company, an interim statement. In the UK the annual report is oriented strongly towards the profit measure with a supplementary funds flow statement and occasionally some statistics of volume of production or a value added statement.

Strong institutional shareholders may have access to some of the internal measures used in the management accounts during visits to their company. Their purpose is to be actively involved with the management and to be able to receive early warning when poor results appear in any section of the company. This is quite different from the largely apathetic small shareholder.

Lenders and creditors tend to be more interested in the cash flow of the company than in profit. A short-term lender needs a measure that will indicate whether or not there is sufficient cash to repay the loan. A long-term lender, however, should be interested also in profit, which may indicate more about the general health of the business.

Bankers advancing longer-term loans have recently become more interested in the internal management accounts used by managers and directors. Internal accounts may show the strengths and weaknesses of certain sectors, may include cash flow measures as well as profit and may indicate to lenders the general quality of information available to management.

INTERNAL USERS

For those inside the business – the managers and directors – the purposes of measurement are different. Broadly there are two facets of the management purpose: (1) control and (2) decision.

MANAGEMENT CONTROL

Management control is a very wide subject on which there is a profusion of literature, especially in USA. There are many definitions. Preferred here is:

A system of organisation and measurement that enables managers to achieve the plans and objectives of the undertaking.

Without measurement one cannot control. Measurement is needed to keep the managers on track, to monitor progress and to assess managerial effectiveness. It is needed also to motivate management to give their best performance. Without some measure of achievement, most managers would feel they were working in the dark.

The measure chosen is terribly important. If, for example, it is 'profit before interest and tax', managers would concentrate on maximising that figure possibly to the detriment of many other aspects of the business, such as cash flow, working capital, and long-term expenditure on training, research, product development and so on.

On the other hand, the measurement used should not be too complicated. Dual measures such as profit and cash flow can be confusing, but may work if the relative importance of each is explained. This may vary from period to period, cash flow, for instance, becoming the prime measure when cash is tight.

Any measure which reflects managerial performance must be clear, well understood and seen to be fair. If the measure is not well explained or is too complex to be understood, there are likely to be arguments about the figures presented, condemnation of the system of measurement, and general ill-feeling which will deaden the motivation of business managers.

INCENTIVE SCHEMES

If the measurement is used as a direct incentive by way of bonus or salary increase, then it is vitally important that it is accepted as fair and just by those entitled to incentive bonus. There is a huge variety of incentive schemes based on the performance of a business or section of a business. And such schemes are becoming more and more fashionable as business profits improve and the complications caused by inflation fade.

While incentive schemes should not be the tail which wags the dog of the measurement system, the measurement used must be appropriate to the kind of incentive offered. It is not the place in this book to recommend measurements for incentive schemes which inevitably are tailored to specific situations, often with very complicated formulae. However, the use of a particular measure for incentive schemes is mentioned and some guidance given on the advantages and disadvantages of the measure for that purpose.

BUDGETARY CONTROL

The classical method of controlling management performance is by setting a budget and monitoring actual results against the budget. The variances between actual and budget are analysed and, where possible, assigned to particular managers as their responsibility.

In many situations the use of budgets has been an effective method of management control, but it is now declining in popularity for many reasons, which are beyond the scope of this book. One of these, however, is undoubtedly the familiarity which may lead to contempt, encouraging managements to fix to some extent their own budgets and to advance or retard revenue or expenditure so that the budget is more nearly achieved.

Variances between actual and budget are not, in the sense of this book, a measure of business performance. The budget, on which the measure depends, is a figure invented by the business itself and therefore has no place in a catalogue of objective performance measures. But it remains essential in the box of tools for business planning.

MANAGEMENT DECISION

Performance measures are needed not only for control but also for decision-making. Control also involves decisions, but strategic decision-making stands out as a particular type of decision which uses the regular performance measure not necessarily to improve the performance, but to change or modify the nature or size of the business itself. Business performance measures can be the basis of decisions to formulate new plans, to alter the course of a business, to expand or contract it, or to develop certain business strategies.

The information provided by statements of past performance, by whatever measure, is unlikely to be sufficient on its own to make strategic decisions, which are affected as much by events outside as events inside, but such statements are usually the starting point for the exploration of alternatives.

The particular measures are thus of vital importance. Managements may easily become hooked on measures which are in fashion at the moment, such as return on capital employed. The situation may require other measures to be considered such as a profit after tax or net cash flow.

For control purposes the measure needs to be regular, simple and acceptable. For strategic decisions the regular measure may be misleading and a variety of measures may need to be considered, doubtless supplemented by some specific information.

In appraising the various measures in detail, the control purpose is naturally foremost. The decision-making purpose is mentioned in later chapters, but the particular measures used are very dependent on the kind of decision to be made.

THE BUSINESS ENTITY

External users of business performance measures generally see only the results for the whole undertaking defined as a legal entity. For a group of companies, though strictly a collection of legal entities, the performance of the whole group is all that external users need to consider.

Internal users look primarily at the performance of each of the businesses comprising the group. These units may be in the form of subsidiary companies, divisions or simply 'business units'. From now on we shall call these constituent parts of a group 'divisions', which is becoming the most common term in use.

A division is defined as:

> A section within the organisation where the divisional chief executive or general manager has responsibility for costs, revenues, profit or loss, and at least some discretion over capital expenditure.

A small independent business carries few problems in choosing objective performance measures. The profit measures are prescribed by law and by its auditors or accountants, bearing in mind the requirements of the Inland Revenue. The measures for internal use in a small business may not be very different from those required outside (although they probably should be more different than they are).

A division, however, is never totally independent in the same way as the owner-managed business.

DIVISIONAL PERFORMANCE

In appraising the performance of a division it is often very difficult to find a measure that reflects the efforts of the division unencumbered, or unassisted, by the activities of other divisions of the same group or of its head office.

For example, two divisions may have common customers. If division A gives special service or discounts to the common customer, division B may be forced to provide them also, although the more generous terms would make the customer's account for B unprofitable. Consultation between the divisions, or in the case of a very important customer intervention by head office, may be needed to resolve the trouble. The two divisions in any event may no longer be able to act independently.

Other examples of constraints on independence of divisional managements are:

- divisions using the same materials with common purchasing
- divisions operating in the same market with implications for selling prices and advertising
- divisions operating on the same site requiring common facilities and welfare benefits
- divisions being partially integrated vertically, where the output of one division is partly the input to another
- divisions making heavy use of group services which cannot be supplied other than from head office

Measurement of performance is not impossible when divisions are not independent, but the true divisional performance is contaminated by the dependence on other divisions.

The performance of division A may be affected by the performance of division B or by edicts from head office constraining the independence of divisions. Intervention by head office also involves head office costs, which may be arbitrarily allocated, thus further polluting the purity of the divisional measurement.

DIVISIONAL AND ENTITY PERFORMANCE

For a fully independent division – and there are some with very few constraints – the same menu of measures is available as for any other business. As independence is lost, however, the measures available become less.

Where there is little independence, any measures have to be treated with great care. In a highly centralised group, with organisational units that are called 'divisions', the true performance measures may be confined to productivity or efficiency, and in some cases even these may be affected by lack of independence.

Fair measures of performance of internal divisions are inevitably constrained by the degree of independence enjoyed.

Measuring performance of completely independent entities has no such problem but demands complete measurement of all costs and revenues, which may include interest and tax. Divisional measurement, however, can stop short of complete accounting and still produce a satisfactory result for management control.

3 Plan of the book

BASIC CLASSIFICATIONS

The main purpose of this book is to sort out the welter of measures of business performance into some kind of order so that each may be considered on its merits.

Chart 3.1 has seven main lines (numbered 5 to 11) and three columns (numbered 13 to 15).

The lines are arranged according to the level of comprehensiveness of the various measures and show, very crudely, the type of revenue and expense taken into account at each level. The measures range from basic revenue at the top to measures which include all transactions of revenue and expense of any kind at the bottom.

Part II of the book is devoted to an appraisal of each of the main line measures. The chapter numbers are those shown on the Chart.

The columns represent three accounting conventions on which any of the line measures may be based. Columns 13 and 14 are profit-based. The profit measures in column 13 are based on the historic or original costs of materials and capital equipment. The column 14 profits are adjusted in a certain way for inflation by using current or replacement costs, which is the basic approach of current cost accounting (CCA). Column 15, the cash flow basis, has little need for cost conventions; only what is received or paid is counted.

Part III explains the merits and use of the conventions, including the 'funds flow basis', which is not shown on the Chart as it is very similar to cash flow.

As this book is being written, the argument which has been raging for many years between historic cost and current cost is reaching a crucial

CHART 3.1

Business performance measures

	Chapter	13 Historic cost basis	14 Current cost basis	15 Cash flow basis
Revenue	**5**	Sales/*turnover* invoiced	Sales/*turnover* invoiced	Receipts from sales
Expenditure deduct		Materials consumed at price purchased	Materials consumed at current prices	Materials paid for
		Other costs varying with output	Other costs varying with output	
you get deduct	**6**	*Gross margin* Costs unrelated to output excluding all employment costs	*Gross margin (CCA)* Costs unrelated to output *excluding* all employment costs	Services and overheads paid for *excluding* all employment costs
		Depreciation on original cost	Depreciation on replacement cost	
you get deduct	**7**	*Value added* Employment costs	*Value added (CCA)* Employment costs	*Cash value added* Employment costs paid
you get deduct	**8**	*Operating profit* Interest	*Operating profit (CCA)* Interest	*Operating cash flow* Interest paid
you get deduct	**9**	*Profit after interest* Taxation on profits	*Profit after interest (CCA)* Taxation on profits	*Cash flow after interest* Taxation paid
you get deduct	**10**	*Profit after taxation* Extraordinary items	*Profit after taxation (CCA)* Extraordinary items	*Cash flow after tax* Other items
you get	**11**	*All-inclusive profit*	*All-inclusive profit (CCA)*	*Net cash flow*

stage. With it there is recourse to methods of accounting for inflation other than by the use of current cost. These other methods are interesting but are not considered here as viable conventions. They are described briefly in Chapter 4.

MEASURES IN DETAIL

Each of the chapters in Part II has a similar format: a brief definition of the measure, a note of the accountancy leading up to it, the philosophy behind it, the kind of business most likely to use it, the sort of organisation most suitable for it, its power to motivate and the probable problems and troubles in using it.

The problems of each measure arise from the particular 'deductions' made from one measure to arrive at the next. The troubles cascade downwards gathering more potential difficulties in using the measure as they reach the lowest level on the chart.

Each of the new difficulties that appear with each lower measure are discussed after that measure. They are called 'trouble spots'.

Turnover has two trouble spots, which apply to all the measures below (if they apply to turnover). Gross margin introduces another trouble spot: stocks and work-in-progress. This again applies to all the other measures below, where the business has stocks or work-in-progress.

There are 14 trouble spots identified. In certain businesses there could be others, but only those applying fairly generally are explained and discussed. The most important trouble spots are 6.1 (Stocks and work-in-progress) and 7.1 (Depreciation). These are given considerable space, while trouble spots such as 10.3 (Group relief) and 11.2 (Goodwill), which do not appear at all in smaller companies, are given only a few pages.

Each trouble spot has a similar format to facilitate reference. More information for those interested is given in a question and answer section. At the head of each trouble spot is a list of measures to which the trouble may apply.

Some trouble spots may hurt only the measures used inside the business (e.g. divisional performance), some may hurt only measures used outside the business (e.g. published accounts) and others may hurt both. Those trouble spots which are common to internal and external measures are generally likely to be the most significant.

ACCOUNTING CONVENTIONS

Part III deals with historic cost, current cost, cash flow and funds flow. Again, a similar format is used to describe and discuss each convention. Historic cost, however, is naturally compared with current cost, and cash flow with funds flow. The cost conventions are from a quite different stable from the 'flow' conventions, with different purposes.

The chapters in Part III attempt to detail what those particular purposes are and to give examples of businesses and situations where particular conventions may be most useful and appropriate. There is no absolute right or wrong in any of the conventions.

Considerable attention is given to cash flow. Inevitably in Part II, the chapters deal largely with the profit measures. A longer Chapter 16 on cash flow is necessary because there are two main uses for the cash flow convention; (1) short-term cash flow which may sometimes be the main objective of the business and primarily internal, and (2) long-term cash flow stretching over several years which can provide a performance measure, primarily external, that avoids many of the trouble spots of the profit-based measures.

Chapter 12 is devoted to an example of the build-up of accounting statements using the different conventions. The same example is used again in Chapters 13 to 16 to illustrate how the statements are likely to appear in practice.

RATIOS

In Part IV we examine ratios, beginning with a warning in Chapter 17 of the snags common to all ratios. All business ratios are then reviewed, from the most general to the most particular and specific.

Chapter 18 is devoted entirely to return on capital employed, which is the ratio most used by top management, and the only ratio which attempts to express profitability.

Chapter 19 introduces the pyramid of other operating ratios which support the return on capital. Chapter 20 deals with earnings per share and price/earnings ratio, which are vital measures for companies quoted on the Stock Exchange.

Ratios which aim to measure productivity and attainment of strategic goals are examined in Chapters 21 and 22. These ratios are based on volumes rather than money revenues and costs. Productivity ratios can provide a simple short-term measure for many businesses while strategic ratios may show the progress towards long-term objectives such as market share, quality and level of service.

CONCLUSION

In the concluding chapters of Part V there is an attempt to gather up the measures which may be particularly appropriate to certain types of businesses or industries. The philosophy and management style may dictate the best measures to be used. Incentive schemes are reviewed overall in the light of the organisational and behavioural aspects.

The book is designed primarily as a reference book in which readers may find something about each of the performance measures that may interest them, and when and where they may be best used.

4 Income, value and cost

A THEORY OF PERFORMANCE MEASUREMENT

This chapter is for the reader who may wish to understand why the measures are as they are and the logic behind the detail of the measures.

This demands a brief excursion into theory. Business performance measurement is clearly akin to profit and income, and inevitably involves the use of capital: topics which have produced a plethora of academic literature both by accountants and economists. Very little of this literature can be referred to in a short chapter, but hopefully there is sufficient to explain the problems of dealing with the concepts of income, value and cost, and how they relate to the measurement of performance.

INCOME

Income, on one definition, is synonymous with profit or earnings (in USA the profit and loss account is called the 'income statement'). On another famous definition (by the economist Hicks),[1] it is the amount of consumption or amount that can be spent to leave you as well off at the end of the period as you were at the beginning.

This Hicksian definition means that you take into account the changes in value of the things you already have. If the value of what you have goes up you can spend more, but you have not 'earned' it. Or have you?

If you are in business, you would not normally think that the increase in the value of your shop or hotel (even assuming no inflation) was any part of your income. You cannot see it and you have not got it. The increase in value is not realised – unless you sell the business.

VALUE

Valuing what you have is nearly always tricky. Even in a perfect market such as the Stock Exchange there are two prices to choose from: the buying price and the selling price.

When you come to assets more specific to the business, such as stocks, unfinished products, plant, machinery and buildings, there are many different valuations possible. If you ask a valuer for a valuation, he will probably say: 'what do you want it for?'

There is a fundamental difference between value in use and value in exchange. If the business is continuing – a going concern – the value in use seems to be what is required. But can such a value be computed? The use of one asset may depend on the use of another. So you may end up only able to value the whole, or a large section, of the assets *en bloc*.

If all the assets of a business have to be valued as a whole, it can only be done by estimating the present value of future cash flows and, to do that, the value of present cash flows is needed, as well as some skill in predicting the future.

Value in exchange is easier. For instance, for vehicles there are published lists of second-hand prices. But again the selling and buying prices are different.

The buying price is used for replacement value and the selling price for realisable value. The difference (or 'turn') depends on the activity in the market. In an active market it is small. In a market where there are infrequent sales and purchases the difference can be very large.

COST

Accountants are not happy with valuation. They regard it as subjective judgement, all rather vague.

Cost is definite, objective, a fact instead of an opinion. The only true cost is the historic original cost – what was paid when the thing was bought.

But historic costs are, in one sense, a kind of value – a past value, which is never kept up to date. If we depart from that value, though, we will be including in income the effects of valuation changes. In the pure accounting convention we must wait until the change in valuation is realised through a sale and then we will know what it really is.

INFLATION

When the general level of prices is rising to the extent that historic cost is expressed in almost a different currency, then something has to be done. The cost of the plant in 1954 is just out of this world in 1984.

The only way to update the 1954 cost is by a valuation – but on what basis? There are three which are possible and all have problems. They are:

(1) Replacement value: the basis of the CCA system, recommended by the accountancy bodies since 1977.
(2) Realisable value: few actual applications, known as COCOA.
(3) Purchasing power value: the basis of the CPP system, recommended by the accountancy bodies in 1974, but never fully put into practice.

REPLACEMENT VALUE (CCA)

For a value in use in the business, replacement value is the obvious answer. The case for replacement value was made in the Sandilands Report of 1975,[2] from which the current cost accounting system (CCA) was developed. The value to the business of an asset, it said, is the value lost if the business were deprived of the asset, called by some others (but not Sandilands) the *deprival value*.

The difficulty with such a valuation is that it cannot separate the wood of specific business from the trees of general inflation. When used in the measurement of income it cannot show how much of income is from inflation and how much is from changes in real value.

In spite of its many disadvantages, CCA remains as the only official and practical alternative to historic cost. It is reviewed more fully in Chapter 13.

REALISABLE VALUE (COCOA)

Market prices tend frequently to be used in any valuation. The selling price obtainable is often the most objective valuation for goods in stock or for assets bought some time ago. Chambers, an Australian professor,[3] advocates values in exchange as the basis of all accounting on the grounds of simplicity and rigour.

His system is known as *continuously contemporary accounting* (COCOA).[4] It is certainly clear, easy to understand and in many cases, where there are published market prices, easily verifiable. The balance sheet shows what the business would look like if all the assets were converted into cash. COCOA is not a *going concern* concept. If the business stopped at the end of the year the figures should be the same.

To most people this seems unrealistic. We are not going to cease business; the realisable value is therefore irrelevant. In any case it is a snapshot value which could change very quickly. Realisable values do not have much to do with income or performance, because in the normal way businesses do not realise their assets.

CURRENT PURCHASING POWER VALUE (CPP)

The third method of revaluing assets for inflation, is to convert all the relevant figures in the accounts to a common base level by use of the retail price index (RPI). The system has for many years had a number of strong advocates.

Myddleton has set out all the advantages of CPP in a recent book.[5] It is 'comparable over time, objective, consistent, comprehensive and practically workable.' It can be applied to all businesses. It uses the original historic costs and applies a fixed arithmetical formula. Only one answer can result, although there are still arguments on the treatment of loans (and a few other minor arguments, set out by Sharp in a recent critique).[6]

The main disadvantage of CPP is that it is not specific to businesses. All the figures are indexed to the RPI, but prices in a particular business may not have gone up in line with the RPI, or may even have gone down. CPP does not revalue any assets individually, but it does provide an income (excluding any change in asset value) which is adjusted for general inflation in a (by now) well known way, called 'indexing'.

CAPITAL MAINTENANCE

Accounting principles require that any business should maintain its capital, i.e. its assets less its liabilities. If the value of its capital goes down, income or profits cannot be left alone as though nothing else had happened.

A fall in the value of any asset must be recognised by charging the amount of the decrease to the profit and loss account, thereby reducing the accounting income. If this is not done, capital is not maintained.

An increase in capital value, on the other hand, is a non-event. Revaluing capital upwards is not allowed – except in the case of inflation.

With inflation came the realisation that capital maintenance in money terms was not good enough. Capital maintenance had to be in real terms so that when the net assets had been corrected for inflation there was still no fall in their value. With current cost accounting (CCA) came the notion of real capital maintenance, later known crudely as *operating capability*.

Still, with CCA, the basic accounting principles apply. Having revalued at current cost, if the market value of any asset is lower than the net book value in the balance sheet, then some provision must be made for the discrepancy in value either by charging more depreciation or by making a special 'write off'. Surpluses over market value do not count. (See trouble spot 6.1, p. 53, on the application of this principle in relation to stocks and work-in-progress.)

ASYMMETRY OF ACCOUNTING VALUES

One major accounting principle is the principle of prudence or conservatism. If the net cost of an asset, be it machinery, building, stocks or work-in-progress, falls below market value, the deficiency becomes a deduction from income. This principle dates from the time when accounts were prepared mainly to monitor the final position of a company. If there were a fall in asset values, this might signal the possibility of insolvency and therefore it should be taken into account.

Prior to 1920, accounts focused on the balance sheet. It was not until 1929 that a profit and loss account became legally obligatory. Today the focus is on the profit measure, the balance sheet being relatively unimportant. The prudence principle means that a fall in a value and a rise in a value are not treated symmetrically. Any loss in value below the cost, known or anticipated, must be provided for. Any increase in value must be left alone. Lee, along with many others, considers the principle of conservatism dubious and 'leads to somewhat misleading and confusing measures of periodic accounting income'.[7]

This principle contradicts to some extent the matching principle, which requires that all the transactions necessary for a sale must be included in the cost. Any transactions which are not related to a sale, for example the purchase of materials for stock, should be left out of the profit and loss account and become an outstanding balance of stock-in-hand in the balance sheet.

A fall in value, for example a reduction in the value of stock below cost, has to be charged to the profit and loss account, although it does not match with anything. The stock may not even have been used or the fall in value may actually have taken place in an earlier period.

There are many views of income. They may or may not take account of changes in value. It depends on the purpose for which the income measure is needed. When the matching principle is paramount, changes in value may defile the income measure.

PERFORMANCE

Income is used as a measurement of performance. Part II of this book covers mostly income-type measures. What sort of income should be used? In this author's view, for a pure measure of performance, it should be income unaffected by changes in the value of capital.

The accounting model, however, is used as the basis of all monetary performance measures and it takes into account any falls in the value of an asset below cost. So we must live with it. Nevertheless it may be possible to pick out the losses in value and show them as a separate item so that matched revenue and expenditure can be clearly seen.

The word 'performance' implies a specific accomplishment – a definite objective pursued and carried out. In general, performance is short-term; it is not too long before the result appears.

If we take the analogy of an actor, the performance may be short, perhaps one evening, or it may be longer as in a continuing TV series. But there will be a point when the performance will be judged or appraised – and it will not go too long before that happens. In business there may be weekly and monthly accounts, but none go more than a year before the performance is measured and communicated to those interested.

If the actor's performance is good, he or she will build up experience, knowledge, further ability and a reputation. This is a kind of capital which enables the actor to obtain more income in the future. But the capital at the time is irrelevant to the comparative quality of the performance.

If the actor is a well known star (with considerable 'capital') his performance is measured in relation to his status as a star. If the actor is young and new to the stage, his performance is measured with that in mind.

The value of the 'capital' in the actor in the short-term is taken as given when measuring performance. A slight fall in his reputation would have no effect until there had been several poor performances.

For businesses, in the short-term, the profit or income-based measures should not be concerned in any way with falls in the value of their assets. In the longer term they probably should, but such a fall may not necessarily be due to bad performances.

For short-term performance measurement then (say, over a year or less) we are not interested in the value of the capital in the business, whether the changes in the values are up or down. The matching principle far outweighs the prudence principle.

In the longer term the matching principle is less important, because over a period of years the unmatched items at the beginning and at the end will be much less significant in relation to the total income for several years. Value of assets over a period of years, whether increased or decreased, may have an effect on the performance. Capital may then have to be taken into account. (This is discussed further under trouble spot 7.1, p. 70 and Chapter 15, p. 192.)

VALUE IN DECISION-MAKING

One caveat should be made in conclusion. Changes in the value of assets (apart from inflation) are not relevant to short-term performance measurement. For making policy or strategic decisions, however, value may be more important than cost. Value is future-oriented while cost concerns the past.

The performance measurement is primarily for monitoring, controlling and motivating. When performance is poor or not up to scratch (or to budget) something may have to be done about it. Management decisions may have to be made on new products, new areas, pricing, marketing, cutbacks, closures, employment of staff, capital investment and so on. The profit and loss account provides only part of the information needed. The *value* of assets that the business possesses, and the *value* of assets and liabilities that may be acquired as a result of the decision, are likely to be essential information.

PART I: REFERENCES

References

1. J. R. Hicks, *Value and Capital* (Clarendon Press, 1946) pp. 171–81.
2. *Inflation Accounting: Report of The Inflation Accounting Committee* (Sandilands Report), Cmnd 6225 (HMSO 1975) pp. 137–55.
3. R. J. Chambers, *Accounting, Evaluation and Economic Behaviour* (Prentice-Hall, 1966) pp. 40–123.
4. R. J. Chambers, *Current Cost Accounting – a Critique of the Sandilands Report*, Paper no. 11 (International Centre for Research in Accounting, University of Lancaster, 1976) pp. 60–77.
5. D. R. Myddelton, *On a cloth untrue: Inflation accounting: the way forward* (Woodhead-Faulkner, 1984).
6. K. Sharp, 'CCA: profession fails in its duty to business', *Accountancy*, April 1984, pp. 125–7.
7. T. A. Lee, *Income and Value Measurement: Theory and Practice* (Nelson, 1974) pp. 44–55.

Part II
The Measures in Detail

'My disports corrupt and taint my business.'—William Shakespeare, *Othello*

'The problem that arises . . . stems largely from misunderstandings of "profit" – misunderstandings on the accounting plane whence considerable argument can and does arise from differences in terminology; and misunderstandings on the sociological plane which are really concerned with the appropriation of the profit earned rather than the factor of profitability in business as such.'—Peter Drucker

5   Turnover

DEFINITION

Turnover is the prime source of income of a business. In the Companies
Act 1981 (relating to published accounts) it is defined as:

> amounts derived from the provision of goods and services falling
> within the company's ordinary activities, after deduction of trade
> discounts, VAT and any other taxes based on turnover (e.g. petrol
> tax).

This legal definition need not necessarily be used for turnover as a
measure of performance. VAT and other taxes which are directly set off
or reclaimed should clearly not be included. It would not be a sensible
measure that allowed performance to be improved simply by an increase
in sales-based taxes.

There are many items of expense directly related to turnover apart from
trade discounts specified above. Items such as cash discounts and
periodic bonuses to customers for reaching a target level of sales may
also be deducted from turnover. If these adjustments are not made,
turnover could be distorted simply by reducing or increasing the related
expenses.

Where commission on sales is universal and sales are received net from
agents, there may be a case for using sales net of commission as the
turnover measure.

Bad debts, being erratic in their incidence, cannot reasonably be
deducted from turnover as a short-term measure. However, a blanket
provision of, say, $1\frac{1}{4}$ per cent of credit sales, could be used, but it would
be unusual.

Turnover covers a much wider range of revenue than sales of goods. It

includes fees for services, commissions on business introduced, amounts
charged for contract work, fares for passenger transport, freight
charges, royalties, subscriptions, hiring fees and rentals.

ACCOUNTANCY

For most businesses, especially where sales are received in cash, the
accounting is simple.

Where there are immediately related expenses, a policy should be
determined which can be operated by the accounting system.

When turnover is used as a short-term measure, the allocation to
particular periods, a week or a month, is crucial. Some system must be
laid down to ensure that invoices are regularly processed and no
backlogs are allowed to build up.

Turnover in cash flow terms (i.e. the actual cash receipts from customers
during a period) may be more reliable than invoiced sales and avoids
appraising the performance of departments or divisions before the cash
is assured.

Turnover is very amenable to statistical interventions, particularly in
ironing out fluctuations in the short-term. Moving averages and
seasonally adjusted turnover may supplement the crude period-by-
period turnover.

UNDERLYING PHILOSOPHY

Almost all businesses are concerned with turnover. It is often the only
revenue and acts as a base from which many other figures follow.

However, there are some businesses with a more sales-oriented philosophy than others. These businesses put a high proportion of their
resources into marketing and advertising with a view to increasing
turnover. The emphasis on marketing may be due to competition, to the
type of customer, or to the general elasticity of demand in relation to
advertising rather than price. But the philosophy behind the business
may be a much more important factor in the emphasis on turnover than

all of these. In the market-driven business, turnover is the key measure of importance. With good control systems on expenditure, margins and profits may almost look after themselves.

BUSINESSES BEST SUITED

In many businesses costs are closely related to turnover. Primarily these are businesses where a large proportion of costs vary directly with output (variable costs) and only a small proportion are fixed in relation to output (fixed costs). Such businesses are found mostly in services where the major costs are staff. They are 'labour-intensive' rather than 'capital intensive'.

Staff costs in many businesses are fixed costs in the short-term, but some businesses have been able to make them largely variable by the use of part-time employees, contract staff and flexible hours.

In mass retailing fixed costs have become relatively small. Provided the expenditure remains stable in relation to sales (i.e. 'margins' of profit do not change greatly), turnover gives a quick guide to the ultimate performance.

There are many businesses where turnover gives a very good indication of the operating profit. Examples are brokers of all kinds, advertising agencies, and travel agencies, whose turnover is largely in the form of commission received. Some small businesses such as restaurants, pubs and hairdressing, where staffing is flexible, can rely to a large extent on turnover as their short-term performance measure.

If results are needed daily or weekly, then turnover is probably the only measure feasible in most businesses, even with the massive speed-up in accounting provided by computers.

ORGANISATIONS BEST SUITED

Turnover can be computed in various ways, and can be of a very different nature in the same organisation. There is therefore a limit to the usefulness of totalling the turnover of large organisations, especially conglomerates involved in various industries.

There is no point, for instance, in adding up car-hire rentals, royalties on books, insurance premiums, sales of flowers and sales of magazines. Turnover is best used in a homogeneous business where profit margins are fairly stable and definitions of turnover are clear and simple.

Many organisations, which technically are not in business, use turnover as a prime measure of performance. Charities look at subscriptions and donations; societies look at the proceeds of their activities; co-operatives (at least producer co-operatives) are more concerned with turnover than with profit. Everyone, even in non-profit-making organisations, needs some measure of their group performance. Turnover is ideal as the first shot.

Turnover is difficult to define in banks, building societies or investment companies. The turnover to which expenses might in any way relate is the revenue obtained from transaction charges, but this is totally obscured by the difference obtained on interest received and interest paid. Banking is one kind of organisation that has no turnover in the accounting sense.

POWER TO MOTIVATE

Turnover, being simple to measure, is used universally as a basis of bonus and incentive schemes. For sales-people the incentive bonus is a natural motivator.

A bonus on turnover can, however, motivate other non-sales staff whose volume of work may be closely related to turnover. The figures are available almost immediately and can be shown on wall charts with ease in a form that everyone can understand.

Staff not associated in any way with selling may be given an incentive based on turnover with an adjustment for stocks (production not sold) at the beginning and end of the period. Another way of expressing this is as the sales value of production (see Chapter 21, p. 256), which may appeal to a wider range of staff.

The cash flow basis of turnover may encourage salesmen to ensure that money for their sales is actually received and that they do not increase sales purely by extending credit.

PROBLEMS AND TROUBLES

Turnover is vulnerable to inflation in the long-term and the money amount may be suspect when annual turnovers are compared. In correcting for inflation, an index of specific prices of the products sold will produce an adjusted sales value figure, but a general price index (such as the RPI) is more suitable where there is a wide variety of products the range of which is continually changing. In the short-term, with low inflation, there is no problem.

When turnover is used as a divisional performance measure there may be problems with interdivisional trading, when one division of a group sells to another. The prices fixed for these sales (i.e. the transfer price) may produce distortions. This is trouble spot 5.1.

Apart from this, the disadvantages of the turnover measure are rarely in the definition or in the accountancy, but in the application:

(1) It may be used too widely because it is simple.
(2) Costs may be ignored when they are very important.
(3) Marketing and selling may take precedence over efficiency.

TRANSFER PRICING

Measures affected

Turnover
Gross margin
Value added
Operating profit
Profit after interest
Profit after tax

Bases of accounting which apply

Historic cost
Current cost
Cash flow
Funds flow

Where found

In divisional accounts only

Source of the trouble

Most large organisations have some central theme or corporate goal. A conglomerate of diverse businesses without any kind of association between them seems to be increasingly rare.

On the other hand, organisations strive to avoid heavy central control, to divide up their businesses into manageable units and to give their divisions considerable autonomy. The divisions, however, are constrained in this autonomy to the extent that they must supply to, or purchase from, other divisions in pursuit of an integrated corporate goal.

These interdivisional sales may be of a service, a process or a material. One division may produce semi-finished goods to be completed by another division, and perhaps sold by yet another. In some cases a major part of the plant and tooling of one division may be specifically dedicated to the requirements of another division. There is then considerable divisional interdependence.

Such interdependence is inevitable if the divisions are organised partly to serve each other. If the divisions were completely independent the organisation would be little more than an investment company leaving the component companies to pursue whatever objectives they wished provided they produced a certain return.

Whenever there is divisional interdependence there is a transfer pricing problem. The seriousness of the problem depends on the extent to which one division trades exclusively with another. If the divisions trade to a large extent outside the group, there is likely to be a market or guideline price for the goods or services, which helps in establishing a fair transfer price.

Some questions answered

1 Are market-based transfer prices the best?

Certainly yes, when there is a good competitive market in the goods or services outside the group.

Where the market is not so good, or the products outside are similar but not quite the same, some adjustment has to be made. An allowance may also be needed for different quality or level of service. A reduction in the market price may be justified by lower selling and delivery costs in the supplying division.

2 Is negotiation between divisions usually needed?

The perfect market exactly corresponding to the sales between divisions is rare. Agreement on adjustments to the market price has to be fairly negotiated between buying and selling divisions if each is to be satisifed. Managers of divisions are then likely to have some faith in the turnover and profit figures embodying these prices.

Negotiation works best when there is some information about whatever market there is. There may, for instance, be a relevant market abroad but not in the UK. The process of negotiation may itself uncover new information pertinent to the prices in question.

3 Can buying outside the group solve the problem?

Buying outside may provide more information about prices, but it is unlikely that the outside price should be the same as the transfer price.

The advantage of freedom to buy outside is that it gives true independence and autonomy to the buying division, while stimulating the selling division to provide good service at a fair price.

The disadvantage lies in the effects on the group as a whole. Capacity in the selling division, for example, may not be fully utilised, in which case buying outside at a higher price than the group supplier's marginal cost would be counter-productive for the group.

4 What happens when negotiation fails?

If external information is hard to come by, the transfer prices agreed tend to be determined more by negotiating skill than by market intelligence. The search for agreement may then involve fierce arguments and prolonged meetings at higher and higher levels. In the end the settlement may become a political one, which is not likely to produce a fair measure of performance in the divisional accounts.

The only other possibility is to base the transfer price on some form of cost.

5 What are the advantages of cost-based pricing?

In theory cost-based transfer prices should produce the optimum result for the group as a whole. Market prices solve the problem of independence of divisions but not of maximum group profit. Costs reflect the internal situations of the various divisions, whereas market prices have little relation to the capacity and capability of particular factories.

There are, of course, different costs for different purposes. In transfer pricing there are three possibilities:

- marginal cost
- fixed fee plus marginal cost
- full cost

6 What are the problems of marginal cost?

Pricing at marginal cost appears attractive, for example, when two divisions are closely dependent on each other; this should lead in theory to optimum profits of the two divisions combined. In practice the method is rarely used, for the following reasons:

(a) Marginal cost is the same as variable cost, i.e. costs which vary according to output. Such costs are often difficult to define precisely and when output is increased substantially extra fixed costs may be incurred (which makes the 'fixed' costs also 'variable').

(b) Turnover, as well as profit, become useless measures of divisional performance when the selling division is compelled to supply at marginal cost.

(c) Audit checks or costs are needed to ensure that the basis of the pricing is correct.

(d) Transfer prices derived from mathematical models rarely succeed owing to difficulties in obtaining correct data and in defining the necessary constraints.

7 How does the fixed fee (plus marginal cost) work?

The fixed fee represents the proportion of fixed cost of the selling division that is attributable to the buying division. It can be regarded as an annual licence fee or subscription to have the supplies at marginal cost.

Fixing the fee may be troublesome, although easier if the capacity and hence fixed costs are agreed with the buying divisions in the light of their own plans. If the selling division has excess 'capacity' that no buying division will be responsible for, then arbitrary allocations may have to be made. The fixed cost must be charged somewhere if the selling division is to survive.

The method may work well in a stable climate where the buying divisions are taking regular supplies from the selling division. But if the buying divisions suffer a recession, they may object to paying the fixed cost fee. If, on the other hand, they have a boom, they are likely to press for expansion of capacity in the selling division and be willing to pay a higher fee.

8 What is wrong with full cost as a basis?

Full cost has the worst of all worlds. It neither produces a theoretical optimum result, nor does it provide any independence for divisions. It entails passing on whatever costs are incurred from one division to another; in which case the divisions have little more than an administrative function to perform.

When to watch out

A considerable volume of interdivisional trading should ring the alarm bell. If the transfer prices used are based throughout on market prices and divisions are allowed also to purchase from outside the group, then there is little fear for the measure of business performance. There may be some fear for the optimum performance of the group as a whole, but that is another matter.

When the transfer prices are based on costs, the alarm should continue ringing. Neither marginal cost nor full cost provide a clear measure of divisional performance. Fixed fee plus marginal cost may be reasonable provided the fixed costs represented by the fee are stable and acceptable.

What should be done – the author's opinion

Cost-based pricing, even with the fee plus arrangement, takes away some of the independence of divisions which is an essential element of a meaningful performance measure. The division which transfers a substantial proportion of its output to other divisions at prices based on cost is scarcely a business, for it has no true turnover.

Market-based pricing is a kind of act of faith. Give people their head and they will respond with greater efforts that will outdo the results of any mathematical model based on present data.

Basically I am a behaviouralist and not a mathematician. Independence and autonomy for the right people with the right guidance may work wonders. The market-based transfer price gives that independence and provides a fair measure of performance as the guidance.

It is interesting that, in two surveys[1,2] of organisations involved in transfer pricing, about 20 per cent based the prices primarily on cost and 80 per cent on market prices of some kind. The cost-based organisations could probably do no other. For them decentralisation to the extent of divisions with independent profit responsibility may have been an impractical dream.

If market prices can replace transfer prices so that the latter term is never used, then the feeling of independence is guaranteed. The division then has most of the attributes of a separate business, the performance of which can be measured in the same way. But there is always a danger that corporate loyalty may suffer.

FOREIGN CURRENCY TRANSLATION

Measures affected

Turnover
Gross margin
Value added
Operating profit
Profit after interest
Profit after tax
All-inclusive profit

Bases of accounting which apply

Historic cost
Current cost
Cash flow
Funds flow

Where found

In published accounts of companies with business abroad
In divisional accounts of such companies

Source of the trouble

When UK companies have, or expect to have, substantial business in an overseas country it is usual for them to set up a branch or subsidiary company in that country. The branch or subsidiary keeps accounts of its revenue and expenditure in the currency of the country.

Take, for example, a subsidiary company in France set up for the purpose of selling and servicing machines exported by the UK company.

In order to measure the performance of the whole business from manufacture to after-sales service, the accounts of the French subsidiary have to be translated from French francs into pounds sterling.

In the days of fixed exchange rates the translation was simple. With floating exchange rates there has been no consensus on what exchange rate should be used, after about ten years of debate.

In October 1983 the Accounting Standards Committee issued SSAP 20.[3] This confirmed that assets and liabilities should be translated at the exchange rate pertaining on the balance sheet date (known as the closing rate). But for the profit and loss account there is a choice: either the closing rate or the average rate can be used (the average can be the average of a daily, weekly, monthly or quarterly rate). Whichever rate is chosen can make a considerable difference to the overall profit. If the closing rate of the French franc is 12 to the £, and the average rate is 11, the choice of average rate improves the profit of the French operation by $8\frac{1}{2}$ per cent.

Some questions answered

1 What are the advantages of the average rate?

   (a) Monthly or quarterly divisional accounts for the foreign operation are simply added together to produce the profit and loss account in sterling for the year.
   (b) The turnover and profit made abroad is likely to reflect the cash flows from abroad as exchanged into sterling when remittances are made to the UK.
   (c) The year need not be sacrosanct. Translations of currency can be made for any period at the rate applicable to the period.

2 What are the advantages of the closing rate?

   (a) Profit for the year is translated at the same rate as the year-end assets and liabilities so that there is no discrepancy or difference on exchange, which occurs if profits are translated at a different rate.
   (b) The closing rate used throughout gives a better valuation of the net investment made abroad.

3 What is the most popular method?

In published accounts about 20 per cent of companies translate profit and loss accounts in foreign currency by the average rate and 80 per cent by the closing rate.[4]

4 Is it necessary to translate at all?

If the foreign operation is an entirely separate business, its performance is best measured in its own currency. Translation may only confuse what is already a clean and clear statement.

If the foreign operation is part of a UK business, as in the example earlier, the foreign accounts have to be translated in order to measure the total performance.

When to watch out

The largest differences between the two methods of translation occur when exchange rates are volatile. If exchange rates are stable, no trouble will arise.

What should be done – the author's opinion

For short-term performance measurement (say, quarterly) the average rate of exchange over the quarter should be used. There is no logic in changing the rate of exchange already used for the quarterly figures to a different rate just because the end of the year has arrived. The rate which rules on 31 December is good for the valuation of the net assets of the overseas branch on that date, but it is of no relevance to the performance of the branch as a business.

6 Gross margin

DEFINITION

Gross margin is the first convenient stage in the hierarchy of profit levels where costs may be deducted from turnover. The costs at this stage are all directly variable and related to turnover. They are not fixed, do not depend on capacity utilised, can be readily identified, are not allocated from a total of indirect costs and exclude anything in the nature of 'overhead'.

Hence the definition is loose and is different for different businesses and in different industries. The term 'gross margin' is not universally used, but seems to be gaining ground as the most popular. Other similar terms are:

(1) *Gross profit*. This has come unfortunately to mean any level of profit from which something can be deducted to make it 'net'. For example profit before tax can be 'gross profit' and profit after tax 'net profit'.
(2) *Contribution*. This is strictly the *contribution to fixed overhead and profit* and is therefore the same as the profit after deducting from turnover *all variable costs* (i.e. costs varying with output). This is not quite the same as gross margin, which may not take in *all* variable costs and which may use a different definition of variable costs from the contribution concept.
(3) *Trading profit*. This is an extremely loose term which, in some cases, may be synonymous with gross margin and, in others, synonymous with operation profit. In merchanting businesses, trading profit is the same as gross margin.
(4) *Gross profit margin*. This is perhaps the best description, but gross profit may have another connotation and the whole term tends more to be used as a ratio than as an amount.

'Gross margin' used here is defined as: turnover less directly related variable costs in producing that turnover. There can be no standard definition of the 'directly related variable costs' that will suit all cases. In

43

accounting 'variable cost' is synonymous with *marginal cost*. The 'gross margin' may be regarded as what is left after taking away from the turnover the 'marginal cost'.

ACCOUNTANCY

Once defined, the ascertainment of gross margins achieved is simple. The data necessary is minimal, requiring only turnover and the directly related variable costs of the goods sold.

Because of the simplicity, requiring no allocations or apportionments, the gross margin can be split down easily into divisions, product groups and individual products. At the product level the gross margin may be used as a basis of pricing, with a 'mark-up' to cover overhead costs and operating profit.

As a measure of performance, the gross margin covers sales volume, selling prices and costs of the sales. When these are separated in accounting statements, it is easy to see how the gross margin has changed compared with previous periods (or with a budget). Changes in gross margin can be analysed by responsibility for sales (salesmen), for selling prices (marketing) and for costs of sales (purchasing and/or manufacturing).

Gross margin is frequently expressed as a ratio to turnover. This can provide an excellent comparison between firms in the same business. A gross margin ratio, however, says nothing about turnover volume. Some firms may have a strategy of high volume at low prices and others a strategy of high prices for a lower volume. Each of these strategies may well exist in otherwise similar businesses. The gross margin ratio is considered further in Chapter 19 (p. 237).

UNDERLYING PHILOSOPHY

The users of gross margin regard it usually as a key measure. If the 'margin' is right, they would say, then the remaining measures will tend to be right. A common rule of thumb is: 'if gross margin is less than x per cent we are working at a loss'. In other words, control of gross margin is the most important control in the business.

This view depends almost as much on the philosophy and style of management as on the type of business. In our recent survey[1] over half of the companies used gross margin as one of the main measures of performance. These included businesses such as commodity dealing, transport, distribution, printing, engineering, construction, brewing and dairying.

The conditions needed for success of the measure are quick reporting and feedback, results produced locally, with an element of self-appraisal. The virtues of accuracy, completeness and attention to detail tend to be spurned in favour of somewhat rough-and-ready home-made measures, which nevertheless carry conviction.

BUSINESSES BEST SUITED

The ideal businesses for gross margin are those in the retail, wholesale and distribution trades, where fixed overheads are a relatively small proportion of total costs. Gross margin is preferable to turnover alone in anything but the very short term. After a few months account must usually be taken of changes in prices of materials, if nothing else.

Gross margin is also used in manufacturing businesses where material costs are high in relation to the process cost, or where the manufacturing is largely in the nature of assembly for distribution. In these situations, again, gross margin accounts for most of the major costs.

Gross margin is not suitable for capital intensive businesses, where ultimate profit may depend on plant utilisation more than on the difference between sales revenue and materials cost. It is not suitable either for pure service businesses which consume almost no materials at all.

ORGANISATIONS BEST SUITED

The organisations making best use of gross margin are those which combine the relevant management style with the suitable businesses.

Again, an organisation of retail or distribution businesses is likely to make the most comprehensive use of the gross margin measure.

Because the definition of gross margin is different for different businesses, it cannot often be compared across businesses. It tends to be useful only for inter-period comparisons in the same business, or where different businesses have similar operating structures and hence gross margin definitions.

To be effective as a measure within an organisation, the businesses should be of similar structures with a common definition of gross margin. A gross margin figure for the organisation as a whole can then carry some useful meaning. When the organisation and the businesses with it are constantly changing, the gross margin measure, which requires a certain stability, is of little use.

If labour or staff costs are included in the variable costs in arriving at gross margin, the gross margin may rise purely due to labour-saving technology and equipment. A new machine, for example, which saves two people, saves the variable cost of those people and increases gross margin. The costs of depreciation and maintenance of the machine, however, are usually charged *after* gross margin, as overheads. In these circumstances only operating profit, where both the old costs and the new costs are accounted for, gives a true picture.

Gross margin is not suitable in businesses or organisations where the balance of fixed and variable costs is changing; and this may be the case today with a large number of enterprises.

POWER TO MOTIVATE

Where overhead costs are largely fixed and not controllable by the people in charge of the business unit, gross margin is ideal as a basis for incentive schemes or simply as a good target to aim for. Almost all the canons of a good motivator are present: proximity of the operation to the accounting results, prompt feedback, controllability of the results, easy to understand and generally easy to produce, except for the one problem of stocks.

For self-contained businesses where fixed overheads are steady, the gross margin is almost all that is required in the short-term. If the management of the business has discretion on selling prices, the whole of the gross margin becomes their responsibility, which should urge them to increase it. The bonus, or at least the kudos, is likely to be there if they do.

PROBLEMS AND TROUBLES

The measure is vulnerable to inflation unless corrected by an index, and a suitable index may be difficult to agree upon.

The greatest problem is the treatment of materials consumed or used in the period, which depends on work-in-progress and stock valuation (trouble spot 6.1). If there are substantial stocks or work-in-progress, differences in the variety of possible methods used can have a drastic effect on the gross margin. A simple example, where stock turns over about every three months, is given below, comparing the month's results using two different stock valuation methods:

Month of . . .	Method 1 LIFO	Method 2 FIFO
Sales	1000	1000
Materials used		
Stock at start of month	2200	1500
Purchased for month	600	600
	2800	2100
Less: Stock at end of month	2000	1350
	800	750
	200	250
Other variable costs	100	100
Gross margin	100	150

A difference of 50 per cent between methods is not uncommon where stock turnover is slow.

STOCKS AND WORK-IN-PROGRESS

Measures affected

Gross margin
Value added
Operating profit
Profit after interest
Profit after tax

Bases of accounting which apply

Historic cost
Current cost
Funds flow

Where found

In published accounts
In private company accounts
In small business accounts
In divisional accounts

Source of the trouble

In computing gross margin, value added or any form of profit, turnover has to be matched with the amount of materials *used* and converted into sales in the period, not with the amount *bought* in the period. If you expect, for example, a gross margin of 40 per cent of sales in a simple process business, materials cost should be 60 per cent of sales (known as the *cost of sales*).

In basic accounts the cost of materials used in the cost of sales is computed from the stock figures and materials bought:

> Materials bought in the period,
> + stock at the beginning of the period,
> − stock at the end of the period.

or:

> materials bought in the period,
> ± change in stock during the period.

The cost of materials used to arrive at value added or profit can depend heavily on the money figures used for stocks at the beginning and end.

Take, for example, a galvanising business, where:

● zinc is bought during the period at £800 a ton,
● stocks at the beginning were bought at £800 a ton,
● the price at the end of the period remains £800 a ton,

there is then no problem of stock valuation. The obvious price at which to value the stock is £800.

Supposing, however, that the price is £1000 at the beginning of the period and £700 at the end. If the stocks are small and turn over fast there is not much difficulty. But consider the following:

zinc bought	10 tons @ £800 = £8 000
stock at beginning	+ 20 tons @ £1 000 = £20 000
stock at end	− 25 tons @ ? = ?
zinc used	5 tons @ ? = ?

There are at least five different methods for dealing with the question marks. None can claim to be the perfect method for all businesses in all circumstances.

The factors involved in choosing a method of stock valuation are:

● the volume and variety of stocks
● the period for which stocks are normally held (stock-turn)
● the volatility of material prices
● the rate of inflation in material prices
● the type of business (e.g. retail or manufacturing)
● the proportion of obsolete stock

- the acceptance by the Inland Revenue of the stock valuation method for tax purposes
- the number of locations where stocks are held
- the extent to which approximation is acceptable
- the system for charging issues from stores to jobs or products
- the system of stock control.

The above apply largely to stocks of materials. With *work-in-progress* and *finished goods* there are further troubles. Apart from the materials used there are two other cost components:

(a) *Labour or staff time.* A rate per hour is generally used, but the elements of cost included can vary from crude ordinary wages to a carefully computed total employment cost.
(b) *Production overheads.* The inclusion of overhead costs associated with the work-in-progress varies from a full allocation of all factory, selling, administrative expenses and depreciation, to no allocation of overheads whatever.

For *long-term contracts* there is yet more trouble. If a contract lasts more than one year, as well as the cost of work-in-progress, an estimate of the profit earned for the year to date should be included. There are about six different methods of estimating the profit to date on a contract. The profit taken is largely a function of the method chosen.

The trouble is that no stock or work-in-progress valuation method is free from problems caused by the turbulence of changing prices and values. If prices of materials were always stable, there would be no problem, but, even without general inflation, prices of basic materials always fluctuate. If stocks are small in relation to turnover (i.e. a fast rate of *stock-turn*), normal price fluctuations have a relatively small effect. If there are large stocks with slow stock-turn, and volatile prices of materials, the problems are compounded. (See Chapter 19, p. 240, for a full explanation of the stock-turn ratio.)

Some questions answered

1   What are the various methods used for valuing stock?

There are seven different methods (the figures in brackets indicate the price for zinc used, replacing the question mark in the table on page 49):

(a) *FIFO* (first in, first out) assumes that the oldest stock is used first (£1000 per ton).

(b) *LIFO* (last in, first out) assumes that the newest stock is used first (£800 per ton).

(c) *Average cost method* calculates the average price of all purchase during the period and of stock at the beginning (£933 per ton, i.e. £28 000 ÷ 30).

(d) *Base stock method* assumes that a certain amount of stock is always retained and materials charged at the latest prices (£800 per ton; base stock, say, 15 tons).

(e) *Standard cost method* fixes a certain price for the period at the outset with changes at appropriate intervals (say, £900 per ton, but the method is not suitable for highly fluctuating prices as in the example).

(f) *Replacement cost method* (or CCA) assumes stocks are replaced at current price (£700 per ton).

(g) *Adjusted selling price* is the current selling price reduced by the gross margin; it is used largely by retail stores (not relevant in the zinc example).

The cost of materials for the period ranges, in the example, from £700 per ton to £1000 per ton. The method chosen clearly has an important impact on the resulting value added, gross margin and profit.

The zinc example is of falling prices, where method (f) produces lower cost and higher profit than method (a). If prices are rising, method (a) would produce lower cost and higher profit than method (f).

2 Can the stock valuation method be changed to suit economic circumstances?

In theory, yes, but in practice it is almost impossible, unless there are only a few items of stock, for the following reasons:

(a) If a stock valuation method is changed, a difference arises between the money amount of the stock at the end of the period from the amount at the beginning of the next period after the change takes place. This difference has to be shown as a prior year adjustment or extraordinary item (see trouble spot 11.1, p. 142). If the new method has the effect of increasing profits in future years with a large debit extraordinary item, it is likely to be regarded as very suspect.

(b) With large and varied stocks the physical process of revaluing, even with a fully computerised system, can be costly and time consuming.

(c) As with all valuations for use in accounts, consistency of method produces understanding, confidence and trust in the results. It may require several years, in a complex area such as stock and work-in-progress valuation, for a new method to become fully credible and acceptable to the users.

3   Are there not occasions, such as in high inflation, when the method has to be changed?

There has to be some shock to the stock valuation method which produces patently misleading results before any change is contemplated. High inflation by itself is not damaging provided a method is used (such as replacement cost) which is suitable for such conditions. But the same method may not be suitable when prices are falling.

Switching from one method to another when there is a sudden rise or sudden fall in prices is scarcely practicable. The alternative is to show the results using a different method, that caters for quickly rising prices, in parallel with the established method.

Inflation affects other elements of business performance as well as stock valuation. It is possible to use replacement or current cost for materials consumed without using current costs throughout the accounts, but there is a strong argument which avers that if the accounts are intended to allow for inflation, which is a general phenonemon, they should account for it all the way through.

Hence replacement or current cost valuation of stock and cost of sales becomes a feature of current cost accounting, which is dealt with as a separate basis of accounting in Chapter 14 (p. 179) in contrast to historic cost.

However, there is one method which comes close to replacement cost and that is method (b) LIFO. This method contrasts vividly with method (a) FIFO, which is the clearest example of pure historic cost.

4 What are the different effects on performance measurement of LIFO and FIFO?

In times of rising prices and active stock movements:

- LIFO provides for the latest prices being used for the cost of materials included in cost of goods sold, thus largely excluding from profit the element of inflationary price rise.
- FIFO provides for the price of the oldest material in stock being used for the cost of materials included in cost of goods sold, thus including in profit an element of inflationary price rise.

In times of rising prices when stocks are falling:

- LIFO may ignore the latest prices because no materials are being bought so that the cost of materials may be charged in cost of goods sold at a lower than current price.
- FIFO may result in current prices being used earlier as old stocks get used up so that the cost of material in cost of sales is increased sooner.

In times of falling prices when stocks are rising:

- LIFO may be charging for materials in cost of sales an amount that is lower than the cost of the materials originally, thus overstating the profits.
- FIFO charges the oldest and hence the highest price, resulting in lower profits.

When prices are falling, however, the principles of stock valuation are modified, and this applies to all the stock valuation methods mentioned. The treatment of stocks in times of inflationary boom and deep recession are not symmetrical and this adds to the difficulty of finding a stock valuation method for all occasions.

5 What are the provisions for falling prices on value of stock?

In 1975 an accounting standard was issued on stock and work-in-progress (SSAP 9).[3] 'Stocks and work-in-progress', it says, 'normally need to be stated at cost, or, if lower, at net realisable value'.

In theory, every item of stock should be ascribed a *net realisable value* and compared with the cost as recorded by whatever normal method of stock valuation is in use. Net realisable value will, of course, be lower than 'cost' when prices of commodities are falling, or when machinery or equipment becomes obsolete, or when clothing becomes out of fashion.

In these cases the stock at the end of an accounting period (for example, the first quarter) is *written down* from cost to net realisable value. This results in the reduction in value – or loss on stocks – being reflected in profits of the first quarter instead of in the second quarter, or whatever later period in which the written down stock is ultimately used and sold. Once written down it cannot be written up again. (This practice tends to make any recession worse by adding to actual losses on sales the assumed losses on future sales.)

The future net realisable value can be highly subjective, especially for large quantities of stocks of finished goods and expensive specialised pieces of equipment. Stock in trade can range from ships, oil rigs, and aircraft to millions of shirts, dresses and calculators.

Different valuers are likely to produce very different valuations. Much depends on whether the goods are assumed to be sold gradually or all at once. In the case of the most expensive products there may be little or no market and it is here that the effect of the valuation on profit is the most significant.

6 What are the snags in work-in-progress?

Work-in-progress comprises all the products, contracts, jobs or assignments undertaken by the business which are not yet completed. At the end of each accounting period work-in-progress has to be valued, or the cost to date ascertained from records of materials used, time spent, services bought out and so on.

The same principle for stocks of 'cost or net realisable value whichever is the lower' applies also to work-in-progress, but it is even more difficult in practice. Market valuation of unfinished products is frequently quite impossible. At 90 per cent completion the products may be worth very little; at $99\frac{1}{2}$ per cent they may be worth virtually the full price.

As well as materials, the cost of labour and (according to SSAP 9[3]) an allocation of overhead cost have to be included in the cost of work-in-progress. If the treatment of labour and overheads is consistent, and work-in-progress does not vary much from period to period, the actual definitions and method are not of great import. The trouble comes when work-in-progress diminishes or increases, especially in relation to overheads.

Production overheads, according to SSAP 9, should include the appropriate depreciation. They are to be 'based on the normal level of activity taking one year with another'.

The scope here for different interpretations is wide. Overhead costs are difficult to define and classify, let alone allocate to particular projects or jobs. 'Normal level of activity' may be, for instance, with or without overtime, or with or without a third shift. Many businesses have no norm. Their hours of production are geared to the level of orders.

In some businesses contracts may require three or four years or more to complete. Over such a long period there may well be considerable changes in 'normal level of activity'. And there is another problem with profits on such contracts.

7 What is the cause of the trouble on long-term contracts?

Before SSAP 9[3], a business engaged in long-term contracts (defined as those lasting more than one year) normally ignored any profit until the contract was completed. As the length of contracts increased, however, no profit or value added could be registered for many years. The profits shown in annual accounts became dependent very much on exactly when contracts were completed.

SSAP 9, since 1976, requires that the profit estimated to be made on the contract, and attributable to the accounting year, is added to work-in-progress, which is to be stated as 'cost plus any attributable profit'. There is a rider which says that profit cannot be added 'until the outcome of the contract can be assessed with reasonable certainty'.

The addition of a profit element to work-in-progress remains controversial. Accounting principles maintain that profit should not be anticipated and current assets (such as work-in-progress) should not be valued higher than cost. This is confirmed in the Companies Act 1981 (Sch. 1, Part II, paragraph 22).

In practice, long-term contracting businesses generally rely on a progress payment (or an invoice for such a payment) being the end of a stage in a large project, effectively dividing the project into sub-projects. This seems to be a reasonably fair method if applied consistently, but there is a danger that the progress payment demands may be issued quite arbitrarily.

For short-term performance measurement some estimate of profit to date is essential. As with stocks, a reasonable method suited to the business should be chosen and applied consistently.

In value added statements

All the troubles above apply equally to value added as to profits.

There is also a slight complication concerning labour or staff time in work-in-progress. If, for example, staff costs for the year are £100 000, but work-in-progress has increased over the year from £50 000 to £110 000, and half of the increase of £60 000 is staff costs; then £30 000 of the year's staff costs is still in work-in-progress. It is not charged against profit (because there is no turnover to correspond) and it should not be counted as a distribution of value-added to staff. However, the staff costs appearing in the value added statement are then less than the actual payments made and the discrepancy may require to be explained.

In divisional accounts

The stock valuation methods in published accounts generally follow from those in internal divisional accounts. The problems are the same for both.

For work-in-progress the methods are usually different. In many companies no allocation of overhead costs is made to work-in-progress. It is quite logical to charge energy costs and other costs which vary directly with production, but it would be very misleading to allocate fixed costs to divisional work-in-progress in the short-term; for example, in monthly accounts. The 'normal level of activity' concept of SSAP 9[3] is no help at all. That would simply mean allocating fixed costs such as administrative expenses and depreciation as a constant percentage. A full discussion of the use of arbitrary allocations in divisional accounts is part of trouble spot 8.2 (p. 94).

When to watch out

In order to produce the sort of profit that is desired for internal, political or fiscal reasons, the classic area in which the profit can best be 'fiddled' is stocks and work-in-progress. Stories of two sets of books were legion, especially from Italy, where one set of books would produce the lowest profit (for the taxman) using one method of stock valuation and another set of books would produce the highest profit (for the directors and private shareholders) using another method.

The scope for 'fiddling' is not as wide as it used to be, but there are a number of points where profit and value added may be distorted:

● change in the stock valuation method for no good reason
● failure to use a different basis of stock valuation when economic factors (such as high inflation) dictate it
● misuse of the highly subjective concept of 'net realisable value'
● allocation of overhead costs to work-in-progress
● addition of estimated profit to work-in-progress on long-term contracts.

The higher and more varied the stocks, the lower the stock-turn, and the larger the work-in-progress, the more is the need to be vigilant in the cause of true measurement of the business performance.

What should be done – the author's view

With inflation never likely to disappear for a long continuous period of years, I favour replacement of current cost for stock valuation in most situations. If price rises are small, LIFO, which is the most usual method in USA, will do equally well. One difficulty in the UK is that LIFO is not recognised by the Inland Revenue as an allowable method of stock valuation although it is one of the acceptable methods listed in the Companies Act 1981.

There are some situations where replacement cost is not appropriate; for example, commodities, farm products, seasonal goods. It is unsuitable also when replacement prices are rapidly falling as with the new technology products such as microcomputers. Once a stock valuations method is chosen for businesses of this kind it should be adopted consistently until the situation radically changes.

The use of net realisable value where prices are falling is a necessary evil in accounts. My own view (see Chapter 4, p. 22) is that any substantial loss on stocks or work-in-progress due to diminution of market value should be shown separately as an extraordinary or exceptional item. The period in which the diminution in value is recognised is likely to be entirely arbitrary. A hidden provision for the loss can easily distort the performance measure of the current period.

Allocation of overhead costs to work-in-progress should be abandoned, as is the case in many management accounts.

7   Value added

DEFINITION

The value added of a business is simply the amount of value created by it (output) less the amount of value put into it (input).

The value of total output of a business is its turnover.

The value of the input to a business is materials purchased, fees for services rendered, payments to contractors, maintenance, repairs, fuel, rentals, licences, etc.: i.e. any goods or services obtained originally from outside the business.

Both output and input are market valuations. Turnover is priced at what customers will pay. Input is priced at what the business will pay. Value added is therefore a measure of creation of wealth as valued in the market place at the time. Those sharing in the wealth are known as 'stakeholders'.

The principal stakeholders are usually:

- the employees (receiving wages, salaries and related benefits)
- the lenders (receiving interest on loans)
- the Government (receiving tax revenue)
- the shareholders (receiving dividends)
- the company itself (retaining the amount held in reserve).

As soon as value added is distributed it may cease to be 'wealth'. In the hands of the stakeholders it becomes their income, which may be spent.

ACCOUNTANCY

The components of the value added account are the same as those of the profit and loss account, assembled in a different way. It can be computed as turnover less materials and bought in services (following the definition); or as operating profit plus wages, salaries and related benefits of employees.

A value added statement cannot be produced unless there is a clear decision at the outset on what items of expense are deductions from value added and what are distributions of value added. The accountancy is largely a matter of analysing the expenses charged to the profit and loss account and allocating them 'above the line' (as an input to value added) or 'below the line' (as a distribution). Once decided, the definitions for the allocation should stick, to ensure consistency between periods.

UNDERLYING PHILOSOPHY

Value added is a measure of performance which avoids most of the wrangles about distribution, particularly those between labour and capital. Labour is not regarded as a cost but as a beneficiary of the value added created.

Discussion of the distribution of value added takes place in a context of what total amount is available and whether the particular slices of the cake appear reasonable compared with previous periods and with other similar businesses.

Value added measures should produce a team spirit that focuses on wider issues than simply wage claims, dividends or earnings per share. Labour and capital are ideally not distinguished.

In measuring productivity (see Chapter 21, p. 252), it is frequently difficult to separate productivity of labour (how hard people work) from productivity of capital (how efficiently plant and machinery is used). If orders are increasing, idle time is reduced and the cost per unit of production is falling; whose productivity is improving? – is it the workers' or the machines'? The increased productivity is due to idle resources being utilised. The nature of those resources is not relevant to the value added concept.

Value added avoids any attempt to divide productivity gains to factors of production. If value added per month or per year has increased, this is sufficient to imply better performance.

However, value added does provide one ratio which is widely used, i.e. value added: employment cost (see Chapter 19, p. 235). It is not strictly a measure of productivity because it can be affected by selling prices, but it does give an impression to the employees of better results for their efforts when the ratio improves.

BUSINESSES BEST SUITED

Like many other measures, value added works best when extremes are avoided.

A business which simply buys and sells materials or commodities with no processing of any kind will show a very low value added in relation to sales. The value added will be very much the same as the gross margin (sales less cost of sales) shown in the profit and loss account. Examples of this are merchanting, commodity dealing, brokerage and so on.

At the other extreme there are businesses with very high value added in relation to sales in which materials are practically nil and equipment is very small. Capital is then comparatively insignificant and almost all the value added is taken by the employees who often have special skills. Examples are hairdressing, designing, professional and consultancy firms.

In both these extreme cases more conventional ratios such as gross margin between sales and purchases (in the first case) and a ratio of employment cost to sales (in the second case) serve better than a value added ratio.

The value added measure demands also some stability to be useful. If components are made in house, when previously they were bought from outside, added value increases in the company now making the components. If work is sent outside by subcontracting, value added falls in the subcontracting company. If switching between manufacturing inside and buying outside is significant, any inter-period comparisons of value added become misleading unless some adjustment is made.

Business that are in the same industry or trade are not necessarily comparable in value added terms, unless the proportions of work undertaken outside and inside are similar. The value added amounts may be true, but it is not possible to say that business A is better than business B because it generates a higher value added, unless the operating proportions of inside and outside work are considered.

Generally the smaller the business unit to which value added is applied the better. In the smaller business changes in structure are less likely and, if they occur, can be easily spotted and taken into account. A fairly stable relationship of employment cost to value added also helps.

ORGANISATIONS BEST SUITED

The organisation which regards employees, shareholders, lenders, customers, suppliers and Government as stakeholders in the enterprise may be the most happy with value added. It is most acceptable where employees are partners with shareholders and management, or are the same people, so that distribution of profit becomes mixed with employee remuneration.

Organisations such as co-operatives, co-partnerships and non-profit-making institutions find that value added produces a measure of performance to which all can relate.

Value added statements are included in the annual report of roughly one-fifth of public companies.[4] Where the company is homogeneous, stable in its operating structure and in one industry, the statement can give a meaningful view from another angle of company performance. It answers the question: what would our accounts look like if we were a producer co-operative?

If the organisation is a large conglomerate, however, a value added statement may be less than helpful. Changes in subsidiaries by acquisition and disposal may radically change the proportions of the factors of production in the group and increase the impact of the various trouble spots described in this part of the book.

POWER TO MOTIVATE

Value added is widely used as a basis of incentive schemes. They work best in small groups where the feedback is quick and frequent.

In many businesses, where numbers employed and wages are not fully under the control of the business manager, added value is a more plausible target than profit. Where employment costs are presented as a share of value added which employees are enjoined to increase, the motivation may move from improving the employees' own remuneration to improving productivity in general – emphasising the size of the cake against the size of the slice.

Where employees are replaced by machines resulting in increased value added, but not necessarily in profit, the case may seem more plausible and acceptable to employees.

A typical value added incentive scheme in a homogeneous business unit starts with an assumption of the distribution of value added. It could be a complex formula or a simple allocation of, say, 70 per cent of value added to employees and 30 per cent to the other stakeholders (i.e. to cover interest, dividend, tax and retention). In this simple case, if value added is increased, the employees would receive 70 per cent of the increase. In practice, of course, no scheme could be that simple and various definitions and rules would have to be agreed and promulgated.

Such schemes have many advantages over incentives based on profits in that they focus on team effort, overall productivity and total performance, avoiding the word 'profit'. Because value added and employee remuneration are generally much larger amounts than profit, the relationship between value added and pay is usually more stable. This tends to make fluctuations of bonus to employees based on value added much smoother than when based on profit.

In 1978 ICI adopted a scheme for annual bonus for all employees based on value added. This use of value added is rare. The main objective of ICI was not to provide a direct incentive but to enhance corporate loyalty and encourage employee involvement and interest in the fortunes of the whole group. The use of value added can assist in spreading a co-operative gospel, but it is of doubtful use as a performance measure to which people can relate on such a large scale.

PROBLEMS AND TROUBLES

The main problems lie in definition. The line between an input to be deducted from value added and a distribution of value added is difficult to draw in many cases, for example:

- certain costs related to employment, such as company cars and low interest loan facilities, which may or may not be regarded as a distribution to employees
- certain taxes such as local rates or vehicle licences, which may be regarded as a distribution to the Government or as an input against value added
- certain payments to people, although not legally employed by the company, may be more logically included as a distribution, e.g. self-employed contractors in the building industry, salesmen on commission

In all these cases the decisions on the definitions may be different for internal and external value added statements. Internal value added statements should tie up with the internal profit and loss statement, which may be different in many particulars from the published statement.

In management accounts value added is used as a divisional or departmental measure, and particularly as a basis for incentive schemes. Definitions have then to be clear and comprehensive. The distribution to employees may be known as employment costs, payroll costs, staff costs, as wages and NI or some other label. It is logical and desirable that any expense which is made as a result of employment of a person should be included, i.e. a total employment cost. Taxes such as local rates and vehicle licences seem best regarded as an unavoidable input. Taxes on profits remain as a distribution, probably not included in the management accounts at all.

There are three important trouble spots which apply specifically to value added:

- Stocks and work-in-progress: trouble spot 6.1
- Depreciation: trouble spot 7.1
- Extraordinary items: trouble spot 11.1

DEPRECIATION

Measures affected

Value added
Operating profit
Profit after interest
Profit after tax
All-inclusive profit

Bases of accounting which apply

Historic cost
Current cost

Where found

In published accounts
In private company accounts
In small business accounts
In divisional accounts

Source of the trouble

Depreciation is the largest and most troublesome weed in the field of performance measurement. The roots go very deep and, for businesses with much capital equipment, cover a large area of the accounting. For the typical industrial business depreciation may be around one-third to one-half of operating profit. (On a replacement cost basis it could be from a half to three-quarters.)

The seeds of the depreciation troubles are the assumptions which have to be made about the long-term future. Some estimate of how long a

65

machine or piece of equipment will last before it becomes worn out or obsolete is essential. This period of years is known as the *economic life* of the machine or the *asset life*.

Often the asset life is little more than a shot in the dark. Over periods of ten years or more the life of a machine may be quite unpredictable. On the one hand, machines are more reliable, have fewer mechanical parts and last longer; on the other hand, new technology makes the machine obsolete sooner. The larger the installation and the longer it is expected to last, the worse is the difficulty of estimating asset life. For short-life assets such as vehicles there is very little problem.

Asset lives are normally estimated conservatively, perhaps on average one-third less than their actual lives. If, for example, all machines are given a 10-year life for depreciation but actually they last 16 years, then operating profit in the typical case (assuming depreciation is one-third of operating profit) would be overstated by 10 per cent. (If depreciation is one-half of operating profit, it would be overstated by $33\frac{1}{3}$ per cent.)

The main purpose of depreciation is to allocate the original cost of the asset over its working/economic life. This matches the *cost* of the asset with the revenue generated by the asset over accounting periods. Asset life is the only problem of this matching principle, although a large one.

However, another even more troublesome problem must be introduced. The *value* of a machine over its life may change. It may go up through inflation or it may go down through recession, new technology, or loss of markets for the product.

The yardstick, with which the external market value of a machine is compared, is the *net book value* or the *written down value* in the balance sheet; that is, the original cost of the machine less all the depreciation instalments that have been charged so far.

What has to be done when the external market value of the machine is materially different from the book value is a matter of accounting convention.

If the external value is lower than the book value, accounting convention has required that the book value be reduced by charging more depreciation. In practice such a reduction is strenuously avoided by most companies, mainly because of the difficulties of valuation. The machine may be unique; professional valuations may vary widely; and it may not be clear whether the valuation is an 'economic value' in the business, a market value on a time-to-spare sale or a realisable value on a forced sale.

If the market value of a machine is higher than the book value, the traditional accounting convention requires that no change is to be made in depreciation. But, if the higher value is due to inflation, then some measure, it is argued, should be taken to correct it.

Inflation and current cost accounting (CCA) is the subject of Chapter 14. It is highly controversial and has caused a great deal of confusion and misunderstanding around the definition and purpose of depreciation.

Depreciation in a situation of rising external values can, however, be dealt with separately, without a comprehensive system such as CCA for accounting for the effects of inflation. Once, though, the basis changes from cost to value, there are troubles.

There has been a slow drift towards *valuation of fixed assets*, particularly of buildings and property (adopted now by about 80 per cent of large companies).[4] And valuation is also used for many plants where buildings can scarcely be distinguished from machinery. (About 20 per cent of large companies make valuations for some of their plant.)[4]

Depreciation is then based on valuation which, with the same asset life, produces, with inflation, a much higher figure than cost, unless the assets are very new.

Valuation can be extended to all kinds of fixed assets: office equipment, plant, machinery, vehicles, ships, aircraft, farms, containers and tools. If they are valued on a replacement cost basis, then the CCA system is in effect adopted for the depreciation.

Unless there is a near-perfect market, valuation is estimated and subjective; cost is actual and objective. Valuation is the science (or art) of a different profession; cost is the profession of the accountant. Accountants are never happy with a change from cost to value and this is perhaps the major reason for the trouble.

Some questions answered

1 What are the costs to which depreciation should apply?

Depreciation applies to fixed assets, i.e. buildings, plant, machinery, equipment or vehicles, which yield a benefit to the business for several years after their acquisition. The definition of fixed assets, however, is a little torn at the edges. For items such as furniture, building alterations, office fittings and office machines, some companies regard them as fixed assets with depreciation; others regard them as an expense of the period.

2 How is asset life estimated?

Engineers usually make estimates for plant and machinery, guided mostly by previous experience. For many assets in the fast changing world of technology there is little or no experience. In computers the speed of change has often caught people unawares, and the asset lives estimated have been too long.

Usually, however, asset lives are estimated very conservatively, that is, too short. If there is any doubt the asset life is rounded down to 15 or 10 years. This conservatism causes a problem later when many assets are fully *written off* even though they have many years of useful life ahead.

3 What happens when assets are fully written off? Does depreciation cease?

A popular estimated life for machines is 10 years. The most popular method of depreciation is the *fixed instalment method*, adopted by almost all large UK companies. For a machine costing £10 000, depreciation is £1000 a year, deducted each year from the cost. After 10 years, all the original cost has been charged and the book value is nil.

In one large company, not untypical in 1980, the plant fully written off (i.e. with nil book value), but still in use, represented 32 per cent of the original historic cost and 44 per cent of its estimated replacement cost. Depreciation on about a third of the plant had therefore ceased, but to a lesser extent in some divisions than in others. Divisions with old plant would be almost free from depreciation while those with new plant would be bearing the full charge.

It is possible to continue charging depreciation in accounts even though the assets are fully written off. Instead of reducing the asset book value (which would be nil) the 'depreciation' is credited to a reserve; it becomes not true accounting depreciation but a substitute charge for the use of the asset.

4 Are there other depreciation methods?

The *reducing balance method* is somewhat old-fashioned, used mostly by smaller companies and the Inland Revenue (in the form of writing-down allowances, see trouble spot 10.1, p. 117). However, it seems slowly to be regaining some adherents largely because of its feature of retaining always some asset value; the asset is never fully written off.

The method applies a fixed percentage, not to the original cost, but to the original cost less depreciation previously charged. An example of a motor van, costing £5000, depreciated at 25 per cent of the reducing balance is shown below:

		Depreciation	
Year	*25% of:*	*For year*	*Cumulative*
	£	£	£
1	5000	1250	1250
2	5000 − 1250	937	2187
3	5000 − 2187	703	2890
4	5000 − 2890	527	3417
5	5000 − 3417	396	3813
6	5000 − 3813	297	4110

No precise estimate of useful life is needed. Six years in this case would be reasonable.

The method, although somewhat unscientific, has a certain logicality in that repairs and maintenance expenses increase as plant and machinery gets older, thereby compensating for the reduced depreciation. The method also lessens the risk of the net book value becoming very much higher than the market value of the asset, because larger chunks of depreciation are taken off at the beginning when a large change in external values is not so likely as it would be later on.

There are a few other methods of depreciation which are very rarely used in practice. There is, however, one method that is used to some extent in USA but not in the UK. It is known as the *compound interest method* and allows for the interest assumed to have been paid or foregone through the investment in the particular fixed asset. Depreciation then increases each year as interest is charged on each depreciation charge.

The compound interest method is similar to the method needed, for example, to arrive at the cost of motoring. When you contemplate buying a car you should include in the annual cost not only the annual depreciation but also the interest lost through taking your money out of the building society to finance the purchase of your car.

5 Should residual value be taken into account in depreciation?

Machines and vehicles, when they come to the end of their useful economic life in the business, are usually sold or part-exchanged. With vehicles particularly there may be a policy to sell the old and buy new every three or four years. A residual value based on the sale proceeds is then assumed. If, for example, a vehicle costing £10 000 is kept for four years, after which it will be sold for £2400, annual depreciation under the fixed instalment system is £1900 (i.e. £7600 ÷ 4).

With less saleable plant, residual value may be almost impossible to estimate. The tendency then is to be conservative and leave it out altogether. When such plant is sold there are likely on average to be large profits on the sales (i.e. the difference between the sale proceeds and the net book value) which have little to do with the business performance of the period when the plant was sold. In internal management accounts such profits are generally regarded as outside the divisional performance measure, treated in effect as an extraordinary item. In published accounts, book profits on the sale of fixed assets are included in operating profit as they are deemed to arise from normal activities of the business, which is convenient, but questionable.

6 Is depreciation in any way similar to the rental charge on leased assets?

When based on valuation, depreciation becomes more akin to a charge for the use of an asset in a similar way to rentals on leasing. Increasingly this is being recognised in management accounts in relation to freehold and leasehold property.

Many companies have adopted schemes whereby divisions are charged a market rent on their buildings irrespective of whether they are legally freehold or on short or long leases. A property profit centre or subsidiary company is set up to own all the freehold properties, be responsible for all repairs and maintenance, pay all the rents of the leasehold property and receive from the divisions a standard rent advised by a surveyor, usually on the basis of a 25-year lease. The divisions carry no depreciation charge on buildings.

For plant and machinery the problems of equating the charge for the use of leased machines and owned machines are more difficult for the following reasons:

(a) There is no profession quite comparable to surveyors who evaluate the market rental for a leased machine on standard conditions.

(b) Rental on leased machines includes interest, whereas depreciation does not (except for the compound interest method, see answer to Question 4).

(c) In published accounts the process of equating the treatment of owned and leased assets has gone the other way. SSAP 21,[3] issue in July 1984, requires that plant and machinery on a finance lease be capitalised as though it were owned, requiring depreciation to be charged (and interest) instead of rental.

For property and buildings, valuation is very common, leading logically to market rents as a charge for use. For plant and machinery historic cost remains paramount and the fixed instalment depreciation to go with it.

In value added statements

If the use of an asset provides income or value added, some charge, whether depreciation or rental, should be made in the accounts in order to provide a meaningful performance measure.

In many value added statements (in fact, the majority which are published) depreciation is taken as a distribution of value added under a caption such as 'Re-invested in the business'. Such treatment throws up an anomaly when assets are leased and rentals are (rightly) deducted from value added. The way in which an asset is financed should not affect the value added (nor the operating profit).

Particularly when value added is used as the basis of incentive schemes, depreciation must be deducted along with materials and bought-out services. Otherwise, value added would increase when new plant or equipment is installed and employees would benefit from the extra bonus on value added which has nothing to do with their efforts.

In divisional accounts

The fixed assets of a large group are likely to be of roughly similar composition from year to year. The proportion of new and old assets, for instance, may not change radically overall, so that depreciation remains fairly comparable.

On a smaller scale, in divisions, depreciation may be affected by a particular new capital investment which increases the depreciation suddenly by 100 per cent or more. Older plant which was previously depreciation-free may be scrapped in favour of new plant with high depreciation. Leased plant too may show a higher cost than depreciation, if not corrected.

Divisional performance essentially requires a short-term measure. The ups and downs of depreciation are most unlikely to come out in the wash in just a year or two.

Items such as exceptional profit or loss on the sale of a fixed asset or the 'writing down' of an asset due to a fall in value should not be included in the profit or loss or the value added statement for a division, except as an extraordinary item.

When to watch out

Depreciation is almost a perpetual trouble spot that requires continuous attention. The scope for different depreciation charges seriously affecting the profit figures are greatest when:

● the business is capital-intensive (with substantial fixed assets)
● the fixed assets have long lives
● the fixed assets are old, and many are fully written off
● there is a mixture of fixed assets that are revalued and assets that are retained at cost
● the valuations used are out of date or inconsistent

The businesses which are *not* likely to have such serious trouble with depreciation are those having few fixed assets, or, if they have many, the assets are short-life, fairly new and steady in value.

What should be done – the author's view

Depreciation is essential in any measure of profit or value added, whether in divisional, small business or published accounts. The cost or the value of the fixed assets used in the business cannot be ignored just because they were acquired in an earlier period than that covered by the accounts.

Depreciation can be looked upon as:

● a charge for the use of a fixed asset
● an allocation of the original cost of fixed assets to accounting periods *or*
● an accumulation of funds for replacement of fixed assets when worn out or obsolete

In the management accounts of a division, depreciation should be regarded as a charge for the use of its assets. No company, as far as I know, has adopted this concept for plant and machinery, but it seems to me to be eminently feasible. The charge:

- could be based on a market rate for long-term hiring
- would cover interest and depreciation
- would be compatible with leasing rentals
- could work in a very similar manner to the notional rent for buildings and property (see answer to Question 6, p. 71)

It could be known perhaps as 'depreciation charge'.

At present when historic cost becomes totally unrealistic, a resort to valuation is made to produce a realistic depreciation that is consistent as far as possible between old and new assets. This involves two separate subjective judgements: the subjectivity of a valuation on top of the subjectivity of an asset life. We might just as well, in my view, make one subjective judgement only, i.e. on a fair charge for the use of the asset.

Depreciation of historic cost may still be suitable for some businesses with short-life fixed assets or with assets such as microcomputers which may be falling in value. If the historic cost depreciation is no more than, say, 20 per cent different from the valuation based depreciation, historic cost could still reasonably be used. The subjective judgements involved in valuation and estimate of asset life could easily be wrong by 20 per cent or more if the assumptions were later compared with the reality.

Accumulation of funds for replacement is not an issue in performance measurement. Depreciation does not and never will guarantee that there are funds available for replacement. Funds can be raised or set aside in very different ways. How it is done is a matter of financial policy.

The balance sheet is important in measuring financial health – hence the more recent emphasis on valuations. But it has very limited use in performance measurement. Neither book values nor professional valuations are relevant.

Depreciation should be consistently calculated and applied from year to year and should not be tied to the balance sheet figures, whether they are gross original cost, original cost less depreciation, gross replacement cost or net replacement cost. When assets are fully written off in the balance sheet, a form of depreciation charge should continue in order to assure a true and fair measure of profits (or value added) for appraisal of the business performance.

REVENUE INVESTMENT

Measures affected

Value added
Operating profit
Profit after interest
Profit after tax

Bases of accounting which apply

Historic cost
Current cost

Where found

In published accounts
In private company accounts
In small business accounts
In divisional accounts

Source of the trouble

Expenditure can be classed as capital or as revenue. Capital expenditure becomes an asset, which is normally subject to depreciation. Revenue expenditure is charged as incurred to the profit and loss account.

The distinction between capital and revenue can often be very blurred. A good definition of capital expenditure is expenditure which will continue to yield benefits after the end of the accounting year. However, the status of an asset requires that it is verifiable and retains a value in each year that it stands in the balance sheet.

Revenue investment is a term given to expenditure which is in the nature of capital because it produces lasting benefits but has not the concrete status of an asset. The most important examples are research, advertising campaigns and staff training.

The expenditure on such *quasi-assets* (except for some research and development costs) is always charged to profit and loss account in the period in which it occurs. But it could be partly carried forward to future periods and thereby give a better measure of the performance in each period.

The trouble is particularly prominent when a large expenditure on a quasi-asset, such as an advertising campaign, is concentrated in one short period, possibly causing a loss in the period in which it occurs purely because the capital investment element is ignored.

Some questions answered

1 What are the quasi-assets which give rise to revenue investment?

They are types of expenditure that produce lasting benefits (say, over more than one year), but are not tangible, not easily computed or verified, and prone to some risk of having in a short time little or no value. Examples are:

- research and development (R & D)
- advertising campaigns
- design and launch of new products
- training and initial cost of employment
- acquisition of renewable business (e.g. insurance policies, rental contracts)
- design, programming and installation of new data processing systems
- management consultancy fees on new systems or re-organisation
- re-organisation implementation costs

2 Why is research and development (R & D) a special case?

R & D can be legitimately capitalised in published accounts, but only for specific development projects. The main conditions, set out in SSAP 13,[3] are:

- a clearly defined project
- separately identifiable expenditure
- certainty as to technical feasibility and ultimate commercial viability of the project
- costs reasonably expected to be covered by revenues
- adequate resources to complete the project

The detailed rules, written in a more legal form, still leave a lot of room for judgement and interpretation.

For the balance sheet the term 'asset' or 'capitalisation' is avoided. The Companies Acts require that all 'research costs' be charged to the profit and loss account as incurred, leaving only *deferred development expenditure* that can be shown in the balance sheet as an asset.

3 Is there any prospect of other quasi-assets being given the status of 'deferred expenditure' in the same way as for specific R & D?

There is no compelling reason why quasi-assets, in internal management accounts, should not be capitalised or recognised as a kind of deferred expenditure. However, there are a number of difficulties:

(a) The extra accounting work involved in isolating the expenditure and depreciating (or amortising) it over the benefit period may not be justified by the small refinements in the performance measure.

(b) Some of the items (e.g. pure research and renewable business) are on-going regular expenditures of almost the same amount in every period, which makes no difference to comparisons of one period with another.

(c) Some items, although not capitalised (e.g. new product expenditure and re-organisation costs), may be treated as exceptional or extraordinary items (see trouble spot 11.1, p. 142) and are thus taken into account in assessing division's performance, with probably some assessment of the likely future benefits arising from the expenditure.

Nevertheless, revenue investment is being increasingly recognised as a distortion of performance measurement, especially in the medium-term (i.e. over two or three years). It is easy for performance to look good with high profits if expenditure for the benefit of the future is cut away. Low profit, on the other hand, may not mean low performance, but may be the result of revenue investment to increase profits in future years.

4   Does this apply to business start-ups?

It is well known that new businesses, often with a cast-iron expectation of profit, make losses in the first two or three years. This is partly due to unused capacity while sales are built up, partly to the gathering of experience and partly to the quasi-assets that have to be acquired. These may take the form of market research, technical research, development of the product, promotion of the business, recruiting and training of the staff and perhaps re-organisation as the business grows. So the 'loss' may be nothing to worry about. The profit and loss account may be showing a too pessimistic picture which can be modified by an assessment of the quasi-assets that will provide benefits in the future.

In published accounts

Apart from specific R & D (i.e. development expenditure) no quasi-assets are shown in published accounts. However, short reports on R & D activities and on employment policies must be included in the annual Directors' Report. The total expenditure for the year on R & D is often given in the report, and some account included of staff training, but with rarely any reference to training costs.

Comparisons of R & D with previous years may give some idea of the extent to which profit includes an element of revenue investment.

In divisional accounts

Revenue investment is often explained by notes and comments on the management accounts, but rarely accounted for as a quasi-asset or by carrying forward specific expenditure. In a few companies new approaches are being developed particularly for large advertising campaigns where it may be possible to estimate the length of time over which the effects of the advertising may endure. The estimates may then be used to amortise (or depreciate) the cost of the campaign over the period of lasting effect.

When to watch out

In any company or division where there is substantial revenue investment a watch should be kept on changes to the amounts expended. If there is a large increase, the profits may be unjustifiably low. If there is a large decrease the profits may be spuriously high.

Without clear information from a system which accounts for quasi-assets as though they were real assets it is not possible to quantify by how much the conventional profit should be adjusted. Any adjustment must inevitably be subjective.

What should be done – the author's view

Wherever feasible, systems should be set up to account for quasi-assets. More could certainly be done in the fields of R & D, advertising, training and other initial costs of employment. Identifying the costs and estimating amortisation periods will become less difficult with more experience of quasi-asset models.

Revenue investment has grown enormously in the last decade as business managers in general have become aware that the soft 'quasi-assets' of expenditure for the future have become as important as the fixed assets of hard plant and machinery. What has happened with computers is happening throughout many businesses. The hardware is relatively cheap and of little consequence. The software is the important key to success.

Accountancy is still in the era of fixed assets when research on the products, marketing the products and providing educated and trained staff for work on the products was of no importance. Today accountancy needs to move away from concentration on the production assets towards the quasi-assets, which are the seed-corn for the harvest of the future.

Any change can only come gradually as the 'soft' or quasi-assets are defined sufficiently well to develop acceptable systems for accounting for them as assets. The initiative must come primarily from management accountants as the designers of divisional accounts. And it is here that the most blatant mismeasurement of performance is likely to take place – where expenditure for the good of the future (even for next year) may produce a very poor result for the present.

Incentive bonuses are based generally on short-term profits or value added. By using these without accounting for the revenue investment we are in danger of living only for today with the morrow having to look after itself.

8 Operating profit

DEFINITION

Operating profit is profit before interest and tax. It is the difference between total revenue and total expenditure. Interest and any items relating to the financing of the business are excluded.

Interest received may be included in operating profit where it arises from the normal activities of the business such as interest on deposits of temporarily surplus cash. A line must be drawn between necessary cash inside the business earning interest and investment outside the business with the aim of making a continuous return.

Operating profit is not precisely defined. Sometimes interest and financial items such as profits on sales of assets are included in operating profit. The word 'operating' may not be appropriate in non-production businesses, such as dealing, consultancy or publishing, where the revenue is commission, fees or subscriptions. But gradually the term 'operating profit' is obtaining a wider acceptance and is applied to many 'non-operating' businesses.

ACCOUNTANCY

All the versions of profit are produced from the profit and loss account, sometimes called the *income statement* (particularly in America) or the *trading and profit and loss account* (especially for small businesses).

The profit and loss account is the most important object of any accounting system. It brings together:

(1) Revenue arising in the period from turnover and other incidental activities normal to the business; and
(2) Expenditure comprising:

(a) All the costs directly or indirectly related to the turnover obtained in the period (known loosely as variable or prime costs); and

(b) All the costs not related or only faintly related to turnover, which are allocated to the period (known loosely as overheads or fixed costs).

The accountancy of revenue and expenditure must follow the matching principle, which requires every item of revenue in a period to bear its corresponding load of expenditure. This is totally irrespective of whether the cash has been received for the sales or turnover in the period, or whether payments have actually been made on the invoices or bills which constitute the expenditure.

The profit and loss account (and normally the value added statement) is based on the *accrual principle*, where the timing of the payments and receipts of money is completely ignored, in contrast to the cash flow principle of Chapter 15.

Revenue and expenditure are invariably analysed by the accounting system into classifications which are useful to management in locating the sources and causes of profit or loss, such as:

(a) Type of expenditure, e.g. materials, rent, rates, gas, electricity, telephone, salaries;

(b) Function, e.g. sales, production, maintenance, administration, training;

(c) Department or cost centre, e.g. printing, personnel, data processing;

(d) Division, e.g. in a chemical company: agrochemicals, timber preservation, building materials, pharmaceuticals.

Operating profit can be derived from the value added statement by deducting the employment costs, shown as a distribution of value added, from the value added. Accounting systems, however, are planned almost always to produce the profit and loss account as the first priority.

UNDERLYING PHILOSOPHY

Operating profit is used overwhelmingly within the business as its principal measure of performance. Internally, where interest and tax are not regarded as the responsibility of the business manager, operating profit is regarded as the key to how well the business unit is performing.

Profit is the prime objective of investors in the business, whether they are lending banks or other institutions, shareholders or co-partners in the business. Directors are responsible for profits to the investors; senior managers are responsible in turn to directors; operating managers responsible to their seniors, and so on.

The profit measure is based on the necessity to provide a reward for the provision of capital in the widest sense. It is almost universally recognised as an essential ingredient of business success. It carries the notion of extra income for someone somewhere. The political arguments are largely about distribution of profits, not about profit itself being a respectable goal.

Operating profit stops short of any distribution problem.

BUSINESSES BEST SUITED

Operating profit is suitable for all businesses where there is turnover, and costs incurred as a result. It is not suitable in businesses such as financial institutions where there is no definable turnover and profit before interest has no meaning.

In small businesses operating profit is often mixed with the owner's remuneration. Without a fair charge for own labour in the business the operating profit may provide a misleading view of the business performance.

In most family limited companies, the directors' remuneration bears no relation to the actual work performed, but is arranged to attract the minimum tax liability. Before the 1984 budget it was generally more beneficial to take out profits in the form of directors' remuneration rather than dividend. After the budget, with low corporation tax rates for small profits and abolition of investment income surcharge, it may be more beneficial to minimise directors' remuneration in order to save national insurance contributions.

Profit before interest and tax is only a good measure where costs:

● are computed at arms' length
● are not mixed with controlling proprietor's remuneration *or*
● are not subject to substantial arbitrary allocation

ORGANISATIONS BEST SUITED

The operating profit measure can be used in all organisations where there are suitable businesses. It can be used in co-operatives, mutual companies, nationalised corporations, trusts and societies, even though ostensibly 'non-profit making'.

Profit is an indicator of funds available for growth, and almost all organisations, regardless of their legal form, wish to grow. Growth is good for management and staff. It provides a measure of security, opportunities for advancement, and the chance of recognition and promotion. Operating profit, which excludes finance costs and profit distribution, is applicable to almost all organisations making financial transactions, except those whose whole business is financial transactions and nothing else.

POWER TO MOTIVATE

The profit motive is well known. It has been the subject of continuous debate for more than a hundred years, both as regards effectiveness and morality. Currently the pendulum has swung towards the virtues of the profit motive. It operates even in Communist countries. China is the latest to embrace profit performance as an important element of its business economy.

In the UK, profit is seen as more important in a highly competitive world. Bonus schemes based on profit apply to 41 per cent of directors and $38\frac{1}{2}$ per cent of managers, according to a recent survey.[5]

Profit is undoubtedly a powerful motivator where the people concerned have some control over it and are aware that they have that control. But profit may not motivate unless it is communicated properly and its meaning explained.

When a business makes a loss, the motivation may be of a different kind. People may look then to survival of the business and their jobs. The negative profit has an effect on the community of managers and staff which might never be produced with positive profits. A strong motivator is the profit and *loss* account when it carries the simple message that we are spending more than our income.

To be effective as a motivator profit must be:

- truly and fairly arrived at
- understandable to the users
- communicated intelligently
- distributed in a manner perceived generally to be fair and reasonable

PROBLEMS AND TROUBLES

The chief problems of operating profit are in the areas of consistency and comparability. Profit is of limited use as a measure of performance if it cannot be compared with earlier periods in the same business, or with similar businesses outside for the same period.

Consistency demands that accounting policies, classifications and methods remain the same from one period to another, or, if there is a change, it requires that the profit and loss account of the previous period be reworked on the new basis.

Comparability between businesses is more difficult to achieve. It can be assisted within a group of companies by the issue of a standard accounting manual, with internal audit to enforce the standard procedures, and between independent companies by statements of standard accounting practice (SSAP), monitored by external audit.

Consistency within the business to some extent conflicts with comparability without. Changes made to improve comparability may damage consistency, and vice versa.

The chief areas in which such changes cause trouble are:

- classifications of expenditure
- methods of cost allocation
- assumptions and methods of depreciation
- stock valuation
- contract work-in-progress
- method of translating accounts in foreign currency to sterling

Under classification of expenditure the main difficulty is the treatment of expenditure which produces benefits extending over more than one year, but which, by convention, is not usually capitalised as an asset.

Profit, being generally only a small percentage of turnover and of costs can be significantly distorted by inconsistent or erroneous treatment of any one item of revenue or expenditure. The trouble spots which apply, in no order of importance, are:

- Transfer pricing   5.1
- Foreign currency translation   5.2
- Stocks and work-in-progress   6.1
- Depreciation   7.1
- Revenue investment   7.2
- Pensions cost   8.1
- Allocation of central costs   8.2
- Extraordinary items   11.1

PENSIONS COSTS

Measures affected

    Value added – distribution only
    Operating profit
    Profit after interest
    Profit after tax

Bases of accountancy which apply

    Historic cost
    Current cost
    Cash flow
    Funds flow

Where found

    In published accounts of companies with own contracted-out pension
      schemes
    In private company accounts with the same
    In divisional accounts of companies with the same

Source of the trouble

A company's own pension scheme is legally under the control of the trustees, the majority of whom are usually appointed by the company board. In practice, in all but a very few cases, the company board can decide on the level of funding necessary to maintain the fund so that it can meet its ultimate liability for the payment of pensions.

The company board is advised by an actuary who values (usually every three years) the assets and liabilities of the fund. In the light of his valuation the actuary makes a recommendation of the amount which the company should contribute to the fund until the next valuation and actuarial report. If the company board wishes to make contributions to the pension fund which are less or more than the actuary's recommendation, it may do so.

The company pension contribution is a charge in the profit and loss account for the year and is actually paid to the pension fund. When profits are low and cash is short, there is an obvious temptation to reduce, or insufficiently increase, the company contribution.

Actuarial valuations can be made on a variety of different objectives, methods and assumptions. Actuaries generally are reluctant to produce precise figures and, if they do, some extra reserve is usually advised.

Actuarial valuation is quite different from the accountant's balance sheet. The actuarial assumptions are made over a very long term (covering up to 60 years). The precise amount required to make up the fund *each year* is impossible to forecast.

Some questions answered

1   What are the objectives of actuarial valuation?

There are basically two:

(a) To establish that the pension fund can meet all its liabilities to potential pensioners (i.e. members of the scheme) if it were closed down at the date of valuation (sometimes known as a discontinuance valuation, a valuation for solvency, or the accrued benefit approach).

(b) To ensure that the on-going ultimate liabilities can be satisfied at the time when pensions have to be paid probably many years ahead (known as the projected benefit or going concern approach).

2   Can these objectives be reconciled or amalgamated?

Not easily. The problem has given rise to a host of valuation methods which aim at a compromise between the two. A recent research study for the Accounting Standards Committee[6] identified five separate projected benefit and discontinuance type methods using seven different formulae for calculating the required contributions to a pension scheme.

3 What are the actuarial assumptions that cause so much trouble?

The projected benefit approaches require assumptions concerning future rates of:

- returns on pension fund investments
- inflation of wages and salaries
- normal progression to higher salary bands
- turnover of staff (i.e. proportion of members of the scheme who leave before retirement age)
- mortality of employees in service (i.e. proportion of members who die before retirement age)
- early retirement (i.e. proportion of members who are given a pension before normal retirement age)

Except for mortality, where there are reliable tables available, the assumptions are built inevitably on shaky foundations.

4 Why is it necessary to look so far ahead if the basic data for the forecast is so inadequate?

Trustees, managers and members of pension schemes do not assume that the scheme will be discontinued. They aim to provide funds for the scheme which will enable all members to be paid the specified benefits on retirement or death. On this view, the short-term ups and downs of return on investment, salary increases and numbers leaving are not likely to be significant in the long-term and should not be considered.

For this purpose, it is argued, what is called *level funding* should be adopted, i.e. a fixed contribution should be paid into the pension fund by the company each year. It is changed only when the actuarial valuation shows definitely and without doubt a substantial change in some trend.

Valuation methods which produce a widely fluctuating contribution (such as some discontinuance methods) are frowned on by many actuaries as conveying a spurious version of what purports to be the correct liability.

5 Do these troubles apply to all pension schemes?

No. If the pension scheme is insured with an insurance company, the employer company pays premiums to insure the pension entitlement. The employer has no influence on the premium calculated.

Insurance companies also manage pension funds on behalf of an employer company. Contributions are paid to the managed fund in the same way as any other pension fund. In this case, the insurance company as manager recommends a company contribution to the fund which is difficult to refute.

6   What about past-service benefits?

These arise when pension schemes have improved their benefits or given credit for previous service with the effect of suddenly increasing the actuarial liabilities of the funds. This may be charged to profit and loss account as a contribution all in one year, or it may be spread over several years (generally no more than 10), or it may be shown as an extraordinary item. The latter is rare.

There is no standard practice on how these past-service benefits should be treated.

In value added statements

Pension contributions are a distribution of value added, not a deduction from it. The company contribution should be included in the distribution to employees. Value added itself is not affected by the troubles of arriving at a true cost of pensions for a particular year.

In divisional accounts

One pension scheme usually covers the pension arrangements of all the divisions or subsidiary companies of a group. Some subsidiaries may have separate schemes and there are often different schemes for different classes of employees (e.g. works, staff, directors).

Company divisions generally are allocated a slice of the group pensions cost, based on total wages and salaries. The composition of workers and staff may, however, differ significantly between one division and another.

For example, division A may have largely young staff, female, with a high turnover rate. Division B, on the other hand, may have largely older staff, male, with a low turnover. In this case, if each division had its own pension scheme, the pension cost per £ of wages and salary would be much lower in division A than in division B.

If the divisions are largely autonomous, the pensions cost to include in the total divisional employment cost should be the cost that would emerge if they each had their own pension schemes but carrying standard group retirement benefits. Otherwise the profit of division A is understated and of division B overstated.

The practical difficulty is in producing actuarial valuations and employer's contribution on a hypothetical basis that reconcile with the actual group valuation.

When to watch out

The different valuation methods can produce very different pensions costs. An actuary, illustrating the results of three different funding plans (the two commonly used and one compromise between them) in a typical example, produced pension costs (i.e. company contributions) as a percentage of salary varying from 10.1 to 16.5 per cent.[7]

There are many service-oriented companies where employment costs (excluding pension costs) are 50 per cent of turnover or more. Take the following example:

	Method 1	*Method 2*
Pension cost as % of salaries	10%	16½%
Turnover	100	100
Salaries	45	45
Other employment costs	5	5
Pensions cost	4.5	7.5
	54.5	57.5
Other expenses	35.5	35.5
	90	93
Profit	10	7
	100	100

In this example a change in the valuation method reduces the profit by 30 per cent.

When employees' remuneration is a high proportion of total costs, that is the time to watch out. Pension contributions disclosed must be related, if possible, to the profile of the scheme in terms of the various ages, sex and turnover of members, and compared with other schemes.

Disclosure of pensions cost information was almost non-existent a few years ago. In the last three years there has been the following, published by the Accounting Standards Committee (ASC):

August 1982:   Pension scheme accounts: ASC discussion paper.
June 1983:   ED 32: Disclosure of pensions information in company accounts.
April 1984:   ED 34: Pension scheme accounts.
November 1984: Statement of intent: Accounting for pension costs.

Pension scheme accounts, when eventually published, should yield a lot of new information. It is suggested that a report on the actuarial valuation should be included. This should give an indication as to whether it has been made on a stringent or a liberal basis.

There is no possibility of standardising the actuarial methods and assumptions, but it will be possible, with some expertise, to judge whether the actuarially recommended contribution looks fair by comparison with others and whether, indeed, the recommended contribution has actually been paid by the company to the fund.

What should be done – the author's view

Pension costs are the longest-term costs in the book. They are therefore bound to be full of assumptions where one man's idea is as good as another.

But, in my view, the projected benefit methods of valuation project too far. Performance measures must assume a going concern, but not a concern going for 50 or 60 years. The maximum time to look ahead for most businesses planning ahead is 10 years – perhaps 20 years at the outside for industries such as electricity generation.

On those grounds I would favour a compromise between discontinuance and going concern methods.

I do not see the need for stability in contributions or 'level funding'. If a pension liability is clearly increased or reduced, it should be reflected in the current profit and loss account. Like any other exceptional item, it can be ignored in the short term but it must be taken to heart in the long term.

Accountants can do all the levelling out if they wish and it seems inappropriate for there to be a large actuarial reserve or extra liability which is not passed into the company accounts. Perhaps the most important thing is that actuaries and accountants should understand each other better.

ALLOCATION OF CENTRAL COSTS

Measures affected

Value added
Operating profit
Profit after interest
Profit after tax
Operating cash flow
Operating funds flow

Bases of accounting which apply

Historic cost
Current cost
Cash flow
Funds flow

Where found

In divisional accounts only

Source of the trouble

Large organisations are difficult to manage, difficult to control, require numerous regulations and instructions, become bureaucratic, out of touch with the people doing the real work, fail to motivate, and so on. The well known solution is decentralisation, dividing the colossus into smaller units or divisions which, as far as possible, are their own masters.

The trouble with decentralisation is that it requires continuous monitoring of the performance of each division to ensure that it is achieving the objectives set out for it, which are usually expressed in some form of profit, or occasionally value added.

Never can the central head office be eliminated altogether, although many large organisations have very small central costs – less than 1 per cent of turnover. The decentralisation fashion has spread to medium-sized and smaller organisations where there tends to be a higher proportion of head office costs with a more significant allocation problem.

Some head office costs, such as management consultancy and central computer services, can be charged to divisions on a usage basis just as though they were bought from outside. But for smaller organisations, with only a few divisions, the cost of setting up a sophisticated charging system may not be worth it, and they fall back on more simple arbitrary allocations of central service costs. These may well be acceptable, but the true measurement of the performance of the division is jeopardised.

Some questions answered:

1 Is it necessary to allocate central costs at all?

   If the costs are relatively small and there is no basis for allocation, as in the case of prestige advertising and board room expenses, non-allocation is a reasonable solution. If the costs are substantial – say, over 5 per cent of turnover – the purposes of allocation need to be fully considered.

2 What are the purposes of allocation?

   In general they are:
   ● to provide a complete picture of a division's performance including all the costs attributable to it
   ● to make divisional management aware of the costs incurred on their behalf
   ● to ensure that, when fixing selling prices, the full cost (including head office cost) is considered
   ● to make divisions as far as possible comparable with one another

3 What is meant exactly by 'allocation'?

   Allocation here means the calculation on an arbitrary basis (e.g. as a percentage of turnover, value added, capital employed, wages or salaries, number of employees) of costs incurred by head office attributable to the division and the inclusion of those costs in the total costs of the division. In some quarters (e.g. ICMA official terminology[8]) allocation as above is defined as 'apportionment', allocation being 'the charging of discrete identifiable items of cost'.

In this book 'charging' is referred to as charging, not as allocation, when a system is set up to charge for a head office service in the same way as if it were purchased from outside the organisation.

4 Does charging for head office services eliminate the problem?

It would do, if:

(a) The head office service is independent of the divisions,
(b) The divisions have discretion to use the services or not, and
(c) The service is charged at a market price.

Usually these conditions are difficult to achieve. A market price may not exist and we are then up against the problems of cost-based transfer pricing discussed in trouble spot 5.1 (p. 34).

Nevertheless charging is usually better than allocation, if the cost of the system is not excessive. At least those divisions using the service more are charged more.

5 Can all head office costs be regarded as services to divisions?

Some costs can, for example

● data processing services
● internal printing
● management consultancy
● legal department
● specific research project

Others cannot, for example

● pension scheme administration
● company secretarial
● board and directors
● general research
● group finance and accounts

The latter group of costs have inevitably to be allocated to divisions or omitted.

6 How wrong is arbitrary allocation likely to be?

Suppose a situation where head office costs are $7\frac{1}{2}$ per cent of turnover – perhaps typical of many medium-sized companies. Central costs are allocated pro rata to turnover so that $7\frac{1}{2}$ per cent is allocated to each division.

In such a situation A may have a much smaller usage of central services than division B, particularly if A's average transaction is £10 000 while B's is £100. If B's usage is double that of A, then the allocation should be on the basis of 5 per cent to A and 10 per cent to B. The difference of 5 per cent profit on turnover could well be the difference between profit and loss at the bottom line.

7 Does management style enter into it?

There is some research evidence that it does.[1] Arbitrary allocations can be accepted by divisional managers where it is clear, understandable and stable, i.e. the method and formulae do not change. The allocation can be regarded as a kind of tax or levy imposed by head office and operations have to be planned with that in mind. Such a philosophy may indeed in some companies motivate managers more than a stream of charges, to be checked and queried, from head office departments.

Divisional independence and the presence of a market price for services perhaps determines the allocation/charging dilemma more than management style. If a charge rate is unrealistic or seen to be unfair, the result may be continually under challenge.

When to watch out

The occasions when the profit of divisions may be badly adrift are when central costs are high and there is considerable arbitrary allocation of those costs, or there may be considerable charging but at artificial rates, producing a result little better than allocation.

The artificial charge rates occur, of course, when there is little independence between divisions (i.e. heavy interdependence) so that head office has in effect to determine the charge rates on transfer prices (as explained in trouble spot 5.1, p. 34).

Arbitrariness may be all right as a means of control and as a means of motivation. Motivationally a simple impression may be better than the detailed truth. But as a means of measuring performance it can simply measure it wrongly, which is no good when one comes to appraising the earning power of particular divisions.

What should be done – the author's opinion

The less independent are the divisions, the more has any performance measure to be examined and appraised. It may be that turnover is not affected by the constraints on independence whereas certain costs are. The measurement may be fair enough at the turnover or gross margin level but not for operating profit.

In my view, there is no simple solution if there is not practically full independence. Measurement can then only be taken as far as it can go without bringing in significant arbitrary allocations. At the point where it gets stuck, explanation and consultation are needed to ensure that those using the results fully understand the position. If there is a lack of independent decision on important revenues and costs at almost all levels, no true measurement of performance is possible, and there is no true decentralisation.

9 Profit after interest

DEFINITION

There are two definitions of the interest that may be deducted from profit before interest to arrive at profit after interest:

(1) Interest actually payable in a period by a company or division on the loans and bank overdraft advanced to it.
(2) Interest that would normally be payable if the company or division were financed entirely by loans at market rates of interest or at a rate that would have some relation (for a division) to the overall cost of finance to the group.

Actual interest (1) is used in annual published accounts. The amount depends on the amount of borrowing, or gearing. If borrowings are large, the company is highly geared; if borrowings are small, gearing is low.

Calculated interest (2) is used in internal management accounts, including subsidiary companies' accounts, which are charged with calculated interest on loans or current accounts with the group head office.

ACCOUNTANCY

Where interest is calculated for internal accounts, there are two numbers needed:

(1) The amount of capital on which interest should be charged.
(2) The rate of interest to be used.

The amount of capital employed in a division or company is derived from a balance sheet or statement of assets and liabilities. The exact assets and liabilities counted in and the value put upon them must be the subject of rules laid down by the accountant. The rules must be set to provide consistency from period to period and, as far as possible, comparability between divisions. The basis of capital employed is described fully in Chapter 18 (p. 214).

The rate of interest used in internal accounts may be:

(a) A market rate, e.g.
  ● bank base rate plus 2 per cent
  ● current rate charged on company overdrafts, or
(b) A composite rate reflecting the group *cost of capital*, which is an average of interest on loans and dividends paid over a year, or
(c) A rate determined by the head office in the light of strategic objectives (in particular, whether it is necessary to reduce or encourage capital spending).

UNDERLYING PHILOSOPHY

The profit after interest in published accounts often has little bearing on business performance, because the interest is only a part of the cost of using the capital employed in the business. Indeed, the profit after interest figure is not always shown in published profit and loss accounts, and it is not legally necessary to do so.

For internal management accounts, capital employed by a division can be taken into account in two ways:

(1) By computing a *residual income*, or profit after interest, the interest being calculated by applying a market or composite rate to capital employed.
(2) By calculating a percentage rate of *return on capital employed* (ROCE), i.e.

$$\frac{\text{Profit before interest}}{\text{Amount of capital employed}}$$

(See Chapter 18, page 215)

Nearly all companies organised in divisions (82 per cent in a recent survey) calculate an ROCE for each division. But a fair number (32 per cent in the survey) use residual income; 23 per cent in the survey used both residual income and ROCE.[1]

Companies using a profit after interest in their internal accounts appear to be those (from the limited survey) which wish to impress on their divisions the cost of finance. They see interest as a cost which, like any other expenditure, divisions can control to some extent through the amount of capital employed.

Companies which are already heavily borrowed may be the most likely to use interest charges in this way. 'Cash rich' companies, with plenty of money for investment, may have little need to discourage increased capital investment in their divisions.

It is also likely that companies promoting autonomous decentralised divisions favour a profit after interest measures. The inclusion of a fair charge for interest on capital may give a feeling of further independence from head office.

BUSINESSES BEST SUITED

Interest paid by companies with a share capital is of little use in measurement of the company performance. This is due to variations of gearing from company to company and from year to year. As a measure of profit available for shareholders, interest must, of course, be taken into account, but not for a measure of the performance of the business, unless the business is the same as the company.

Profit after interest, calculated on total capital employed in the business, is a most suitable measure when there is a considerable amount of capital employed in the business and particularly if a large part of it is working capital, i.e. stocks and debtors, less creditors.

Profit after interest, calculated on capital employed, is *not* useful where there is:

● no ready means of evaluating consistently the assets in use
● a new business, or a recently acquired business, where the capacity is known to be in excess of what is required
● a large capital project, extending over several years, which would suffer an interest charge without any corresponding revenue
● very little capital employed, as in many service businesses, e.g. window cleaning, painting and decorating
● a position of low or even negative capital employed due to customer payments in advance, e.g. in some construction businesses, magazine publishing by subscription

ORGANISATIONS BEST SUITED

An interest charge on divisional capital appears to work best in organisations which have a considerable capital requirement in each of its divisions, preferably of working capital, rather than long-term fixed capital.

The organisation needs to have considerable knowledge and financial expertise in order to work out the most acceptable and yet rigorous formula that can endure through substantial changes in capital employed, interest rates and profit or loss.

POWER TO MOTIVATE

Where capital available is scarce and interest rates are high, there is a need to economise on the use of capital. An interest charge related to capital used does encourage managers to use capital efficiently. If bonuses are based on profit after interest the motivation can be very strong.

Fixed assets, such as long-life plant and machinery, cannot easily be controlled by a manager so that the interest charge may just be regarded as an imposition that cannot be changed. A charge on working capital, however, can have a significant effect and certainly encourages managers to reduce stocks and debtors where it can be done without damaging turnover.

PROBLEMS AND TROUBLES

The problems of interest in internal management accounts arise in three areas:

(1) The amount of capital employed: what assets should be included (see Chapter 18, p. 218).
(2) The basis on which the assets included in the capital employed should be valued: whether they should be at historic or replacement cost and gross or net of depreciation (see Chapter 18, p. 219).
(3) The interest rate to be applied: whether it should be based on market rates or on the average cost of capital of the company.

In published accounts the problems of computing a useful profit after interest usually prevent it being taken as a viable performance measure. In the accounts of companies with a simple capital structure, where interest paid is back interest only, there are few problems provided that the financial structure remains the same. A new problem has arisen for companies obtaining loans for major capital projects the interest on which can be capitalised; the details are in trouble spot 9.2 (p. 108).

The full list of trouble spots that could apply to profit at this level is given below:

- Transfer pricing   5.1
- Foreign currency translation   5.2
- Stocks and work-in-progress   6.1
- Depreciation   7.1
- Revenue investment   7.2
- Pensions cost   8.1
- Allocation of central costs   8.2
- Interest and cost of capital   9.1
- Capitalisation of interest   9.2
- Extraordinary items   11.1

INTEREST AND COST OF CAPITAL

Measures affected

> Profit after interest
> Profit after tax

Bases of accounting which apply

> Historic cost
> Current cost

Where found

> In divisional accounts

Source of the trouble

Interest charges are sometimes included in divisional management accounts and sometimes not. If interest is included, it is being regarded as a cost of the division. The division needs capital to operate and capital has to be financed from somewhere; therefore it is right that interest be charged – so the argument goes.

This is all very well, but the division is not the same as a self-contained business. It may have full autonomy in pricing, purchasing, personnel, selling, marketing and operating, but it cannot have in the long-term autonomy in finance. Because the division is part of a large group, it can never know what it would have to pay in interest and/or dividends if it were on its own, without that backing.

Therefore, a rate of interest has to be assumed or calculated on the basis of what the group may pay. If each division were on its own, as a separate business under separate ownership, the costs of finance would be different in each business. The interest and dividends which the independent business pays would depend on its past profits and its ability to obtain loans. In theory each division should be charged interest at different rates according to its record and the risk involved in its business, but that is impossible in practice. Nobody in the UK, as far as we know, does it.

Some questions answered

1 What methods are used in charging interest?

There are basically only two which seem practical:

(a) A market rate of interest, or
(b) A group cost of capital rate.

2 How is a market rate arrived at?

The market interest rate may be the current bank overdraft rate charged to the group, or bank base rate plus a certain percentage, or, to save altering the rate frequently, a rate which appears to be reasonable over three or six months. It is not a rate which a division or group will actually have paid on its total borrowings, unless they are financed totally by bank overdraft and the rate is changed exactly in time with the changes in bank base-rate.

3 How is a group cost of capital calculated?

It is technical and complicated. It recognises that the capital of a group is usually a mixture of loans, retained profits and share capital; to put it in terms of finance, a mixture of debt and equity.

The interest on the loan (or debt) part of it is fairly easy, except where old loans carry unrealistic fixed rates of interest. The loans may then be valued at the market price.

The equity part is difficult and controversial. Clearly the dividend paid to shareholders is not a sufficient measure. They own, in theory,

the retained profits from previous years which could have been paid
in dividend, but have gone to increase the value of the group. These
retained profits are part of the capital which must earn a return.

The value of profits retained as capital rather than paid out as
dividend is reflected, in the case of a public company, in its share
price quoted on the Stock Exchange. The price/earnings ratio (P/E,
see Chapter 20, p. 243 could be taken as an indicator of the value of
retained profits and the cost of finance to the company. (The higher
the P/E, the lower the cost of capital.) But then we make the cost of
capital rate depend on the earnings, i.e. profit after taxation. If we
then deduct the cost of capital from profits of divisions, we are going
round in a circle.

In any case, not all groups with divisions are quoted companies. In
private or unquoted companies valuation of retained profits is full of
problems (and very expensive if it has to be done professionally).

Stock market prices too are volatile, going up and down from day to
day. The price to be used is largely a matter of convenience, e.g. a
weekly or monthly average, or the mean between high and low?

Even if we can solve all these problems, the cost of equity capital
must be combined with the interest on loans to arrive at an average
cost of capital. This has to be weighted as the example below:

	Amount £m	Average rate	Total cost
Equity: Share capital and retained profits	60	8%	= 4.8
Loans: Debentures and bank overdraft	40	11%	= 4.4
	100		9.2

The weighted average cost of capital is 9.2 per cent.

This 9.2 per cent rate would be applied to the capital employed in
each division and deducted from operating profit to produce a profit
after interest. It is more likely to be called a capital charge than an
interest charge, the connection with interest being somewhat remote.

4   Which method is better: market rate or group cost of capital?

The capital charge may seem to be remote to the divisions. Managers may not be able to understand its basis and, if they do, may query why that particular capital structure of equity and loans should apply to their division. In one survey[1], out of 18 companies showing a profit after interest or capital charge in their divisional accounts, only seven used an average cost of capital.

An interest charge based on market rates is simple to understand and is clearly realistic in the case of working capital, which is often financed by bank overdraft.

The capital charge based on the group cost of capital is an attempt to allocate the cost over divisions. Like many allocations it produces questionable results.

When to watch out

Any interest or capital charge chosen is artificial. Care must be taken to ensure that the profit after interest is not applied too strictly.

With a large new capital investment, for example, the interest charge to a division may increase dramatically. This is not to say that the investment is bad or that the charge is wrong. The result has to be considered in the light of the time taken for the investment to bear fruit in the form of increased profit.

What should be done – the author's view

Where capital is scarce, the use of it must be accounted for and the cost included in the performance measurement. How the capital is financed is irrelevant and therefore a charge for capital has to be made that fits the situation.

The charge made can only be approximate and somewhat arbitrary, but it is worth making to show that the cost exists. It is probably less arbitrary than depreciation.

Generally, I believe that the interest or capital charge is a better way of accounting for capital employed than the percentage return on capital employed. The issue is discussed further in Chapter 18 (p. 214).

CAPITALISATION OF INTEREST

Measures affected

Profit after interest
Profit after tax

Bases of accounting which apply

Historic cost
Current cost

Where found

In published accounts of construction companies and new companies
In divisional accounts of such companies where interest is charged

Source of the trouble

Many European countries and the USA have for many years allowed interest paid on loans raised to finance large capital projects to be capitalised along with all the other costs of the project. The interest so included in the capital cost is not then charged in the profit and loss account as interest payable.

The EEC Fourth Directive on published accounts included specifically the feature of capitalised interest, and this has been incorporated in the Companies Act 1981 (Schedule 1, clause 26(3)(4)). The Act says only that interest on capital borrowed *may* be included in the production cost of the asset, provided that it is disclosed in a note to the accounts.

With high interest rates the interest paid to finance a capital project lasting three years could be very substantial, perhaps 20–25 per cent of the production cost. The capitalisation would increase the profit after interest by considerable amounts if all such interest were capitalised. The interest, being part of a fixed asset, is subject to depreciation, which is charged in the profit and loss account, but this would reduce the benefit to profits by only 5 or 10 per cent of the interest.

Some questions answered

1 How is the rate of interest applicable to the project determined?

Rarely is it possible to earmark a loan for a specific project. The weighted average rate of interest on all loans and overdrafts in existence during the period of the project has to be applied to the capital cost. It is not possible to capitalise interest which has not been paid. Equity cost of capital may not be taken as interest.

2 What companies can use the option to capitalise interest?

It can be used by any company with sufficiently large long-term projects financed by borrowing. There is as yet no accounting standard on the subject which circumscribes the use or method of capitalising the interest.

In divisional accounts

Interest could be capitalised, but it should be part of a comprehensive scheme for charging interest on capital employed in the division (see trouble spot 9.1, p. 104).

When to watch out

A business which is capitalising interest will show higher profits than otherwise and may well convert a loss into a profit. When capitalisation is first used, the profit will not be consistent with earlier years and may be difficult to adjust in order to show a fair comparison.

What should be done – the author's opinion

Capitalisation of interest, prior to the 1981 Act, was forbidden on the grounds that it was not part of a fixed asset, but only a means of financing it. This was perhaps a conservative view, but in line with many other conservative conventions in UK accounts. To be logical, other conservative practices, such as excessive depreciation and writing down asset costs to net realisable value, should also be abandoned.

Ironically the capitalisation of interest, in increasing the cost of the fixed asset, makes it more exposed in theory to a market value that is lower than cost. In large construction projects, of course, this is well nigh impossible to prove – the value of the project, or lack of it, will not be established until some years later.

10 Profit after taxation

DEFINITION

Profit after tax means profit after deducting tax based on that profit for the period in question.

The tax based on profit in the UK is corporation tax. In a group of companies with overseas branches or subsidiaries, similar taxes are levied overseas. Tax on profits made abroad is then included.

There are many taxes paid by businesses which are not included in the tax charge shown in accounts. Examples are local rates, employer's national insurance contributions, vehicle licence duties, development land tax, stamp duty and VAT in excess of what has been charged to customers. These taxes are regarded as business costs and therefore charged against operating profit.

Corporation tax is not generally regarded as a cost. It is not, however, based entirely on profit. Dividends paid cause a charge to corporation tax irrespective of profit. If a dividend is higher than the taxable profit, the corporation tax payable becomes based on the dividend, not the profit.

Capital gains tax is included in corporation tax. Although not part of normal activities, capital gains are generally included in published profit and loss accounts. They may be included as an extraordinary item (see trouble spot 11.1, p. 142) in which case the relative tax is usually deducted from the extraordinary item. Otherwise it is included in the tax charge.

The tax charged in accounts is not likely to be tax actually paid or even the tax which the Inland Revenue will demand for the year covered by the accounts. In the case of capital gains particularly, the actual tax on the gain may not be paid for many years, if ever.

In many published accounts the word 'taxation' is used rather than 'tax'. Taxation conveys the idea of a process leading to some estimate of tax to be paid, which may distinguish it from 'tax' that is regarded as a cost.

Government grants, although sometimes regarded as negative taxation, are never deducted from taxes. They are usually deducted from the cost of the building or plant for which the grant is given, or credited directly to profit and loss account over several years, according to the expected life of the grant-aided asset.

UNDERLYING PHILOSOPHY

Profit after taxation is the key to company performance from the point of view of the stock market and dividend distribution. It is the basis of the two main financial ratios: earnings per share and price/earnings ratio, explained in Chapter 20 (p. 243).

It is normally the bottom line of the profit and loss account with nothing further to add or deduct except extraordinary items. It is probably the figure which most readers of published accounts look for, in particular when compared with last year.

Until taxation is taken into account, the 'distributable profit' or the 'profit attributable to the shareholders' cannot be known. Profit after taxation is what the shareholders can take home when everyone else has had their pick.

But as a measure of performance, profit after taxation is not very useful. Profit before taxation is likely to be more comparable from year to year. Tax rates and tax allowances can change and this can play havoc with comparisons. Business performance is clearly not improved just because tax rates are reduced, or diminished just because a tax allowance is withdrawn.

If there were no special tax allowances, and all capital allowances for plant and equipment were the same as accounting depreciation, and provided the corporation tax rate is not changed, the comparison of pre-tax profits would show exactly the same picture as the comparison of post-tax profits. Profit before tax would be all that is needed; everyone would know that 50 per cent, or whatever the rate is, would be dedicated to the taxman.

The corporation tax system, which started in 1965 as fairly simple, became more and more complex until accounting profits became wildly different from taxable profits. The taxation charge in accounts became more important because no one could guess what it was until the accountants had sorted out the problems of first-year capital allowances, stock relief, large losses brought forward and the tax on dividend (known as ACT), to name but a few.

The taxation charge, though nothing to do with company performance, became in some way a measure of the company's efficiency in tax planning and its ability not only to use all the tax devices available but also to interpret the accounting standards on tax charges in the most favourable light for the 'bottom line' in the company's profit and loss account.

BUSINESSES BEST SUITED

Profit after taxation is essential to businesses needing to know the final 'take-home pay'.

In small businesses, however, where profit may be taken out as dividend or as directors' or owners' remuneration, the taxation charge on profit may convey nothing except the manner in which the profit has been distributed. Indeed, everything should have been arranged in advance to obtain the lowest tax liability.

In divisions or business units of large groups a taxation charge may be far from straightforward. There are two snags here. One is 'group relief'; the other is when the tax is not determined by profit, but by dividend – the problem of ACT. Both these snags are discussed in trouble spots 10.2 and 10.3 (pp. 125 and 135).

In our survey only 5 per cent of companies calculated a profit after taxation for divisions.[1] The reasons were basically that the allocation of tax to divisions was too difficult, that the impact of tax on divisional managers was too remote, or that the group tax liability was not anyway based on profit, most usually because of dividends being higher than *taxable* profit.

ORGANISATIONS BEST SUITED

Organisations which must use profit after taxation are public companies quoted on the Stock Exchange. All other organisations should regard it with some scepticism.

Even as a measure of distributable profit, profit after taxation may be misleading. No company should decide on a dividend on profit after taxation without considering cash flow (see Chapter 15, p. 188).

POWER TO MOTIVATE

Profit after taxation has little motivational effect unless there are managers and other employees interested in company dividends or distributable profit. This may be the case where there is a profit sharing scheme based on after-tax profit or where employees hold shares. Generally, however, cash schemes (as opposed to share schemes) are based on profit before taxation, which is much closer to the understanding of employees.[9]

In the few companies in the survey[1] where a profit after taxation was computed for each division in spite of the difficulties, it was said to be useful. The 'bottom line' gave a feeling of greater independence simulating more faithfully the accounts of an independent company. The advantage of divisional managers being able to see the whole picture may outweigh any trouble caused by an arbitrary allocation of tax.

PROBLEMS AND TROUBLES

The main problems of profit after taxation arise from the necessity of expenditure to match with revenue all the way down the profit and loss account. When it gets to the bottom line, this 'matching principle' becomes highly debatable, but it has, up to now, been maintained in accounting standards.

Profit before taxation represents the difference between matching revenue and expenditure. When a further expenditure is entered, i.e. corporation tax, it too must match with profit before taxation, so the argument goes.

As corporation tax is based on a very different concept of profit (i.e. taxable profit) from the accounting profit, the problems of computing the tax that would have been paid if the tax rules were the same as the conventions of the profit and loss accounts are legion. Some of these are listed below:

- capital allowances greatly in excess of accounting depreciation
- 'deferred tax' arising from the excess allowances
- 'rollover relief' on capital gains
- irrecoverable ACT due to dividends being in excess of taxable profit
- tax losses in previous years
- double taxation relief on profits overseas

Capital allowances and deferred taxation are explained at some length in trouble spot 10.1 (p. 117); surplus ACT in trouble spot 10.2 (p. 128).

Profit after taxation for divisions of a group raises a further complication known as group relief. This is explained in trouble spot 10.3 (p. 135).

There are many other points where the matching of tax charge with profit hits snags, but they are either of minor significance or apply with force only in particular situations. A short check-list, not by any means comprehensive, is given below:

- entertaining expenses other than for overseas visitors
- professional charges of a capital nature
- general provisions for bad debts
- political and charitable donations
- certain installations (especially in offices) not qualifying for capital allowances although subject to depreciation
- restrictions on capital allowances for expensive motor cars
- sales of assets on which capital allowances have been given
- Government employment and other subsidies

The 1984 Budget has eliminated some problems but made others, in the medium term, worse.

Stock relief, which was given to alleviate the extra costs of acquiring materials due to inflation, has been abolished completely. It no longer should appear in any list of differences between accounting and taxable profit.

The radical changes, however, in capital allowances and future rates of corporation tax will make the problems of matching profit and taxation more difficult over the next few years.

The full list of trouble spots affecting profit after taxation in published and private company accounts is:

- Foreign currency translation   5.2
- Stocks and work-in-progress   6.1
- Depreciation   7.1
- Revenue investment   7.2
- Pensions cost   8.1
- Capitalisation of interest   9.2
- Capital allowances and deferred taxation   10.1
- Dividends, surplus ACT and losses   10.2
- Extraordinary items   11.1

CAPITAL ALLOWANCES AND DEFERRED TAXATION

Measures affected

Value added (distribution only)
Profit after taxation
All-inclusive profit

Bases of accounting which apply

Historic cost
Current cost

Where found

In published accounts
In private company accounts
In small business accounts (sometimes)
In divisional accounts (rarely)

Source of the trouble

Depreciation in accounts is not the same as depreciation for tax purposes:

(1) Depreciation in accounts is based on the useful life of the asset in the business, taking into consideration obsolescence as well as wear and tear.

(2) Depreciation for tax purposes is based on fiscal and economic policy, depending particularly on whether the Government wishes to encourage capital investment, to retard it or to be neutral. This purpose is reflected in the term *capital allowance*, which in 1970 replaced the term 'wear and tear' allowance.

The beginning of the real trouble was in 1972 when the capital allowance for plant and machinery was increased to 100 per cent in the year when it was acquired. This meant, of course, that the whole cost of any plant and machinery was charged against profits for tax purposes immediately. Depreciation in accounts, however, continued as before.

There was thus a yawning gap between accounting depreciation and the capital allowance for tax. The tax payable for any particular year became totally unrelated to the profit before tax and the profit and loss account.

Something had to be done about making the tax charge in the accounts match the profit shown in the accounts. The result was a series of edicts by the Accounting Standards Committee: SSAP 11 in 1976, followed by SSAP 15 in 1978 and ED 33 in 1983.[3] Each caused a considerable amount of controversy and disagreement. There is still no consensus on the matter.

There have been for many years other cases where profit for tax purposes does not match accounting profit, requiring a provision to be made for *deferred taxation*. But these cases are usually what are known as short-term timing differences compared with 100 per cent first-year capital allowances (FYA), which cause long-term timing differences.

The treatment of short-term timing differences is not very controversial. Usually they make little difference to the tax charge in the profit and loss account. On occasions, however, there may be a substantial effect on profit after taxation.

Some questions answered

1   What is a timing difference?

A timing difference comes about when an item of revenue or expenditure is put into a different year in the profit and loss account from that required for profit for corporation tax.

Interest received is a simple case of timing difference. In the profit and loss account it is shown on an *accruals basis*; for tax purposes only actual receipts are counted.

For example, if interest is received half-yearly on 31 March and 30 September, and the company accounts year-end is 31 December 1984, the three months' interest to 31 December (not yet received) has 'accrued', and must therefore be included in revenue for the year 1984. The interest in the accounts is then usually called interest receivable. The interest for tax purposes is the interest received without any accrual of the unpaid three months.

There is a timing difference due to the three months' interest to 31 December being included in the profit and loss account for the year 1984, while for tax purposes it is included in 1985 (being received on 31 March 1985).

Suppose the annual interest in this example is £120, corporation tax is 50 per cent and the deposit of £1000 on which 12 per cent interest is received was made on 1 April. For tax purposes the interest received for the year 1984 is £60 (half-year to September 30). For accounts purposes the interest receivable is £90 (nine months to December 31).

On the £30 difference, tax is payable at 50 per cent, i.e. £15. As the accounts include £30 accrued revenue in 1984, they must also include the £15 tax in 1984. But the Inland Revenue does not ask for it until 1985, when it is received.

The unwanted £15 is therefore regarded as deferred tax. It has to be paid because the £30 has been earned, but not paid yet.

Such differences as these on interest received are usually referred to in published accounts as 'short-term and other timing differences'. Generally with these there is no problem. The amounts involved are usually small and certain, with only a one-year overlap.

2 How are capital allowances different?

With capital allowances the problem is much more complex. They come in a variety of colours, with different allowances for plant and machinery, motor cars, industrial buildings, small business workshops, hotels, mines and agricultural works.

All the capital allowances, except those for motor cars, have some element of investment incentive, providing a much higher allowance in the year when the asset is brought into use than normal depreciation. Hence these capital allowances are sometimes referred to as *accelerated depreciation*.

3 What did the 1984 Budget do?

The 1984 Budget changed the system radically as is shown in the table below:

First year capital allowances (FYA)

% of capital cost	*Before 14/3/84*	*14/3/84 to 31/3/85*	*1/4/85 to 31/3/86*	*After 1/4/86*
Plant, machinery and vehicles (except cars)	100	75	50	25
Industrial buildings	75	50	25	4
Hotels	20	20	20	4
Agricultural works	20	20	20	10

After 1/4/86 the allowances shown are annual allowances. Accelerated capital allowances disappear. In the case of plant, machinery and vehicles the annual allowance is calculated on the same basis as reducing balance depreciation (see trouble spot 7.1, p. 69). For companies using fixed instalment depreciation (almost all large companies) there will remain a difference between the annual capital allowance and the accounting depreciation for several years to come.

4 How does deferred taxation arise from the FYA?

Let us take as an example a company with one fixed asset (e.g. a specialised concrete mixing lorry) which is purchased and is expected to have a life of four years.

The lorry cost £100 000 in 1983; depreciation is therefore £25 000 per annum.

In the first year:

£100 000 is deducted from taxable profit.
£25 000 is deducted from accounting profit.

In the second year:

> *Nil* is deducted from taxable profit.
> £25 000 continues to be deducted from accounting profit.

To put this anomaly right the taxation charge in the accounts would be calculated as if the tax allowance was £25 000 each year and not £100 000 in the first year only.

Assuming corporation tax at 50 per cent, there is £50 000 less tax to pay on account of the purchase of the lorry. This would not be deducted from the tax charge all at once but would be taken at £12 500 each year, exactly matching the depreciation.

At the end of the first year there would be £37 500 corporation tax relief which belongs to the next three years in the accounting sense. This £37 500 is *deferred tax*, the result of a timing difference between the depreciation period for tax purposes (one year) and the depreciation period for the accounts (four years).

5 How is deferred taxation affected by a change in the tax rate?

The 1984 Budget changed not only capital allowances but also the corporation tax rates. For companies with more than £500 000 annual taxable profit the corporation tax rates will be:

Financial year	Rate per cent
1982	52
1983	50
1984	45
1985	40
1986	35

For 1984 deferred tax provided at 52 or 50 per cent is excessive, when the corporation rate will be only 45 per cent. In the case of the lorry, instead of £12 500 each year, the amounts of deferred tax should be:

1984	£11 250
1985	£10 000
1986	£8 750

This is the case where full provision for deferred taxation has been made. But in many companies this is not so.

6   What companies do not provide for full deferred taxation?

If a company is expanding and making new capital investment each year, with 100 per cent capital allowances the tax relief before the Budget could continue almost indefinitely. The tax relief could become almost permanent and should, it was argued, be treated as a permanent exemption.

If the company owning the concrete mixer lorry, for example, was expanding and purchased a second lorry after two years, the company would have obtained another £100 000 capital allowance with a further £12 500 a year deferred tax, making the combined provision for the two lorries £25 000 a year. If there was continued expansion of the lorry fleet, deferred tax would pile up with very little chance of it ever being needed.

To cover this situation an accounting standard (SSAP 15), *Accounting for deferred taxation* was issued.[3] It ruled that deferred tax need not be provided where 'the tax benefit can be expected with reasonable probability to be retained in the future'. This exemption from providing deferred taxation was hedged by further detailed requirements, but the key criteria remained extremely vague.

The result was that companies could provide or not provide for deferred taxation almost at will. The tax charge in the profit and loss account could vary by very large sums according to the opinion of a very few people as to whether there was a 'reasonable probability' or not. The after-tax profit was, in many cases, no longer trusted as a measure of performance. Companies making substantial capital expenditures seemed to divide into those which provided for deferred taxation and those which did not. In an economic climate as uncertain as that of 1981 it was impossible to foresee the future with any confidence for more than a few months ahead.

In June 1983 a new standard was proposed (in the shape of an exposure draft ED 33, *Accounting for deferred tax*[3]) with the intention of tightening up the rules for exemption from providing for deferred taxation. The wording of the basic criteria was to be improved and there was to be a requirement that management intentions and financial plans should be considered. Then in March 1984 came the Budget.

7 How does the 1984 Budget affect provision for deferred taxation?

The effect of the changes in the capital allowances and corporation tax rates on deferred taxation are profound. There are two possible cases:

(1) Where deferred taxation has been provided, the provision becomes excessive, as we have seen with our one mixer lorry. The 100 per cent capital allowance carried forward to cover the same number of years as depreciation is not worth as much as it was in terms of tax.

(2) Where, relying on SSAP 15,[3] deferred taxation has not been provided, the assumption that new investment and 100 per cent capital allowances will continue in the future becomes untenable. Deferred taxation of some kind suddenly becomes required because there are no further accelerated capital allowances to justify continued exemption.

Let us suppose that there is continued expansion in the mixer lorry company and it is decided that no deferred taxation need be provided. The other assumptions for this exercise are:

(a) A new lorry is purchased every year at a cost of £100 000.
(b) Depreciation is 25 per cent per annum.
(c) Each new lorry produces an operating profit of £15 000.
(d) The company earns a steady operating profit of £70 000 on other activities with negligible fixed assets – therefore no depreciation, no capital allowances.
(e) Inflation is zero.

Before the 1984 Budget, as long as the company continued to buy new lorries, the 100 per cent capital allowance provided a 'tax shield' for the other activities, leaving no corporation tax to pay (except ACT, see trouble spot 10.2, p. 128).

For this company, however, the party is over in 1986, when there is £52 000 corporation tax to pay notwithstanding the lower rate of tax, as shown in the table overleaf.

Profits and tax

(£'000)	1983	1984	1985	1986
(1) Operating profit	85	100	115	130
(2) Interest payable	10	20	30	40
(3) Profit after interest (1−2)	75	80	85	90
(4) *Add*: Depreciation	25	50	75	100
(5) Profit before taxation and depreciation (3 + 4)	100	130	160	190
Capital allowances on:				
(6) New lorries	100	75	50	25
(7) Old lorries	—	—	6	17
(8) Total (6 + 7)	100	75	56	42
(9) Taxable profit (5−8)	—	55	104	148
(10) Corporation tax rate	50%	45%	40%	35%
(11) Tax payable	—	25	42	52

If the company had provided for deferred taxation, this large increase in the tax charge would not have arisen. Should we then provide for it now? Without the tax shield of capital allowances on the new lorries, the £70 000 profit on other activities would have attracted tax in 1983 of £35 000. In 1986 £25 000 will have to be paid certainly – if the figures can be projected so far. It could be argued that much of the increase belongs to 1986, not to any earlier years.

Unfortunately for accounting the Chancellor of the Exchequer told us of his plans three years in advance. If it had come as a sudden shock each year the liability could be adjusted each year.

8 What are the new rules (post-Budget) on deferred taxation?

The troubles will not finish entirely in 1986. Projecting the capital allowances for a further period, assuming now a fleet of four lorries replaced every four years, a stable situation will not be reached until 1989. In the last column of the table above it will be noted that in 1986 the capital allowances are only £42 000 for four lorries. To match depreciation they should be £100 000.

A *schedule of capital allowances* is required to see this clearly. The lorries are numbered 1, 2, 3, 4 . . . (It is assumed that after four years each lorry is sold for its tax written-down value.)

Year of purchase	Lorry number							Total capital allowances (£'000)
	1	*2*	*3*	*4*	*5*	*6*	*7*	
1983	100							100
1984		75						75
1985		6	50					56
1986		5	12	25				42
1987	===	4	10	19	25			58
1988		===	7	14	19	25		65
1989			===	10	14	19	25	68

The difficulty arises obviously from the lorries still running which have had the high accelerated allowances. Until these drop out and are replaced by new ones accounting depreciation will be higher than the tax allowances – the reverse situation from the pre-1984 Budget. (Assuming a constant tax rate from 1986 onwards, tax payable will not be reduced to normal until 1989.)

9 Will there still be timing differences on capital allowances even when a 'steady state' is reached?

Yes, because nearly all companies use the fixed instalment system for depreciation in accounts while the Inland Revenue will continue to use the reducing balance system. In the case of lorry 4, for example, only £68 000 capital allowance is given over the four years instead of £100 000 under the fixed instalment depreciation system. (Another example is given, with some further explanation, in trouble spot 7.1, p. 69.)

The 'depreciation' allowed by the Inland Revenue is known as the *writing-down allowance*, which is based on the cost of the capital equipment less the allowances already given. The writing-down allowance is at a standard rate of 25 per cent per annum. For long-life assets the writing-down allowance in the early years is much larger than the fixed instalment depreciation. Later in the life of the asset it will be much less.

Where deferred tax has not been provided, as in the case of the mixer lorries, the Accounting Standards Committee ruled (May 1984) that the additional tax up to 1986 should be provided for immediately as an extraordinary item. The taxation charged against profit is then to some extent smoothed out over the next three years. There will be discrepancies between taxable profit and accounting profit after 1986, but they will be much smaller than hitherto. The day when accounting depreciation equals capital allowances is a long way off yet.

It all depends, of course, on the business concerned. The lorry example is probably the worst situation. It could be not unlike the position of banks with a leasing business, backed by substantial profits on the main business that has few fixed assets qualifying for capital allowances and little depreciation. A company which is all services on the one hand, or all regular investment in long-life plant and machines on the other, may not be hit so hard.

When to watch out

Before the 1984 Budget reductions in capital allowances, the provision of deferred taxation was very much at the discretion of directors and management. The tax charge had to be scrutinised to find the extent to which deferred taxation was included.

Following SSAP 15,[3] the full possible liability for deferred taxation has to be shown in a note to the accounts so that the tax charge can be computed hypothetically either with full deferred taxation provided or with no deferred taxation provided at all. In comparing after-tax performance of companies or annual after-tax profits of the same company, the treatment of deferred taxation must be examined and put on to a common basis for true comparison.

After the 1984 Budget the discretion is much more limited but still sufficient to show results that are not comparable.

What should be done – the author's view

The subject really requires a book on its own. In my view the profit after taxation in many companies (but not in all) will continue to be based on subjective assumptions and remain very unreliable as a measure of performance for many years. In the meantime it would be better simply to make the tax charge correspond with the tax payable on the profits for the year (without any deferrals or timing difference adjustments) and forget about any attempts to match tax and profit as long as they are fundamentally not matchable.

Eventually the new regime of annual writing-down allowances may have settled down sufficiently for the profit after taxation in most companies to appear roughly as 65 per cent of the profit before taxation (with a 35 per cent corporation tax rate) without any dubious adjustments. But for companies with major assets lasting for 15 to 20 years with changing patterns of investment, the gremlins of deferred tax and the 1984 Budget could be alive in the profit after taxation until the next century.

DIVIDENDS, SURPLUS ACT AND LOSSES

Measures affected

Profit after taxation
All-inclusive profit

Bases of accounting

Historic cost
Current cost

Where found

In published accounts
In private company accounts

Source of the trouble

Whenever a dividend is paid by a company, a special tax has to be paid soon afterwards (four months later at the most). This tax is known as ACT (the letters stand for Advance Corporation Tax, but this full name is very rarely used).

Currently the ACT rate is 30 per cent on the dividend plus the ACT, which is 42.86 per cent on the dividend (i.e. $100 \times 3/7 = 42.86$).

If the company is paying corporation tax on profits (known as mainstream corporation tax) the ACT paid is set off against the mainstream corporation tax payable (subject to a proviso that the ACT set off must not exceed 30 per cent of the profits for corporation tax).

When a company is making reasonable profits and distributing a conventional one-third as dividend, ACT can usually be set off fully against the tax on profits. Within reason the amount of the dividend has no effect on the total tax payable. This was the intention of the *imputation system* of company taxation introduced in 1972, by which tax on dividend (ACT) was 'imputed' to the shareholders, and the company would pay the same tax irrespective of the dividend.

When companies are making losses for corporation tax or only low profits the ACT picture is quite different. It cannot be set off against mainstream corporation tax because there is none payable.

Losses for corporation tax are not the same as losses in the profit and loss account. In recent years the main difference has been the 100 per cent first year capital allowance (see trouble spot 10.1, p. 118). This is deduced from profits for tax purposes causing a build-up of tax losses even though the company may be producing accounting profits.

To the extent that ACT cannot be set off against mainstream corporation tax in any one year, the *surplus ACT* can be applied against mainstream corporation tax already paid in past years or against mainstream tax to be paid in future years. The 'carry back' (since the 1984 Budget) is permitted up to six years (against any of which the ACT paid can be refunded).

Both tax losses on trading and surplus ACT can be carried forward indefinitely and set off against future trading profits for tax and mainstream corporation tax respectively. They are two separate carry-forwards, although clearly if a company has tax losses from capital allowances it is likely also to have surplus ACT.

Both these carry-forwards produce distortions in the tax charge. When a company starts to make profits for tax purposes, its tax liability will be cushioned by losses and surplus ACT 'brought forward'. Only when the losses brought forward and the surplus ACT are eliminated by continued profits will the tax charge begin to bite.

The trouble is that neither the losses carried forward nor the surplus ACT (for more than one year) are regarded as assets. When they eventually can be set off against profits, they are treated for accounting as windfalls.

The accounting treatment is asymmetrical. Tax that you might have to pay one day is provided for as deferred taxation. Tax that you might not have to pay one day is just not counted at all.

Some questions answered

1 Is there a connection between ACT and the basic rate of income tax?

The ACT rate is the same as the basic rate of income tax for individuals, presently 30 per cent. When applied to the dividend, however, the dividend is 'grossed up' so that ACT is at 30 per cent on the total of dividend plus ACT.

For a shareholder receiving a dividend the position is exactly as if basic rate tax had been deducted, although it is legally known as dividend payment with tax credit.

Suppose, for example, one shareholder to whom the company pays a dividend of £100 with ACT and basic rate of income tax 30 per cent.

Company:	dividend paid	£100
	ACT paid	42.86
Shareholder:	dividend payment	£100
	tax credit	42.86

2 What are the accounting rules for ACT paid by companies?

Although for tax purposes surplus ACT can be carried forward indefinitely, for accounting purposes it is restricted by accounting standard SSAP 8, *The treatment of taxation under the imputation system in the accounts of companies.*[3] Surplus ACT, it says, can be set off in accounts against a provision for deferred taxation (see trouble spot 10.1, p. 120) which means that it can be applied in reducing the tax charge in the profit and loss account. But, if a company has no deferred taxation provision and cannot carry back the surplus ACT, it can carry it forward in the accounts only for one year. In the words of the standard, it must be 'expected to be recoverable taking into account expected profits and dividends – normally those of the next accounting period only'.

Only one year's surplus ACT can then be regarded as a current asset in accounts and the remainder of surplus ACT becomes, in the accounting terminology, *irrecoverable ACT*. This means that it cannot be used in reducing the tax charge in accounts until it is set off against mainstream tax.

With high accelerated capital allowances this situation has been very common. Although a company is showing a reasonable profit in the accounts, it may have large losses for corporation tax when the 100 per cent capital allowances have been deducted. Particularly is this the case with companies installing new plant and machinery on a continuous programme – the sort of situation when deferred taxation has not been provided for.

3   Is ACT really a tax on dividends or a tax on profits?

If a company has large losses for tax purposes it will not pay mainstream corporation tax until all the losses have been set off against taxable profits. Until then, which may be many years ahead, the ACT paid cannot be set off against anything. The higher the dividend, the higher the ACT. ACT is then just a tax on dividends.

In the profit and loss account the ACT paid may be the only taxation to be charged. The caption may state 'tax on profit' or 'tax on profit for the year'; but it is not a tax on profit, it is a tax on the dividend.

If the company is making taxable profits and paying mainstream corporation tax, ACT is set off against it. Unless the dividend is higher than the taxable profit, ACT becomes simply part of the corporation tax on profit. It is not then a tax on dividends.

4   Will there be a tendency for ACT to become more of a tax on profit and less of a tax on dividend?

Yes. There are several factors which in the long run should bring back ACT to its original role of a tax on company profits paid in advance:

(a) Phased abolition of capital allowances in the 1984 Budget will reduce substantially the losses for corporation tax.
(b) The increased period (six years) for carry-back of surplus ACT enhances the possibilities of set-off.
(c) The restriction of ACT set-off to the ACT rate on taxable profit

will become much less significant when the rate of corporation tax becomes 35 per cent (in 1986) against 30 per cent for ACT (assuming the current rate continues).

(d) As profits increase in most companies, the taxable profit may become more in line with dividends.

No doubt these factors will take several years to work through. When surplus ACT is used up, ACT will no longer be a tax on dividends and the tax charge in accounts will more nearly represent the tax on accounting profits.

5   Is there any difference for companies with small profits?

Yes. For companies with taxable profits of less than £100 000, the mainstream corporation tax rate is 30 per cent – the same as the ACT rate. This means that ACT can be set off completely against any mainstream corporation tax payable.

Above £100 000 but below £500 000, there is a tapering reduction in the rate (in 1984) from 45 per cent at £500 000 to 30 per cent at £100 000.

6   What is the difference between surplus ACT and losses carried forward?

Both are amounts which can be carried forward from one year to another in order to obtain corporation tax relief in the future. 'Surplus ACT' is a strange term, which simply means ACT carried forward.

The differences are:

(a) *Surplus ACT* is an amount of tax paid – an amount of money – that can be refunded:
Losses carried forward are an amount of negative taxable profit.

(b) *Surplus ACT* can be set off in accounts against deferred taxation:
Losses carried forward are brought into account only in calculating the deferred tax amount.

(c) *Surplus ACT* can be treated in accounts as an asset that can remain for one year only:
Losses carried forward can never be regarded in accounts as an asset of any kind.

In both cases, the amounts that can be carried forward can also be carried back; that is, they can be set off against ACT paid or profits made in a previous year. For ACT, the carry-back extends five years; for losses carried back only one year is allowed normally (with three years for unused capital allowances).

7   What happens to the tax charge in accounts when profits of the year are set off against losses brought forward?

When tax losses from earlier years are set off against profits for the current year, the tax charge is simply reduced accordingly.

This produces a mismatch of the tax charge with accounting profit. No adjustment is made to bring the tax charge into line with profit. Tax losses, although often of substantial value, are not an asset to be carried forward in the company accounts. They are only in the files of the Inland Revenue.

When to watch out

The time to watch out for distorted tax charges in accounts due to surplus ACT or losses carried forward is when profits are picking up and surplus ACT and previous losses can be used to reduce the tax that otherwise would be paid.

Companies do not normally disclose remaining losses carried forward, so the start of full taxable profits being charged may be difficult to foresee. Surplus ACT, however, although 'irrecoverable', is often disclosed in the notes on deferred taxation, and it may be used as a means of predicting when the benefit from using surplus ACT against current ACT will come to an end.

What should be done – the author's view

Some of the troubles described here will diminish as the new regime of the 1984 Budget on capital allowances gets under way. Taxable profits will increase and the use of tax losses from previous years will gradually wither away so that in most companies the taxable profit will be more like the accounting profit.

But it will probably take several years for the rough equation of taxation and accounting profit to come about for most companies, and still there will be the distortions caused by surplus ACT and losses carried forward being utilised to reduce current taxable profit.

In my view surplus ACT should always be an asset in accounts. Not to allow it to be carried forward in accounts for more than one year is far too prudent. Indefinite carry-forward in line with the Inland Revenue, will avoid a current tax charge being reduced by surplus ACT (previously written off as of no value) when it is repaid or set off.

Tax losses carried forward cannot easily be set up as an asset. They may never be used and their value depends on the tax rate at the time of use. However, when tax losses brought forward are used to reduce the tax charge based on current profit, the tax reduction obtained should be shown separately, possibly as an extraordinary or prior year item. In my view, the reduction due to previous losses should not be included in the 'Taxation on profit on ordinary activities for the year'.

GROUP RELIEF

Measures affected

Profit after tax

Bases of accounting

Historic cost

Where found

In divisional accounts

Source of the trouble

Divisions of large groups (and of some smaller ones) are often organised in subsidiary companies. The companies are given as much autonomy as possible so that they may appear almost independent of the holding company. Measurement of the performance of the subsidiaries is then carried all the way down the list of profit measures, ending with profit after tax.

However, a subsidiary company, as a member of a group, does not always have its own tax. Each company has its own profit (or loss) for corporation tax, computed from the company accounts. Only the individual subsidiary companies are the legal entities which are legally responsible for payment of the tax. The 'group' is not a legal entity. But the group is recognised in tax law for certain concessions and restrictions. One of these is 'group relief'.

Group relief allows tax losses in one subsidiary to be set off against taxable profits in another. This results in the tax charge in one subsidiary being too low and in another too high in relation to their pre-tax profits. The way group relief is used is quite arbitrary, depending on the likely future distribution of losses (including capital allowances) among the companies, having little to do with current performance.

Some questions answered

1 What are the conditions which govern group relief?

The main conditions are:

(a) The relief applies only to profits and losses of the same current year. Losses carried forward from a previous year cannot be used in the set off.

(b) The subsidiary companies must be at least 75 per cent owned.

(c) The relief does not apply to subsidiary companies outside the UK.

(d) The relief will work only when the group structure is not on a temporary basis and there is no fiddling with the ownership of a subsidiary (this summarises a very long 'anti-avoidance' clause in the Finance Act 1973).

2 How does group relief work in practice?

The tax losses that can be used in the relief are not put into a group pool but are exchanged individually with companies having taxable profits. (Technically company A, with a loss, 'surrenders' its loss to company B, with a profit, which 'claims' the loss from company A.) The best deal has to be worked out which will minimise the total corporation tax borne by the group. This usually involves forecasting the future pattern of profits and losses in the subsidiaries.

3 Does the use of profit after tax but before group relief solve the problem?

It is possible to show the divisional accounts, derived from the subsidiary company accounts, the tax charge as though it were not a subsidiary company and there were no group relief. The disadvantages of this are:

(a) The use of group relief reduced the overall tax bills of the group. Without it the tax charge on some subsidiaries would be too high.

(b) In order to maximise the benefits of group relief to the group, it may be advantageous to plan particular capital expenditure in subsidiaries on a group basis. The tax liability, even though excluding group relief, may still be determined by the group.

However, a tax charge ex-group-relief may have its merits in simplicity and motivation.

4 Will the problem of group relief diminish with lower capital allowances?

Certainly, yes. The large losses that are swapped around are primarily due to 100 per cent first year allowances. As tax losses begin to fall away following the 1984 Budget, group relief is likely to have much less significance.

When to watch out

The distortions of group relief apply only in subsidiary company accounts used as a divisional performance measure. Where an after-tax profit is used, the effects of group relief on tax losses must be watched.

What should be done – the author's view

The use of profit after tax in divisional performance is comparatively rare. As long as there are large losses in some divisions affecting tax charges in others, it is best to stick with profit before taxation. There is no way in which total group tax can be satisfactorily allocated, and a tax charge which ignores group relief could be misleading.

11　All-inclusive profit

DEFINITION

In published accounts there is generally a further deduction (or addition) for extraordinary items following the profit after tax. The final figure shown for profit after extraordinary items is named in the Companies Act 1981 (sch. 1, Part I) *profit (or loss) for the financial year*, and in the accounting standard as *profit after extraordinary items*. In annual accounts other names are used such as *attributable profit* (meaning profit attributable to the shareholders). None of these names usefully describe the concept, the worst being the Companies Act name.

Although not in general use, *all-inclusive profit* is the best description. It is the profit after taking into account *all* the transactions which have taken place during the year excluding only those that are classified as capital expenditure (but including profits and losses on disposal of fixed capital assets).

The ideal of separating expenditure or income which did not belong in the normal way to the year when it actually occurred was implemented in the UK in 1975. The purpose was to show a true profit for the accounting period excluding items which relate to a previous period or which come into the current period by change, unrelated to the *ordinary activities*. This makes the *profit after taxation* line the *profit for the year*. The very bottom line in published accounts is now in fact the 'profit *in* the year' including *all* the business transactions except capital spending, or what is called here the 'all-inclusive profit'.

UNDERLYING PHILOSOPHY

In a short period such as a month there are likely to be many items of expenditure and income that land in that month purely at random. There may be large claims involving legal damages or heavy write-offs of obsolete stock. These may make the monthly profit and loss statement show a heavy loss which totally absorbs the operating profit for the month. There is then a natural tendency to look at the ordinary profit without the extraordinary or exceptional item.

The all-inclusive concept has no place in such short-term appraisals. The seeds of the extraordinary income or expenditure may have been sown many months or years ago. The fact that they finally came out in a particular month is a matter of chance, nothing to do with the performance of the business in that month.

On the other hand, in the long term the extraordinary items must be taken into account. It may be that there are many such items, some recurring until they almost cease to be extraordinary. No business should be appraised over a period of, say, five years without including the extraordinary expenditure and income. There may be a tendency, with too much emphasis on the short-term, to forget about the incidence of these items over the long-term.

BUSINESSES BEST SUITED

Extraordinary expenditure has to be financed and, in most cases, is concomitant with a cash outflow. For businesses where finance is easy it can be safe to omit extraordinary expenditure on the grounds that it is not part of the business and any excess of extraordinary expenditure over income can be handled as a matured contingency for which funds are available. With this proviso in mind, the trends of profit and loss can be studied more sensibly if they are free from the erratic swings caused by extraordinary items.

Nevertheless, all businesses which habitually show extraordinary items in their accounts must also consider the all-inclusive profit. Where an extraordinary charge or credit is a genuine once-and-for-all, the all-inclusive profit is less important.

In small independent businesses, with perhaps little backing of reserves, the all-inclusive concept is essential. Whether the extraordinary item reflects a disaster or a bonanza, it should be included in long-term business performance. In presenting the measured performance to proprietors, financiers, customers or suppliers, the extraordinary items are bound to be taken into account.

For divisional performance measurement, which concentrates on the short-term, extraordinary and exceptional items, if included in the accounts, are shown separately or are the subject of a special note or comment. The all-inclusive concept is not valid.

ORGANISATIONS BEST SUITED

Large organisations have in recent years made widespread changes in a grand scale. They have incurred heavy redundancy and reorganisation costs and have sold less profitable subsidiaries. These have been taken as extraordinary items, leaving a large gap between the all-inclusive profit and the ordinary profit after taxation.

This gap has come under some suspicion and there has been some reversion towards a more all-inclusive approach. Many large groups of companies, more than ever before, continue to change their composition and often the very businesses they are in. In these circumstances the all-inclusive concept is needed for long-term *group* performance measurement, but not for the individual businesses.

In single business organisations the all-inclusive profit cannot be ignored in the long term as the bottom line measure.

POWER TO MOTIVATE

The all-inclusive profit has no power to motivate. By definition it includes items which are nobody's responsibility except possibly the chief executive or managing director.

PROBLEMS AND TROUBLES

After all-inclusive profit there is still one place where accounting items in the year can be lodged. They can be credited to or charged against reserves of profit built up from previous years and not shown in the profit and loss account at all. An example is the treatment of goodwill: trouble spot 11.2 (p. 147). A direct credit or debit to reserves is also used for 'prior year adjustments', usually in relation to a change in accounting policy for stocks (trouble spot 6.1, p. 51) or depreciation (trouble spot 7.1, p. 65).

The main problem, however, lies in the definition of extraordinary item which is discussed in trouble spot 11.1 (p. 142).

The all-inclusive profit in published accounts hits the same trouble spots as earlier levels of profit, with the new ones added. They are:

- Foreign currency translation — 5.2
- Stocks and work-in-progress — 6.1
- Depreciation — 7.1
- Revenue investment — 7.2
- Pensions cost — 8.1
- Capitalisation of interest — 9.2
- Capital allowances and deferred taxation — 10.1
- Dividends, surplus ACT and losses — 10.2
- Extraordinary items — 11.1
- Goodwill — 11.2

EXTRAORDINARY ITEMS

Measures affected

Value added
Operating profit
Profit after interest
Profit after taxation
All-inclusive profit
Operating cash flow
Operating funds flow

Bases of accounting which apply

Historic cost
Current cost
Cash flow
Funds flow

Where found

In published accounts
In private company accounts
In divisional accounts

Source of the trouble

When faced with a profit and loss account which shows unexpected results, there is always a tendency to ask: Is there anything extraordinary here? A budget should foresee most unusual expenditure or income, but the reason for the unusual actual result may not be recorded. When comparisons are made from period to period, it helps if the reasons for major differences are noted in the accounts or in an adjoining paper.

In a small business the owner/manager may know all about extraordinary debits or credits; indeed they may be printed indelibly on the mind. So too will the manager of a cost centre or division of a larger company.

When accounts are examined by directors or others more remote from the scene, something more formal and permanent has to be done to incorporate the reasons for the extraordinary results into the system. This may be done by a written report or commentary on the results, which, to some managements, is more acceptable than tables or figures. The larger the organisation, however, the more is a formal system needed with some definition of what constitutes an extraordinary or abnormal item.

Some questions answered

1 What are the rules for published accounts?

In 1974 an accounting standard (SSAP 6)[3] was issued which defines extraordinary items as 'items which derive from events or transactions outside the ordinary activities of the business and which are both material, and expected not to recur frequently or regularly'. They should be 'shown separately in the profit and loss account for the year after the results derived from ordinary activities'.

2 Can the rules be easily fiddled?

Up to now there has been a tendency for the rather vague definition of 'extraordinary items' to be exploited. In cases of doubt, unusual expenditure tends to be shown as an extraordinary item while unusual income is included in ordinary revenue, so that the profit of the year is shown as high as it can be stretched.

In January 1985 a proposed new standard of accounting practice was issued - ED 36.[3] This will limit the items which can be classified as extraordinary, not by changing the definition, but by changing the interpretation and citing specific cases.

The following items, for example, are no longer to be treated as extraordinary:

- redundancy costs
- re-organisation costs
- profits and losses on disposals of fixed assets

Extraordinary items would be confined to situations such as:

- closure of a division or business unit
- sale of a subsidiary company
- sale of substantial shareholding in associated company
- heavy loss on fixed asset value through unusual events or expropriation

Generally, extraordinary items should be confined to cases where particular businesses cease trading or are sold or taken over by others. In this way the profit for the year will once again include almost all income and expenditure for the year incurred by continuing businesses – back to an all-inclusive profit concept.

3   How is taxation treated?

In published accounts the extraordinary income or expenditure is expressed after deducting the tax charged on the extra income or the tax saved on the extra expenditure. This follows the ruling in SSAP.[3]

In practice the calculation of the tax charge attributed to a particular item may be fraught with difficulty. If a company is paying full rate corporation tax on profits, there is no problem. But if there are losses brought forward, surplus ACT, deferred taxation provisions, double taxation relief, or group relief on losses (see trouble spots 10.1–10.3), the full rate cannot properly be used. Strictly, computations should then be made of the tax payable with and without each extraordinary item and the difference charged or credited.

4   What about exceptional items?

Exceptional item is a term used in SSAP 6 and ED 36[3] to mean an item of abnormal size and incidence which derives from the *ordinary* activities of the business. It is not isolated from normal expenditure or income but it has to be disclosed in the accounts by way of a specific note or as an item in the profit and loss account. The figures, unlike extraordinary items, are before taxation.

Exceptional items, after ED 36 becomes a standard, are likely to be significant amounts of:

- redundancy costs
- re-organisation costs
- profits or losses on sales of fixed assets
- bad debts
- stocks heavily written down
- surplus on insurance claims
- surplus pensions contributions
- contribution to new employee share scheme

In value added statements

Extraordinary items pose the same problem for value added as in profit and loss accounts. Items which have no relation at all to current turnover, such as an exceptional capital loss, redundancy or closure costs, should be shown as a separate distribution of value added or not included at all. Extraordinary income similarly should be treated as a separate item.

In divisional accounts

Because these concentrate on short-term performance, extraordinary and exceptional items should be shown separately. Often this is done by means of notes or comments on the management accounts.

When to watch out

In published accounts extraordinary items are picked out from normal revenue or expenditure by a judgement which may not be entirely unbiased. Where it is suspect, an estimate should be made of the operating profit (and other key measures) had the judgement been the other way.

What should be done – the author's opinion

Both exceptional and extraordinary items need to be taken into account in all of the performance measures for the purpose of identifying important deviations from a normal trend. Whether the deviant item arises from normal or abnormal activities is not very relevant for this purpose.

In my view, the distinction should be abolished and any items which are seriously 'out of trend' should be shown separately. In the short-term these can be ignored. In the longer-term they can be taken in and averaged out.

There are two ways of measuring distance travelled. On a short distance by country road the distance includes all the bends and bumps (the exceptional variations). On a longer distance by motorway the bends and exceptions are ironed out. Each measure of the distance has its uses.

Both, however, are measured in miles. It seems incongruous that a few rather undefined journeys (the extraordinary items) have a different unit of measurement – £s after taxation instead of £s before taxation. If taxation has to be taken into account in business performance, it should be an integral charge on the total business so that the measures can be seen clearly without corporation tax, and with corporation tax.

GOODWILL

Measures affected

Operating profit
Profit after interest
Profit after taxation
All-inclusive profit

Bases of accounting

Historic cost

Where found

In published accounts

Source of the trouble

Anyone purchasing a business has usually to pay for goodwill – an amount over and above the value of the physical assets. When the buyer of the business comes to record the purchase in his own accounts, the goodwill must be included somewhere. And there is no argument that the goodwill then is also an asset, albeit an intangible one.

However, if goodwill is acquired through starting a business from scratch, such goodwill is never an asset in the accounting sense. This is because it has never been bought and it is impossible to measure. Advertising which generates goodwill could be regarded as an asset, but this is too vague and uncertain to be counted (see trouble spot 7.2, p. 76).

The problem then arises as to what should be done with the goodwill that is set up as an asset. It may decay or it may grow, but its value cannot be measured and it will before long get inextricably mixed with the goodwill internally generated. The only solution is to 'write off' the goodwill as an asset as soon as possible. Then the balance sheet showing the business assets will at least be consistent – no goodwill of any kind shown.

To write off goodwill as soon as it arises is the most consistent policy, but, in some cases, large amounts have been paid for goodwill and to charge it against profits all in one year would have a crippling effect. So concessions have to be made. In what circumstances a gradual write-off can be allowed, and over how many years, has exercised accountants for ages.

In December 1984 the Accounting Standards Committee published SSAP 22 *Accounting for goodwill*,[3] which states that purchased goodwill can be written off over its 'useful economic life', but 'normally' it should be eliminated immediately from the accounts by deduction from reserves.

The decision to write off goodwill and over what period is effectively in the hands of the company directors. This means generally that companies with substantial retained profits may write it off immediately, and those without such profits may extend the writing-off period for as long as seems respectable.

Some questions answered

1   When does purchased goodwill most often arise?

On a small scale, people may buy businesses with a considerable amount of goodwill, especially in retail shops where the customer base has a considerable value. In this case goodwill may be retained in the balance sheet without spoiling the profit as a measure of performance. To the next buyer of the shop the goodwill as an asset will presumably still be there.

On a large scale, a large company may purchase a smaller company by acquiring all the shares from the existing shareholders. This is likely to involve the payment of an amount to the shareholders which in total is much more than the total net book values in the balance sheet. The excess paid over the net assets so valued is known as 'goodwill'. When group accounts are prepared consolidating the holding company and its new subsidiary, an amount for goodwill will appear in the consolidated (or group) balance sheet, unless it is written off immediately.

2   When goodwill is written off, where is it shown in the profit and loss account?

If it is written off straight away, it must be deducted from retained profits or reserves; it is then not shown in the profit and loss account.

If goodwill is written off over a period, the instalment written off should be treated as depreciation (under the Companies Act 1981) and deducted from operating profit. As depreciation of goodwill is entirely arbitrary and discretionary, the operating profit (and the profit levels below) can be badly polluted by the inclusion of goodwill.

3   What happens when a subsidiary company is sold?

The holding company selling the shares in its subsidiary normally receives goodwill as the excess of the selling price over the net asset values. This 'goodwill' sold is usually credited to reserves, but it is possible to include it in operating profit, which then could badly distort the true figure.

When to watch out

The danger points are when goodwill is retained in the balance sheet and depreciated, and when subsidiaries are sold involving a receipt of goodwill. In measuring current business performance all transactions relating to goodwill are best excluded.

What should be done – the author's opinion

In small business accounts purchased goodwill should be retained at cost as long as there is no clear evidence that it is not losing its value.

In consolidated accounts 'goodwill' is a misnomer. It is usually only part of the cost of a portfolio of customers, reputation or expertise. Most of the excess may be simply a premium necessary to be paid in order to buy complete control of a company. Such a premium should be financed from reserves and should have nothing to do with current profits.

PART II: REFERENCES

1. E. A. Whiting and K. Gee, *Decentralisation, Divisional Interdependence and the Treatment of Central Costs and Interest as Charges or Allocations* (Financial Control Research Institute, 1984).
2. R. W. Scapens, J. T. Sale and P. A. Tikkas, *Financial Control of Divisional Capital Investment* (Institute of Cost and Management Accountants, 1982).
3. Publications of the Accounting Standards Committee of the Consultative Committee of Accountancy Bodies:

SSAP 6	*Extraordinary items and prior-year adjustments*	1975
SSAP 8	*The treatment of taxation under the imputation system in the accounts of companies*	1977
SSAP 9	*Stocks and work in progress*	1975
SSAP 11	*Accounting for deferred taxation*	1976
SSAP 13	*Accounting for research and development*	1977
SSAP 15	*Accounting for deferred taxation*	1978
SSAP 20	*Foreign currency translation*	1983
SSAP 21	*Accounting for leasing*	1984
SSAP 22	*Accounting for goodwill*	1984
ED 33	*Accounting for deferred tax*	1983
ED 36	*Extraordinary items and prior year adjustments*	1985

4. *Financial Reporting 1983/84: A Survey of UK Published Accounts* (Institute of Chartered Accountants in England & Wales, 1984).
5. 1984 *BIM National Management Salary Survey* (Remuneration Economics, 1984).
6. C. J. Napier, *Accounting for the Cost of Pensions* (Institute of Chartered Accountants in England & Wales, 1983).
7. S. Carnel, 'Accountants and actuaries still not in step', *Accountancy*, March 1984, pp. 101–2.
8. *Management Accounting: Official terminology of the ICMA* (Institute of Cost and Management Accountants, 1982).
9. *Profit Sharing & Share Options*, IDS Study 306 (Incomes Data Services, 1984).

151

Part III
Bases of Accounting

'For any accounting information to be worth reporting it must be material in amount, relevant to an understanding of the accounts and the costs of preparing the information should not exceed the benefits of providing it.'—Accounting Standards Committee, Preface to ED 35

'Essentially, understanding represents the highway from knowledge to wisdom'.—C. W. Churchman, University of California

12 Accounting mechanics

INTRODUCTION

This short chapter is for those who may wish to trace the mechanics of the accounting conventions in practice: how they differ and how they tie up.

An example is used in the form of the accounts of a fictitious company called Printapress plc. It has two divisions: the Printing Division and the Magazine Publishing Division.

Chart 12.1 (p. 158) shows the accounts of the company on the four different bases. Chart 12.2 (p. 161) shows the accounts of the two divisions on a historic cost basis and a cash flow basis.

The same accounts are developed as further examples in the four chapters that follow.

COMPARATIVE BASES OF COMPANY ACCOUNTS

The layout of Chart 12.1 is similar to the summary chart of business performance measures in Chapter 3 (p. 14). The one noticeable exception is the treatment of employment costs, which in Chart 12.1 are added to operating profit to obtain value added and then taken out again in the next line. This is done in order to show a number for each performance measure without breaking the arithmetical sequence.

None of the four accounts shown are likely to appear in exactly the same form as Chart 12.1 in any published accounts. Examples of the accounts, as they are most likely to be published by Printapress, are shown in the chapters that follow:

*These statements only are legally compulsory or are required by
 accounting standards.

The historic cost, cash flow and funds flow accounts are each based on
common accounting data, rearranged in different ways. The current cost
account usually requires new data, such as cost and price indices, to
produce the necessary adjustments.

Company accounting systems are almost always based on historic cost,
leading to the traditional profit and loss account and balance sheet.
Each of the three other accounts have therefore to be founded on the
historic cost accounts, which themselves need no explanatory notes or
adjustment.

The current cost profit and loss account is not, under the latest proposed
accounting standard, to be published as such. Only the adjustments will
need to be published along with the effect of those adjustments at two
levels of profit.

Cash flow statements have no prescribed form and are rarely published.
The example in Chart 12.1 is based on a form used by Professor G. H.
Lawson with some extra lines to tie up easily with the historic cost profit
and loss account. The cash flow adjustments are all concerned with
converting the revenue and expense (computed according to the
matching principle of the historic cost convention) into cash actually
received and paid.

The comparison of the cash and funds flow statements with the profit
and loss account ends in Chart 12.1 with the all-inclusive profit/net cash
flow/net funds flow line. Beyond this point any use of the cash flow or
funds flow as a performance measure probably ceases. The statements,
however, continue downwards to show the total use of all cash or funds,
ending with the increase (or decrease) in cash balances or the increase (or
decrease) in funds. No balance sheet of Printapress is presented.

DIVISIONAL ACCOUNTS

Current cost (CCA) is rarely used as a complete system in divisional accounts. Funds flow is sometimes used, but cash flow is most common as a kind of second opinion to the historic cost profit and loss account.

In Chart 12.2 the divisional accounts would seem to be fouled by the high proportion of interdivisional turnover, involving a transfer pricing problem (see trouble spot 5.1, p. 34) and by the arbitrary allocation of head office overhead costs (see trouble spot 8.2, p. 92). The cash flow statements are tainted with these troubles in exactly the same way as the profit and loss accounts.

However, the cash flow statement for the Printing Division shows a net cash outflow (or deficit) for the year against a small surplus on the profit and loss account, due largely to the slower collection of cash from debtors while paying creditors apparently faster than the Publishing Division. The example does confirm that the cash flow statement adds a dimension to business performance which is not found in the profit and loss account.

CHART 12.1

Printapress plc
Accounts 1983
(comparative bases)

| | Profit and loss accounts | | | Cash/Funds flow statements | | | |
| | Historic cost | Current cost | | Cash flow | | Funds flow | |
	(£'000)	(Notes) and new titles	(£'000)	(Notes) and new titles	(£'000)	(Notes) and new titles	(£'000)
Turnover	6370		6370	Receipts from sales (1)	6036	Turnover	6370
Deduct: Materials	3445	(1)	3465	(2)	3362		3445
Other variable costs	1690		1690	(3)	1603		1690
		MWCA (2)	10				
	5135		5165				
	1235		1205				
Gross Margin							
Deduct: Overhead costs	585	(3)	585	(4)	545	(1)	585
Depreciation	165		205	(5)	—		—
	750		790		5510		5720
Operating profit	485		415	*Operating cash flow*	526	*Funds from operations*	650
Add: Employment costs	1950		1950		1950		
Value added	2435		2365	*Cash value added*	2476		

	1995	1980	1992	
Deduct: Employment costs	1950	1950	1950	1950
Interest payable *(Interest paid (6) / Interest payable)*	45	30	42	45
	Equity profit (4)		*Cash flow after interest*	*Funds flow after interest*
Profit after interest	440	385	484	605
Deduct: Taxation *(Tax paid)*	150	150	124	124
Profit after taxation *(Net cash flow / Net funds flow)*	290	235	360	481
Add/Deduct: Extraordinary item	60	60	—	—
All-inclusive profit	230	175	360	481
Deduct: Net capital investment			435	435
Cash flow after investment *(Funds flow after investment)*			(75)	46
Deduct: Dividend paid			104	104
Equity cash flow *(Equity funds flow)*			(179)	(58)
Add: New loans/shares issued			650	650
Deduct: Loans repaid			(160)	(160)
Increase in cash balances *(Increase in funds)*			311	432

Notes on p. 160

NOTES ON CHART 12.1   Printapress plc

Current cost

(1) The materials cost is increased by a cost of sales adjustment of £20 000, which is the extra amount needed to charge the cost of goods sold at the current cost of the materials at the time of sale instead of the historic cost.

(2) The monetary working capital adjustment (MWCA) of £10 000 is made to allow for the fact that debts to the company (a monetary asset) and creditors of the company (a monetary liability) reduce in real value with inflation.

(3) Depreciation is increased by £40 000 when replacement cost of fixed assets, such as plant and vehicles, is taken as the basis of depreciation instead of historic cost.

(4) A gearing adjustment of £15 000 is made to reflect the gain obtained by loans which reduce in real terms during inflation. In this case the adjustment is deducted from the interest charge.

Funds flow

(1) Depreciation is not a fund and depreciation charges; therefore do not involve a funds flow.

Cash flow

(1) Debtors have increased over the year by £334 000. This means that actual receipts from sales in cash during the year are that much less than the turnover.

(2) Creditors for materials have increased by £150 000 over the year. Stocks have also increased by £67 000 which has been paid for and not included in material costs. The net adjustment is £83 000, being the increase in the year of materials used but not paid for.

(3) Creditors for other variable costs have increased by £87 000 during the years.

(4) Creditors for overhead costs have increased by £40 000.

(5) Depreciation is an allocation of cost not involving any cash payment or receipt.

(6) Interest paid out during the year is £3000 less than the interest actually due for the year.
Total creditors have increased by:

		£000
(2)	Materials	150
(3)	Other variable costs	87
(4)	Overhead costs	40
(6)	Interest accrued	3
		280

CHART 12.2

Printapress plc
Divisional accounts 1983

	Profit and loss accounts			Cash flow statements			
	Group (£000)	Printing Division (£000)	Publishing Division (£000)	Group (£000)	Notes	Printing Division (£000)	Publishing Division (£000)
Turnover							
External		2420	3950		(1)	2124	3912
Interdivisional		1515	—			1515	—
Total turnover	6370	3935	3950	6036		3639	3912
Deduct: Materials	3445	2740	705	3362	(2)	2680	682
Interdivision printing		—	1515			—	1515
Other variable costs	1690	770	920	1603	(3)	737	866
	5135	3510	3140				
Gross margin	1235	425	810				
Deduct: Overhead costs							
of division (specific)	284	104	180	244	(4)	94	150
of H.O. (allocated)	301	150	151	301		150	151
Depreciation	165	130	35	—		—	—
	750	384	366	5510		3661	3364
Operating profit/Cash flow	485	41	444	526		(22)	548
Add back: Employment costs	1950	850	1100				
Value added	2435	891	1544				

Notes on p. 162

Use of divisional accounts

Printapress has two divisions set up as subsidiary companies. The Printing Division carries out work for external customers and for the Magazine Publishing Division. Printing for the Publishing Division is charged at the same price as for external customers, but the Publishing Division manager considers that the price should be lower.

Overhead costs incurred by the Head Office are allocated in proportion to turnover (roughly 50/50 in 1983).

For divisional performance measurement, the Group uses turnover, gross margin, operating profit and value added. It also considers the operating cash flow of each division. Although the Group pays interest it does not charge any interest to divisions and it does not prepare a cash value added statement (i.e. value added based on cash flow).

For interdivisional trading and the allocation of Head Office overheads, accounting entries are made which are regarded as cash flow.

Cash flow notes

(1) Debtors in the Printing Division have increased by £296 000 and in Publishing by £38 000.

(2) The increase in creditors for materials was £107 000 in the Printing Division and £43 000 in Publishing. Stocks in the Printing Division increased by £47 000 in Printing and £20 000 in Publishing. The net adjustment for materials not yet paid for was £60 000 for Printing and £23 000 for Publishing.

(3) Creditors for other variable costs increased over the year by £33 000 for Printing and £54 000 for Publishing.

(4) Creditors for specific overhead costs increased by £10 000 in Printing and £30 000 in Publishing.

13 Historic cost

ORIGIN AND DEFINITION

From 1921 to 1939 there was no inflation. Retail prices actually fell during the 1920s and remained almost stable during the 1930s. In those days there was only one cost convention. The cost of a machine was what you paid for it, and so it would remain.

Early in the 1950s, however, when prices had more than doubled since 1939, some accountants became concerned with the anomaly arising when pre-war plant would appear in accounts at half the cost of identical post-war plant. As time went on, and price inflation increased, there evolved a 'purchasing power adjusted cost' along with an 'original cost'. It was not until the 1970s that the term 'historic cost' became widely used – in contrast to 'current cost'.

Historic cost is simply the cost which has been used in accounts for decades. It needs no explanation and is well understood by almost everyone. Without inflation no adjective describing the basis of cost would have been needed.

ACCOUNTING STATEMENTS

An example of a historic cost profit and loss account following the Companies Act 1981, is shown in Statement 13.1 (p. 170). It is familiar to anyone who reads accounts, and it requires no 'historic cost' caption.

Statement 13.2 (p. 171) shows a value added statement on the historic cost basis. Value added statements can be prepared also on a current cost basis and on a cash flow basis (see Statement 15.3, p. 199) but in practice almost all value added statements are based on historic cost.

In published accounts, the term 'historic cost' is hardly ever mentioned, until the auditor's report, which usually refers to the accounts 'which have been prepared under the historical cost convention'. When, and only when, another 'cost convention' is used and reference to both is made in the same document does the description 'historic (or historical) cost' have to be given.

In divisional accounts the historic cost basis is again taken for granted. However, some companies use CCA selectively, for example for depreciation or cost of sales. The basis may be noted, for example 'current cost depreciation', when historic cost is not used. After a long period using current cost, it may no longer need to be described as such on the statements. But long-standing use of CCA alone, without historic cost figures also, is extremely rare.

FEATURES OF PURE HISTORIC COST

Historic cost is based firmly on transactions. A purchase or a sale is made for a certain sum of money which is recorded in the books of account (or, more likely, a computer file) and that sum of money is not changed throughout any classification, analysis, manipulation or aggregation, as long as it remains 'on the books'.

Fixed assets, such as plant, machinery and vehicles, remain at the cost when they were purchased until they are scrapped, sold or otherwise disposed of. Depreciation is calculated on the same basis, truly an allocation of the cost over the working life of the asset.

Stock and work-in-progress are retained strictly at cost. Historic cost is associated naturally with the FIFO method for charging out the cost of materials (see trouble spot 6.1, p. 51). Only if the oldest stock is assumed to be used first in every case, is it sure that the remaining stock is kept at its historic cost, i.e. the price at which it was purchased.

In foreign currency translation, historic cost demands that fixed assets held abroad in foreign currency should be translated to sterling at the rate of exchange when the fixed asset was purchased, and depreciation should be translated similarly. This ensures that the original cost is maintained throughout, regardless of any subsequent changes in the exchange rate. (This historic cost concept is known as the *temporal method* of exchange translation, which is now rarely used.)

VALUATION

Pure historic cost, without any resort to valuation, has not existed for many years. The early accounting principle of conservatism (or prudence) required that when the market value of an asset was lower than cost, market (or realisable) value should be substituted for historic cost. The substitution could be made only when market value was lower – never, in those days, when it was higher.

However, after the Second World War, when general price levels began to lose their pre-war stability, market value came gradually to be used for certain assets, whether the value was lower or *higher* than the original cost. The pure historic cost then became badly polluted.

First, market value of investments had to be shown as a note and later as a substitute for cost in the actual balance sheet, the differences from period to period being charged or credited to profit and loss account or reserves.

Then, as the historic cost of buildings became wildly out of line with current values, buildings and property were valued by surveyors and the valuation used in the accounts instead of cost. This was an almost inevitable reaction to the 'asset stripping' of the 1960s, which was the result of exploiting the very low historic cost figures for property shown in company balance sheets.

Contract work-in-progress (see trouble spot 6.1, p. 55) is another example of valuations being used that are higher than historic cost. The inclusion of anticipated profit is in effect putting a value on the profit before it is realised.

Foreign currency translation, with SSAP 20,[2] has become almost entirely based on the closing rate, i.e. the market exchange rate at the time of the accounts, in place of the historic rate.

Departures from pure historic cost cause trouble, but they seem to be inevitable when current costs are such a long way off from historic costs. Historic cost has in fact become 'modified historic cost' – modified to suit the changing economic environment.

ADVANTAGES OF HISTORIC COST

(1)   It is well known and corresponds with the popular conception of cost.
(2)   Historic cost accounts are simply analyses and summaries of actual transactions made by the business with comparatively few assumptions or estimation.
(3)   Historic cost is completely objective in its pure form; it has no problems of valuation.
(4)   It provides continuity over many years, being the basis of accounts since time immemorial.
(5)   It is widely used in commercial contracts, as the basis of bonus or commission and as the basis of tax assessment and economic statistics.

DISADVANTAGES OF HISTORIC COST

(1)   It depends on stable general price levels.
(2)   It may be modified to cope with the most glaring distortions of asset costs caused by inflation, but it then loses many of its advantages.
(3)   Unless older assets are revalued, or some other provision made, depreciation on historic cost in times of inflation becomes inadequate to provide the funds for replacement of the asset at the end of its economic life.
(4)   Inflation on a moderate scale can seriously erode the historic cost depreciation over a period of years and, even if it falls to zero, the historic cost of the older long-life assets will remain an unrealistic basis for depreciation for as long as they are in use.

WHERE HISTORIC COST IS GOOD

The drawbacks of historic cost are most evident when inflation is high. At 26 per cent (the highest point reached in 1975) historic cost becomes misleading for almost all businesses. The only exceptions are those which work almost entirely on a cash basis with negligible fixed assets in the way of buildings or machines. Examples are betting shops and auction markets where the cash is very quickly in and out. There is no 'time lag error' (as a leading authority on inflation accounting would put it[1]).

At five per cent inflation many businesses can use the performance measures based on historic cost without any serious damage. Such businesses are likely to have small working capital in relation to turnover and small fixed assets in relation to operating profit.

Working capital comprises stocks plus debtors minus creditors. A small working capital requirement implies quick turn-over of stock and/or cash transactions, with minimum credit to customers, but extended credit given by suppliers. In some businesses, by careful control of the three elements, working capital can be slightly negative, the stocks and debtors (if any) being financed totally by creditors. Such businesses should be quite happy using historic cost.

If the fixed assets are small in amount, depreciation will be small. Any error or defect in the depreciation charge will therefore have little effect on the profit-based measures of performance. It is difficult to say how small the fixed assets should be to make the profit measure immune from inadequate depreciation. We have postulated later, with little firm evidence, that this should be a state when gross fixed assets (i.e. their original cost without depreciation) are less than twice average operating profit.

As well as the size of the amount of fixed assets affecting depreciation it is also affected, in times of inflation, by the age of the assets. The historic cost of new assets is not likely to be widely different, in moderate inflation, from the current cost, so that historic cost depreciation remains reasonable. For older assets, however, the historic cost as a basis for depreciation may be quite unrealistic especially when there has been high inflation at some time during the life of the asset.

The simple algorithm overleaf shows some conditions on which historic cost (HC) may be used as a basis of performance measurement.

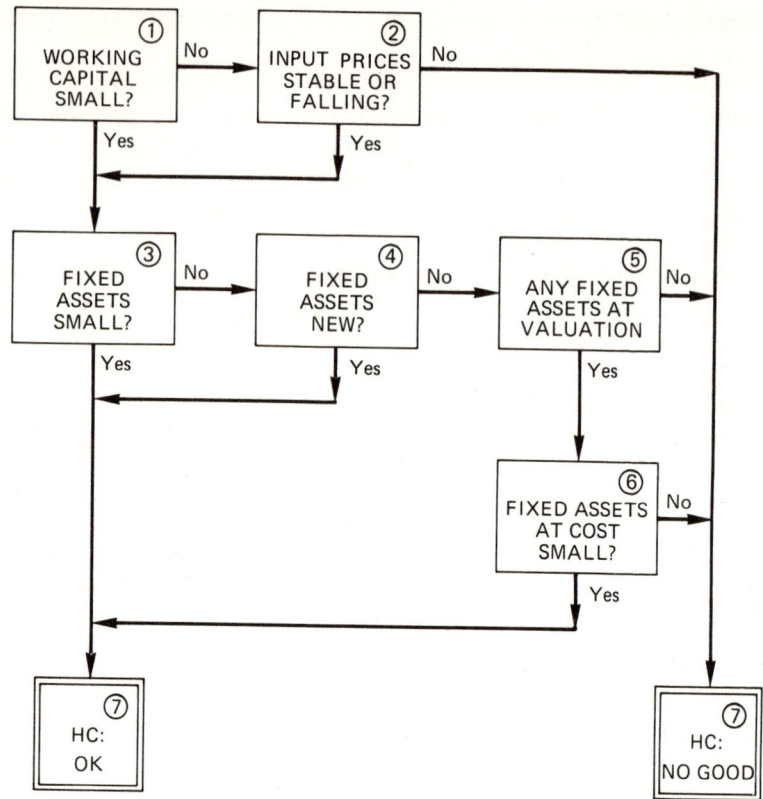

NOTES

(1) Small in relation to turnover: say, less than 20 per cent of annual turnover.
(2) Input prices = prices paid by the business for materials, components or goods for resale.
(3) Small in relation to operating profit: say, gross fixed assets less than twice average operating profit.
(4) New assets: say, on average less than five years old.
(5) Property and buildings carried in the accounts at valuation.
(6) Fixed assets at cost (excluding assets at valuation): say, gross fixed assets less than twice average operating profit.
(7) The above parameters are extremely simplified, are not based on research findings and do not cover all conditions.

CONCLUSION

Pure historic cost is objective. It is based on transactions made in the period. It is well known and understood.

But it has not proved adequate in a changing world, especially changing price levels. As historic cost has become 'out of date', valuations have become more prevalent. Property and buildings, contract work-in-progress and overseas assets are examples.

These departures from historic cost damage its clear objectivity and produce 'hotch-potch' accounts. In using historic cost as a basis of performance measurement the valuations used have to be examined to ensure consistency and fairness.

For businesses with few, or new, fixed assets historic cost should be a reasonable measurement basis, provided inflation is not so high as to affect stocks and charging out of materials.

STATEMENT 13.1   *Historic cost based accounts as they would be published*

PRINTAPRESS plc

GROUP PROFIT AND LOSS ACCOUNT
Year ended 31st December 1983

	1983		1982
	£'000	£'000	£'000
Turnover		6370	5420
Materials consumed	3445		2925
*Staff costs (employment costs)	1950		1755
*Depreciation	165		130
Other operating charges	325		250
		5885	5060
Operating profit		485	360
Interest payable		45	40
Profit on ordinary activities before taxation		440	320
*Taxation on profit on ordinary activities		150	130
Profit on ordinary activities after taxation		290	190
*Extraordinary items		60	—
Profit attributable to shareholders		230	190
Dividends		110	95
Retained profit for the year		120	95

---

*Further details of these items would be found in Notes to the accounts.

STATEMENT 13.2 *Historic cost based accounts as they would be published*

PRINTAPRESS plc

VALUE ADDED STATEMENT
Year ended 31st December 1983

	1983		1982	
	£'000	%	£'000	%
Turnover	6370	100.0	5420	100.0
Bought-in materials, services and depreciation	3935	61.8	3305	61.0
Value added	2435	38.2	2115	39.0
Distribution:				
To employees as wages, salaries, national insurance and pension contributions	1950	82.1	1755	83.0
To lenders as interest	45	1.9	40	1.9
To government as taxation	150	6.4	130	6.1
To shareholders as dividends	110	4.6	95	4.5
	2255	95.0	2020	95.5
Retained in the business	120	5.0	95	4.5
	2375	100.0	2115	100.0
Extraordinary expenditure	60		—	
	2435		2115	

14   Current cost

ORIGIN AND DEFINITION

When historic cost became misleading because of inflation, other bases of accounting were invented in an attempt to produce profit and loss statements that were 'translated', 'adjusted' or 'corrected' for inflation. In 1973 the two main contending bases were:

- current purchasing power (CPP)
- current cost accounting (CCA)

In 1974 a version of CPP was promulgated as a 'provisional' accounting standard (SSAP 7).[2] It was not mandatory, and only a few accounts were published on the CPP basis. The standard was only partly accepted and caused considerable controversy.

To arbitrate on the matter a Government Committee was appointed, known after its chairman as the *Sandilands Committee*.[3] It settled, in 1975, for CCA. In many respects the Sandilands arguments were weak, and the controversy between CPP and CCA simmers on. Myddleton in a new book (see Chapter 4, p. 21) revives the case for CPP, which he has rechristened '*constant purchasing power*'.[4]

The weaknesses of CCA have led to continual changes in the concept and in the accounting methods and presentation to be used. Since 1975 there have been five different versions. But still CCA remains dominant as the most acceptable basis of providing for inflation in accounts.

The many changes in CCA, however, make it difficult to define what it really is.

Sandilands[3] confined CCA to changing the historic cost figures in two areas:

(1)   The valuation of all fixed assets at current value or replacement cost, and hence depreciation based on the replacement cost.

(2) The value of stocks at replacement cost, and hence cost of sales based on the up-to-date prices of materials used.

These two main adjustments (for depreciation and cost of sales) have continued as the essence of CCA. They apply only to physical assets. They are not concerned with what are called *monetary items*, i.e. debtors, creditors and loans, the amount of which is fixed in money terms (although Sandilands did suggest that the gain to the shareholders' interest from financing by fixed loans should be shown in the current cost balance sheet).[5] CCA at this stage was concerned only with movements in prices *specific* to the business (or, in Baxter's terms, *special price change*[1]).

In 1976 the Sandilands recommendations were translated into a long and complex draft accounting standard (ED 18) with a 400-page *Guidance Manual*.[5] (In order, probably, to satisfy the supporters of CPP, it included two extra statements, not mentioned by Sandilands, concerning the change in shareholder's equity at constant purchasing power and the gain or loss on monetary assets and liabilities.) All this was plainly too much for ordinary accountants (never mind the users of accounts) and ED 18 was rejected.

On re-examination by a new Committee the troublesome question of the *purchasing power gain* from loans was raised again, having been dismissed by Sandilands as 'irrelevant'.[3] The Committee decided that it *was* relevant and included a new feature, the *gearing adjustment*. CCA according to Sandilands plus gearing adjustment was launched in 1977 as an 'interim recommendation' (not mandatory), known as the *Hyde Guidelines*, after the Committee chairman.[2]

The fourth version of CCA was ED 24, 1979.[2] Many of the finicky details of the pure CCA in ED 18 were dropped, but a balance sheet as well as a profit and loss account had to be produced. The gearing adjustment introduced by Hyde was retained, but was considered to be one-sided. What about the 'purchasing power *loss*' from debtors and loans made *by* the company? In answer to this question a *monetary working capital adjustment* (MWCA) was included to allow for the net loss or gain, caused by inflation, on net debtors or net creditors.

A further development was the concept of *operating capability*. This assumes that present assets will always be replaced by similar assets producing 'the same amount of goods and services'. If operating capability is not maintained, it was declared, then capital has not been maintained in real terms. Companies following this concept were saddled with depreciation of replacement cost on a set of assets which may be totally different, due to change in technology, markets or economic circumstances, when the time comes. They may well be in a different business altogether.

In March 1980, the main provisions of ED 24 were incorporated in SSAP 16,[2] which became mandatory for quoted companies and other large companies not quoted. As the cost of preparation, usefulness and relevance of the new standard was assessed by companies, there were a growing number expressing their general dissatisfaction and many refusing to produce current cost accounts at all.

The fifth version of CCA was published in June 1984, as ED 35, with a different title, *Accounting for the effects of changing prices*.[2] The term 'current cost' is used in the text but 'current cost accounting' has been dropped, although the four adjustments of depreciation, cost of sales, MWCA and gearing remain as in SSAP 16. The 'maintenance of operating capability' is emphasised with even more force.

However, only the depreciation and cost of sales adjustments are needed to restate operating costs on a replacement cost basis instead of a historic cost basis. A pure and simple definition of current cost is: 'a cost of assets consumed in a period that is based on what it would cost to replace them at present prices'. The other adjustments, MWCA and gearing, belong more properly in the CPP camp.

ACCOUNTING STATEMENTS

In published accounts the statement of profit and loss on a current cost basis will be as prescribed by ED 35[2] (if it is accepted). An example is shown in Statement 14.1 (p. 187). There is no current cost profit and loss account as such and no balance sheet; only the effect of the adjustments on the historic cost profit or loss need to be shown and a few balance sheet figures.

Statement 14.1 is based on one example out of three in ED 35. It emphasises that these are 'illustrative and in no way prescriptive'. The statement appears as a note to the main accounts, showing primarily what the profit after taxation (and any figures below that level such as extraordinary items) would have been if it had been based on current cost.

In published accounts there has been a steady downgrading of CCA since the Sandilands report when a full set of accounts on a current cost basis was envisaged to replace historic cost as the main basis of accounting.

In divisional accounts CCA is used by some companies on a selective basis. The gearing adjustment, naturally, is never used. MWCA seems to be used by only a handful of companies. The cost of sales and depreciation adjustments are likely to be those given most attention. Cost of sales on a replacement cost of LIFO basis may be used in divisional accounting statements without any reference being made to CCA or current cost.

Depreciation on a current cost basis is clearly useful when divisions have a mixture of old and new assets. A consistent basis for valuing assets for the purpose of return on capital employed (ROCE) is highly desirable (see Chapter 18, p. 219). Current cost is certainly more logical than historic cost, although comparatively few companies use current cost for ROCE (only 10 per cent in a recent survey). Generally, according to most surveys,[6] current cost has not taken hold on any substantial scale in management accounts.

FEATURES OF CURRENT COST

There are two features of pure current cost, i.e. depreciation and cost of sales adjustments, and there are two features added to cater for effects of inflation outside the costs of physical assets, i.e. monetary working capital and gearing adjustments.

Depreciation on a current cost basis is an obvious means of correcting the anomaly between new and old assets. For example, on a historic cost basis, depreciation of plant purchased this year is charged, with 5 per cent inflation, about $1\frac{1}{2}$ times the depreciation of identical plant purchased 8 years ago. But current cost depreciation does not get rid of all the snags in historic cost depreciation – and there is at least one new one.

(1) *Economic life of asset.* Estimation has the same problem. Under historic cost asset lives are deliberately conservative partly to allow for higher replacement cost. Under current cost there is a tendency not to be conservative and to reduce estimated asset lives.

(2) *Assets fully written off.* On a current cost basis fixed assets do not become fully written off, as they are revalued every year, but depreciation can be very low.

(3) *Recoverable amount* (used when net realisable value or 'economic value' is below current cost). The necessary values are difficult to estimate and use of 'recoverable amount', which occurs much more often than on the historic cost basis, is avoided as far as possible; there are further complications if the current cost of an asset in future years *exceeds* the 'recoverable amount'.

(4) *Backlog depreciation* (an illustration is needed to explain):

asset purchased at start of year 1	£1000	
asset life 10 years, therefore		
10 per cent p.a. depreciation		
replacement cost at end of year 1	£1080	
depreciation, year 1		£108
replacement cost at end of year 2	£1166	
depreciation, year 2		£117
total depreciation		£225
but two years depreciation on current cost is 20% of £1166 =		£233
'backlog' depreciation not provided for =		£8

(Assuming replacement cost continues to rise by 8 per cent each year, the replacement cost in year 9 will be £2000 and the total backlog £750.)

If depreciation is intended to provide funds for replacement of the asset at the end of its life, the backlog depreciation should be charged each year (in the illustration, £8 in year 2 for the undercharge in year 1).

ED 18 (1976) proposed that backlog depreciation should be provided.[5] SSAP 16 (1980) and ED 35 (1984), imply that it can be ignored.[2]

Cost of sales on a replacement cost basis has much to commend it when general price levels are rising. The logic would be denied by very few. But it does have problems in certain cases:

(1) *Seasonal products.* At the end of a season there is no replacement cost available until the following season, which cannot be relevant to the profit of the current season.

(2) *Commodities.* Basic materials are subject to considerable price variations downwards as well as upwards. Replacement cost is irrelevant. Stocks are often held for dealing rather than for subsequent manufacture.

(3) *Falling prices.* When prices are falling, the cost of sales adjustment to replacement cost will become a credit, producing an increase in profit. This offends the prudence principle in accounting by anticipating a profit on the lower-priced materials before it is realised.

If inflation is low and stocks are not very large, the cost of sales adjustment for most businesses becomes immaterial.

The *monetary working capital adjustment* is similar. Low levels of inflation will produce very small adjustments which may not be worth making. MWCA is sound enough in theory, but it is not part of current cost accounting and has severe problems of definition, for example:

(1) *Trade debtors and creditors.* Debtors and creditors relating to capital transactions should be excluded, but it is not always easy to distinguish.

(2) *Cash in hand.* Normally cash should be excluded, but some cash may be necessary working capital.

(3) *Bank overdrafts.* Overdrafts to cover seasonal working capital or special stocks should be included, but are often difficult to separate from a permanent loan.

The *gearing adjustment* is the most controversial adjustment of all of the extensions to the current cost basis. There are two main questions:

(1) Should the gain in purchasing power (or the 'inflationary profit') on loans be taken into account in current cost accounts or not?

(2) If so, how should the adjustment be calculated?

Sandilands was against any recognition of the *inflationary gains on loans*.[3] Since 1977 the supporters of such an adjustment have won the day, but the method of calculation carried into SSAP 16 has been subject to widespread criticism, with the result that ED 35 allows any one of three possible methods of calculation, which could produce very different profits.[2]

Originally the inflationary gain on borrowing was regarded as an offset to interest, the theory being that interest included a certain allowance for inflation. With the evidence of the past ten years that actual rates of interest have little correlation with inflation, the gearing adjustment becomes even less convincing, and in ED 35 is divorced from interest in two of the three methods allowed.

Any gain in purchasing power on loans is not realised and could easily disappear if inflation falls sharply. The gearing adjustment, although probably remaining mandatory for public companies, is becoming increasingly regarded as irrelevant. Its effect, if any, can only be taken into account over a long period. It has little place in business performance measurement.

VALUATION

For Sandilands 'current cost' is synonymous with *value to the business*, which is 'in the great majority of cases,' the Report says,

> represented by the current purchase price (replacement cost) of the asset; but may in certain circumstances be represented by its net realisable value or 'economic value'.[3]

The 'circumstances' are when either of these two latter values are lower than replacement cost.

Land and buildings in CCA are valued normally at open market value for existing use. More specialised buildings, rarely sold, are valued at estimated replacement cost.

Plant and machinery are valued at the cost incurred if they had to be replaced. The replacement should be by a piece of plant or machine with a similar output or capacity. Often, because of technological advance or more efficient designs, such a similar plant or machine does not exist. One way of getting over this problem is to find what is called a *modern equivalent asset*, which would have a higher output, larger capacity, or lower operating costs than the present plant or machine, and reduce the current cost of that asset in proportion to its extra economic performance. In very many cases, sufficient information is not readily available or the calculations become too complex to be practicable.

Instead, index numbers applied to the historic cost of plant and machinery have been used overwhelmingly. (In one survey, only 2 per cent used the 'modern equivalent asset' approach and 72 per cent used indices[6].) Over 100 specific indices relating to fixed assets are published by the Central Statistical Office, but they do not provide the same accuracy as using the individual replacement cost of each major piece of plant or machinery.

Stocks are valued at the current replacement cost, unless net realisable value is lower. Replacement cost of materials, in most businesses, is easy to ascertain and is probably recorded as an important piece of management information. Where stock is not to be replaced in the same form, an index can be used.

Dealing or commodity stocks subject to fluctuating prices are, according to SSAP 16, to be treated as monetary working capital and subject therefore to MWCA.[2] If no adjustment is made, it is said, the 'operating capability' of the business will be impaired, but this is hardly relevant in businesses engaged in dealing and speculation as objectives. A similar MWCA approach is recommended for seasonal stocks.

Work-in-progress is valued at replacement cost of the elements within it. Where these are difficult to find, index numbers can be used.

Monetary working capital is not revalued in the balance sheet, although the MWCA produces the same effect on the current cost profit and loss account as if it were.

Valuation of assets for CCA (as laid down in SSAP 16) is a messy process, involving usually a mixture of indices, market valuations and current prices. The result is that no one has a 'feel' for what the answer ought to be. What comes out of the pot tends to be accepted, because it is difficult to refer back and examine all the ingredients in detail.

ADVANTAGES OF CURRENT COST

(1) It ensures that profit measures take into account the up-to-date costs of assets used.

(2) It uses price adjustments specific to the business and may therefore be relevant and useful to business managements.

(3) It retains the monetary unit as £s of the day, which involves no translation into £s of other periods or of other purchasing power.

(4) It matches sales revenue at the same price level as the costs incurred in making those sales.

(5) It provides, on a replacement basis, some measure of real capital maintenance.

(6) It indicates, to some extent, the cover available for dividends.

DISADVANTAGES OF CURRENT COST

(1) It does not account for general inflation; current cost accounts remain in £s of the year so that the profits of different years are not comparable in real terms.

(2) It relies on values which may be highly subjective, superimposing a judgement on asset life on to a judgement on replacement cost.

(3) It cannot be applied to all businesses (examples of businesses unsuitable for CCA are commodity dealing, seasonal foods, shipping, mining, and 'value-based businesses' such as insurance and investment companies).

(4) It does not properly indicate the cover available for dividends, although an improvement on historic cost.

(5) It is costly to implement and involves continuing extra costs as long as it is a supplement to historic cost accounts.

(6) It cannot cope adequately with falling prices without offending normal accounting principles.

(7) It is complex, and appears to have no simple overall rationale.

In addition

(8) The operating capability concept assumes a static structure of operations and capacity – an assumption, for most companies, which is very unrealistic in today's turbulent environment.

(9) The recoverable amount is almost impossible to estimate and yet the incidence of this value is much more frequent under replacement cost than under historic cost.

(10) The MWCA lacks precise definition.

(11) The gearing adjustment in its original form (Hyde guidelines) was totally illogical, but is retained as one of the options in the latest version (ED 35).

(12) The three options of gearing adjustment proposed will produce such widely different results for highly geared companies as to be useless for many company comparisons.

(13) The MWCA and gearing adjustments are very difficult to understand for the non-accountant.

WHERE CURRENT COST IS GOOD

In some businesses current cost is of no use at all. In others it can be a great improvement on historic cost in particular circumstances.

First, the businesses where current cost is *bad* or simply inappropriate:

(1) *No physical assets.* Businesses with no stocks or work-in-progress and negligible fixed assets have nothing on which replacement cost can be based. Typical of such businesses are financial institutions dealing only with money coming in and going out. They may own land and buildings, but usually these are treated as an investment rather than an operating asset.

Particular examples are:
- insurance companies
- investment and property companies
- factoring businesses
- leasing businesses
- banks (for their core business)

(2) *Wasting assets*. Oil, coal and precious metals are wasting assets. Companies which extract these materials from the earth or the sea do not expect to replace their mines or wells when they are exhausted. As oil gradually runs out, the oil companies intend probably to go into other businesses. Replacement cost of oil, for example, is scarcely indicative of 'value to the business'. The value of reserves of oil increase because oilfields are seen to become exhausted, not because of inflation.

In some extractive industries there is almost an unlimited supply of raw material, although in practice limited by planning rules. Stone, sand, gravel and clay are examples where there is a continual renewal of resources and where CCA could therefore be useful. Particular examples of where the use of CCA is dubious are:

- oil-wells
- gas-fields
- coal-mining
- metals mining

(3) *Single purpose businesses*. There are many businesses which have a single objective for a certain period, and do not intend to replace their major assets after the objective is fulfilled. When the main assets are worn out, the business may stop. Sometimes such businesses are formed to exploit certain supplies of materials, or certain processes, patents or particular events.

Small businesses are often of the kind that have no objective beyond the working life of the owner/manager. Maintenance of operating capability is then of no interest.

Declining businesses may continue for a period, even though their historic cost profit is modest, until major renewal or investment is required. Such businesses have been called 'cash cows'; they exist

only as long as the cow is alive to produce the milk. No new cow will be obtained. Such businesses may show a loss on a current cost basis, but that does not mean that they should be closed.
Particular examples are:

- small shops
- single project consortia
- glass bottle manufacture (being replaced by plastic or cans)
- linoleum manufacture (being replaced by vinyl)

(4) *Fluctuating asset values.* Large expensive assets such as ships and aircraft can vary widely in value from year to year according to the demand for transport and travel. Ships, for instance, can easily go from the replacement cost category to the 'unrecoverable amount' category due to a slump, and back again when the demand for shipping picks up. This makes nonsense of CCA depreciation, and produces misleading, widely fluctuating, profits as a result.
Particular examples are:

- tankers
- large aircraft of middle age

(5) *Fluctuating stock values.* Replacement cost is an impossible concept when prices of materials go up and down like yo-yos. Seasonal crops may be of this kind: one year there may be drought causing high prices; next year a bumper crop may lead to rock-bottom prices. Commodity prices vary according to factors which have nothing to do with inflation. CCA is not at all happy in the situation when prices are falling.

Fluctuating values promote speculative activities. Speculative profits can in no way be adjusted for inflation. The objective of the speculator is to make profits from inflation as well as from the ups and downs of commodity prices. In practice the two cannot be separated.
Particular examples are:

- fruit farming
- potato farming
- Christmas and post-Christmas sales
- commodity dealing

In what situations then is current cost useful? In general, it is most necessary when inflation is high. But again, it depends on the business. If the business has few fixed assets and negligible working capital, historic cost may be good enough, even in high inflation. If, however, the business has substantial fixed assets of considerable age, current cost could be essential, even when inflation is low.

The largest CCA adjustment in capital-intensive businesses is invariably the extra depreciation. If a high proportion of the assets have been acquired before the high inflation of 1974 to 1979, a large depreciation adjustment will be needed until these pre-1979 assets have been disposed of, no matter how low inflation is now.

Even if inflation becomes negative, a depreciation adjustment may still be necessary for the businesses with old assets. The short-term adjustments, on the other hand (i.e. cost of sales and monetary working capital), would produce awkward results when material prices are steadily falling.

The simple algorithm opposite shows the main conditions in which the use of the primary CCA adjustments, rather than pure historic cost, should be considered.

Notes on algorithm

(1) High inflation: say, over 7 per cent.
(2) High inflation in the past: say, averaging over 7 per cent in the last 10 years.
(3) Capital intensive: say, gross fixed assets more than twice average operating profit on historic cost basis.
(4) Old fixed assets: say, more than 50 per cent of assets more than four years old.
(5) Large stocks: say, stocks and work-in-progress more than 25 per cent of turnover.
(6) The above parameters are extremely simplified. In the case of depreciation the current rate of inflation, the age of fixed assets and the record of inflation relevant to the old assets should be reviewed each year. In accounts for the year 1984, with an increase in fixed asset prices of 5 per cent in that year, it can be shown, using the record of inflation rates for earlier years, that it is not worth charging CCA depreciation on assets less than 7 years old, because the difference of 27 per cent between historic cost and current cost depreciation does not seem to be sufficiently material in view of the uncertain features of historic cost – particularly the tendency to use conservative asset lives. In 1985, if inflation remains low, the threshold of asset age above which CCA depreciation should be charged will be extended from 7 years old to 8 years old. As time goes by, with continued low inflation, only very old assets will be affected. However, in 1984, for assets acquired 16 years ago (in 1967), historic cost depreciation needs to be tripled to convert it to current cost.

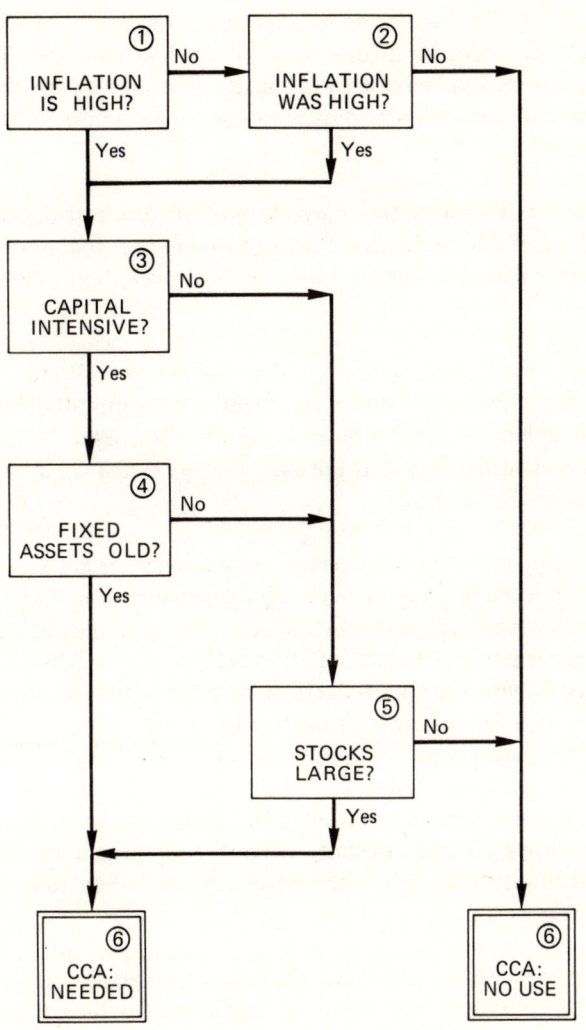

CONCLUSION

The catalogue of drawbacks, disadvantages and defects of CCA is large and heavy: valuation anomalies; depreciation problems; 'recoverable amounts'; illogical adjustments; extreme complexity; lack of universal application, overall rationale and inter-period comparison. Most of all, it is difficult to understand and each of the five changes since its inception ten years ago increase the difficulty. Through all the changes, however, the true current cost adjustments for depreciation and cost of sales have stuck.

The necessity for a depreciation correction of historic cost depends on the size and age of the fixed assets. Present low inflation does not remove the distortion if there are substantial fixed assets over about seven years old.

Depreciation is an important ingredient of profit or value added measures of performance. Wherever there is a continuing business intending to replace assets when worn out or obsolete, depreciation must be computed in such a way that the age of assets is neutral in order to assure a fair profit measure.

The cost of sales adjustment is necessary only when there are substantial stocks and/or work-in-progress with significant inflation. In practice, the system of accounting for stocks and cost of sales cannot be changed every year according to whether inflation is high or low. Some form of current cost of stocks and materials consumed should be adopted so that the result is not far different from the CCA type of cost of sales adjustment to historic cost.

In the management accounts of company divisions the treatment of rising price levels should normally follow these principles, using a current cost adjustment only when necessary and when fully understood.

In published accounts the use of current cost is regulated by accounting standards, which, largely because of the many changes, have taken on a political aspect. Unfortunately the selective use of appropriate current cost adjustments to the historic cost accounts is unlikely to win favour. Published accounts seem doomed to a messy combination of historic cost accounts with some isolated illogical adjustments which may give a view of company performance that is far from true and fair.

STATEMENT 14.1   *Current cost based accounts as prescribed by ED 35*
(Example B)

PRINTAPRESS plc

ADJUSTMENTS TO GROUP PROFIT AND LOSS ACCOUNT
Year ended 31st December 1983

	1983		1982	
	£'000	£'000	£'000	£'000
Operating profit (historic cost basis)		485		360
Cost of sales adjustment	20		22	
Monetary working capital adjustment	10		12	
Depreciation adjustment	40		35	
		70		69
		415		291
Interest payable	45		40	
Less: Gearing adjustment	15		13	
		30		27
Current cost profit on ordinary activities before taxation		385		264
Taxation		150		130
Current cost profit on ordinary activities after taxation		235		134

No adjustment is required for extraordinary items

15   Cash flow

ORIGIN AND DEFINITION

Cash flow is the oldest form of accounting, predating historic cost by many centuries. It is extremely simple. All cash payments and all cash receipts are recorded in a book (now probably on a computer). The balance at the end of the week or month is the cash amount in hand, or in the bank. When the balance at the beginning of the month is compared with the balance at the end of the month, a cash surplus or a cash deficit for the month appears.

The periodic cash surplus or deficit is similar in its function to profit or loss, but its basis is quite different. Profit separates out capital payments and adjusts the cash surplus or deficit for transactions not yet paid for or not received in cash, so as to match up revenue (not receipts) with costs (not payments). The profit measure 'accrues' the costs incurred but not yet paid for, and the sales or fees invoiced but not yet received in cash.

Cash flow can be analysed in exactly the same way as profit. Cash spent on capital items can be singled out. Other payments can be classified into wages or salaries, materials bought, interest paid, tax paid and so on. The problems of classification are exactly the same for cash flow as for profit. Clearly, when both measures are used (as is usually the case), the classification rules should be the same.

The definition of cash is not so simple as the concept. Purest cash is cash in your pocket. Cash in a bank current account is next. Cash in a deposit account, such as seven-day money, is 'near cash'. Deposits requiring longer notice are doubtful.

On the negative side, a fluctuating overdraft is generally negative cash. A short-term loan is probably not. And there are shades of loan in the middle which may or may not be negative cash.

Ideally the definition should match on either side, short-term deposits, if included, being the counterpart of short-term borrowings. When these are included, the result may not be termed 'cash', but *net liquid funds*.

As more items are included, cash deteriorates from pure money in the pocket to a funds flow concept (Chapter 16). Cash is normally defined as money which is available almost immediately for an absolutely certain amount. Liquidity is different and there is no easy definition of 'liquid funds'. In some definitions it would include short-term investments.

Certainty is an essential element of cash flow accounting. If any kind of valuation has to be used, the clear objectivity of cash flow is prejudiced.

Unfortunately the term 'cash flow' is not always given to mean the flow in and out of the business of pure cash. In many textbooks cash flow is defined as 'profit before tax plus depreciation' or instead of 'depreciation', the wider term: 'items not involving the movement of funds'. The result, of course, is not 'cash flow' but 'funds flow', which is defined more precisely in Chapter 16 (p. 200).

Cash flow can be defined as an adjustment to profit, thus:

> operating profit
> plus depreciation
> plus sundry provisions
> plus or minus change in working capital, comprising
>   stocks, debtors and creditors

ACCOUNTING STATEMENTS

There is no statute or accounting standard that requires a cash flow statement to be published or produced. Hence the statements that exist take on various forms, depending on the type and position of the business and the emphasis required on particular aspects.

Statement 15.1 (p. 196) shows a simple presentation of a cash flow account, like a profit and loss account but on a different accounting basis. Depreciation and change in stocks and work-in-progress, two major trouble spots, do not feature in any cash flow account. Tax paid in the year is factual and avoids the trouble spots of deferred taxation, surplus ACT and losses brought forward.

Operating cash flow is the cash flow equivalent of operating profit without the troubles of depreciation, stocks and so on, mentioned earlier. Depreciation particularly may be a very unfair charge and not very relevant if the assets concerned are not likely to be replaced. Some divisions of companies may be 'managed for cash', in which case operating cash flow is the most appropriate performance measure.

Where cash is short, operating cash flow is a vital measure. When comparing the performance of divisions, the cash generated by a division may be more important than profit and divisions may be judged, at least partially, on their operating cash flows.

The longer the period covered the better is the cash flow basis for a performance measure. Over a period of ten years, for example, in businesses with fairly short-life fixed assets, cash receipts may more or less 'match' with cash payments (including capital expenditure). Over twenty years, if the same business can exist that long, the cash flow basis could be even more useful and probably the most truthful measure of long-term performance.

Statement 15.3 (p. 198) shows the cash flow performance of Printapress for five years, as an example. The statement is divided into two halves: (1) the actual cash flow and (2) the cash flow in 'real terms' as restated at 1983 prices throughout, by application of the RPI. Inflation can be logically and acceptably taken into account in this way because cash is always received and paid at a particular date. There is no hangover or 'timing difference' from one period to another.

There is, however, a little problem with loans. Loans at fixed interest rates are repaid at the original amount and it may not be right that the repayments should be indexed. Bank overdrafts are regarded as loans in the statement, because they are used as an alternative to a loan, and not as a negative cash balance. Within this definition the statement shows how much in current terms (1983 prices) the company has needed to borrow in order to maintain and expand its business.

Statement 15.2 (p. 197) shows cash flow in value added format. Again there is no depreciation, no stock movement, and no deferred tax. Strictly speaking the statement should not be labelled 'value added' as the 'value' in debtors, stocks and work-in-progress is not shown. But the statement avoids the mysteries to many people of 'accrual' accounting. For this reason the cash flow approach is sometimes used in a value added statement in simplified form for employees. It can show 'how the money was spent' without any fear of misunderstanding.

FEATURES OF CASH FLOW

Because cash flow is basically so simple there are few features that need to be described or commented upon.

However, there is one central feature which distinguishes cash flow from all other bases of accounting. That is the facility to assess whether the business performance is sufficiently good to enable it to survive. None of the profit measures, or funds flow, shed much light on the ability of a business to generate sufficient cash to continue. Lee, an advocate of cash flow reporting, says 'A business cannot survive, progress, repay loans and other debts, or pay dividends without cash'.[7] Lawson, in a similar vein, says 'Taking one year with another, operating cash flow is the fund from which all capital expenditure, all tax payments and all liquidity adjustments must be financed, not to mention risk-commensurate returns to lenders and shareholders'.[8]

But is the cash flow measure really a measure of business performance? Lawson again, 'The trend of an entity's operating cash flow must be regarded as a paramount index of its financial performance.'[8] In other words, depreciation, stocks and accruals should be omitted. This is clearly too drastic for all except very long-term measures. And neither Lee nor Lawson would maintain that the profit and loss account should be abolished.

Cash flow is sometimes referred to as the 'life blood of the business'. The amount of petrol in a motor car is perhaps a better analogy. The performance of a motor car is not affected by the amount in the tank, except that, when it is empty, the car stops.

Cash flow is totally objective. Having decided on its definition there are no estimations, assumptions or judgements. The petrol gauge in a car is likewise objective; the amount in the tank can be measured with complete accuracy. But the measures of performance for motor cars are various (e.g. m.p.g., top speed, seconds to reach x m.p.h.) and cannot reasonably be combined.

Cash flow, however, can be one of the collection of business performance measures for certain businesses in certain circumstances. It is analogous to blood or petrol only in its role as a long stop.

VALUATION

Pure cash flow entails no valuation of assets or liabilities. As a check on solvency, ensuring enough cash for survival, only pure cash flow is relevant.

When used in performance measurement, cash flow tends to be analysed, and capital expenditure in particular is shown separately (as in Statements 15.2 and 15.3) or not at all (as in Statement 15.1). Payments for capital equipment are 'cash outflow', just as are payments for materials or wages, but capital payments are regarded as something different, in deference possibly to the normal accounting conventions.

It cannot be denied that capital payments do have a *value* for future periods. But if this value is recognised, it re-introduces all the weakness and subjectivity of 'accrual' accounting. If it is not recognised, it ignores an essential element of performance measurement.

Lawson suggests that, in the case of public companies, the value of capital investment is 'impounded' in the market value of the shares.[9] But clearly there are many other factors which affect Stock Exchange values. No valuation method has been discovered which does not damage the intrinsic factual basis of cash flow.

Valuation could be used at the beginning and end of a long-term cash flow performance statement, but all the old controversies of historic, replacement or market value would rear their ugly heads once more. The exercise would scarcely be worth all the trouble, unless there were a very large difference between fixed assets at the beginning and at the end. And then it would probably be more sensible to use the CCA figures. But that would not be cash flow.

ADVANTAGES OF CASH FLOW

(1)   It is entirely objective, factual and clear-cut.
(2)   Cash flow statements are cheap and easy to prepare.

(3) It is essential to ensure short-term business health and can be extended for use as a performance measure.

(4) It has no problems of valuation.

(5) It is simple to understand, requiring no accounting jargon.

For the long term

(6) Cash flow can be indexed for inflation, and thus converted to 'real terms', with few logistic problems.

(7) It can show objectively how both historic and current cost can be misleading in times of inflation.

(8) It can show the real extent to which borrowing has been used to make up deficiencies in operating cash flow.

DISADVANTAGES OF CASH FLOW

(1) It takes no account of the long lasting use and benefits of capital equipment and buildings.

(2) It takes no account of amounts paid for working capital necessary for future periods.

(3) It is generally too erratic to be used as a short-term performance measure.

(4) It has no clear agreed definition.

For the long-term

(5) It becomes tempting to introduce valuation of the worth of capital expenditure, which negates most of the advantages.

WHERE CASH FLOW IS GOOD

As a short-term measure of performance (not for survival) cash flow is useful only in a very stable situation, where:

● credit transactions are few, or very steady
● stocks are small, or regularly come in and go out
● capital expenditure is small
● sales and production are regular
● there are no seasonal fluctuations
● input and output prices are steady

This means a very simple business without fluctuating prices.

In the long-term, ideally ten years, cash flow is useful, where:

- the business has not undergone major changes in structure or strategy
- capital expenditure has been fairly steady
- capital investment has been mostly in short-life assets
- there has been inflation on a significant scale (say, over 5 per cent) requiring adjustment to real terms

Such a long-term measure, indexed for inflation, as illustrated in Statement 15.3, undoubtedly provides the best overall picture of business performance. However, it does include financial performance which begs the question: what was the *business* performance regardless of how good or bad were the *financial* decisions?

Statement 15.3 can be looked at in two ways:

either (1)   The operating cash flow was not sufficient to support all the capital expenditure, tax, interest and dividends paid without (apparently) excessive borrowing.

or   (2)   The capital expenditure and dividends (both discretionary) should have been cut to match the cash resources generated internally.

Only (1) is relevant to this book. The operating cash flow is the crucial measure. The rest of the statement is primarily financial, showing the difficulties (or benefits) resulting. But, as with value added, the distribution of cash flow may have an effect on the motivation to improve the performance.

CONCLUSION

Cash flow is not a good measure of performance in the short-term except in cases where the cash receipts and payments are not unlike the revenue and expense of the profit and loss account.

In cash flow accounting there are no assets or liabilities. Nothing is allocated, accrued, or carried forward to another period. Stocks, debtors, creditors and fixed assets are ignored. So there are no problems of valuation. Cash is cash is cash.

Cash is certain, simple and clear. There may be a little difficulty in defining what it is, but it is no problem provided it is consistent. The objectivity and certainty of cash and the fact that a payment or receipt can always be precisely dated, make it good for indexing the figures for inflation, and this enables a long-term view of cash flow performance to be obtained. To complete the long-term picture, some kind of valuation of fixed assets at the beginning and end of the period may have to be made; but that would damage the clear portrayal of cash flow.

Cash flow comes into its own when times are bad, through high inflation or severe recession. When survival is at stake, profits may go by the board. The only relevant measure of performance becomes the amount of cash available.

Cash flow statements and forecasts continue to be used in some form in every business, primarily to ensure that cash is always available to finance the operations. It is a planning tool rather than a performance measurement tool, until the worst conditions should happen.

In the short-term, under severe economic conditions, a cash flow based measurement is essential. Otherwise for the short-term it is not suitable; but for the long-term it can be indexed and used to appraise the total financial position that results.

STATEMENT 15.1   *Cash flow based accounts as they might be published*

PRINTAPRESS plc

CASH FLOW STATEMENT
Year ended 31st December 1983

	1983 £000	1983 £000	1982 £000	1982 £000
Receipts from sales		6036		5170
Payments for:				
Materials	3362		2835	
Wages, salaries and contributions	1950		1735	
Other goods and services	198		235	
		5510		4805
Operating cash flow		526		365
Interest paid		42		37
		484		328
Tax paid		124		94
Net cash flow		360		234

STATEMENT 15.2   *Cash flow based accounts as they might be published*

PRINTAPRESS plc

CASH VALUE ADDED STATEMENT
Year ended 31st December 1983

	1983		1982	
	£000	%	£000	%
Receipts from sales	6036	100.0	5170	100.0
Payments for materials and services	3560	59.0	3070	59.4
Cash value added	2476	41.0	2100	40.6
Distribution:				
Paid to employees as wages or salaries, plus national insurance and pension contributions	1950	87.8	1735	88.8
Paid to lenders as interest	42	1.9	37	1.9
Paid to Government as tax	124	5.6	94	4.8
Paid to shareholders as dividend	104	4.7	87	4.5
	2220	100.0	1953	100.0
Paid to lenders to redeem loan	160		—	
	2380		1953	
Paid for new plant and equipment	435		352	
	2815		2305	
Received from shareholders by new issue	650		—	
	2165		2305	
Addition to cash held in bank	311		(205)	
	2476		2100	

STATEMENT 15.3 *Cash flow accounts as they might be published*

PRINTAPRESS plc

LONG-TERM TOTAL CASH FLOW STATEMENT

£000's	*Actual cash*				
	1983	*1982*	*1981*	*1980*	*1979*
Operating profit	485	360	241	340	335
Depreciation	165	130	134	120	105
Increase/(decrease) in working capital	(124)	(125)	(70)	80	130
Operating cash flow	526	365	305	540	570
Fixed assets bought, less sold	435	378	430	320	600
	91	(13)	(125)	220	(30)
Less: Interest paid	42	55	40	20	22
	49	(68)	(165)	200	(52)
Less: Tax paid	124	87	60	85	34
	(75)	(155)	(225)	115	(86)
(Increase)/decrease in cash balance	(311)	94	208	45	(104)
	(386)	(61)	(17)	160	(190)
Less Dividend paid	104	95	80	90	90
	(490)	(156)	(97)	70	(280)
Financed by:					
Proceeds of new share issue	650				
Increase/(decrease) in overdraft	(160)	156	97	(70)	280
	490	156	97	(70)	280

Restated at 1983 prices					
1983	*1982*	*1981*	*1980*	*1979*	*Total*
526	381	346	686	854	2793
435	395	488	407	899	2624
91	(14)	(142)	279	(45)	169
42	57	45	25	33	202
49	(71)	(187)	254	(78)	(33)
124	91	68	108	51	442
(75)	(162)	(255)	146	(129)	(475)
(311)	98	236	57	(156)	(76)
(386)	(64)	(19)	203	(285)	(551)
104	99	91	114	135	543
(490)	(163)	(110)	89	(420)	(1094)
650					650
(160)	163	110	(89)	420	444
490	163	110	(89)	420	1094

16 Funds flow

ORIGIN AND DEFINITION

Balance sheets are rather formidable documents to people not versed in the jargon and conventions of accountancy. The balance sheet is intended to show the financial position of a company, but that objective is rarely possible without some standard of comparison. Businesses tend to be very different in the resources they employ, the operations that they carry out, the financial structure that they have inherited and the accounting policies that they adopt.

The only reasonable comparison is of the previous balance sheet with the current balance sheet. This shows in effect where the money has come from and how it has been used.

A statement based on the difference between balance sheets shows the retained all-inclusive profit for the year, the debt incurred (or repaid), the increase or decrease in working capital (comprising debtors, creditors and stocks, and usually including cash balances), the amount spent on new fixed assets (and realised on sales) and the depreciation for the year. This kind of statement was used first in USA where it became generally known (after a period of many titles being used) as the 'Statement of changes in financial position'.

In the UK the statement is usually entitled 'Statement of source and application of funds', but many other titles are used such as 'Source and use of funds', 'Movement of funds statement', or simply 'Funds statement'. An accounting standard (SSAP 10) on the subject was issued in 1975,[2] but it prescribed little more than the requirement that a statement of source and application of funds should be included in all annual accounts, except for very small companies. The content and format of the statement were left largely to the discretion of the company. The problem areas were reduced somewhat by a book published two years later.[10]

The word 'funds' is invariably used in every statement, although it has no agreed definition. It could mean, at one extreme, all the available resources of the company, or at the other, simply cash in hand. The most usual definition is 'net current assets', or, what is the same thing, 'working capital including cash'. 'Funds' therefore mean assets that are fairly quickly turned into cash. In effect, funds defined thus are cash and things around the business which are getting close to cash.

ACCOUNTING STATEMENTS

Since 1975 the funds statement has become more standardised. The most usual form is illustrated in Statement 16.1 (p. 205).

The statement almost invariably starts with profit before taxation, showing taxation paid and dividends paid as applications of funds. A figure for 'Funds generated from operations' or 'Operating funds flow' can then be shown (the third line of the statement), being profit before taxation, plus depreciation and any other provisions above that level.

Note that in this statement interest is charged against operating funds flow. This is misleading as interest is not related to operations, although it is the general practice. Chart 12.1 (p. 158) illustrates the logic of interest being shown as a deduction from operating profit, operating cash flow *and* operating funds flow.

Statement 16.1 focuses on the movement in funds (as defined above), which is the increase/(decrease) in working capital. In this format it is simple to convert the statement into a cash flow statement, ending with the increase/decrease in net liquid funds, which may be acceptable as the 'change in cash balance'.

Funds flow statements can be produced more frequently than annually. In some companies funds flow statements are produced monthly for each division. Dividends, taxation, and long-term loans would then be omitted.

FEATURES OF FUNDS FLOW

Funds flow can be used as a measure of performance in the same way as cash or near-cash (e.g. becoming pure cash in seven days). Funds flow comprises cash flow plus the working capital 'fund' flow, which becomes cash in anything up to one year.

As regards capital expenditure the position is exactly the same for cash flow as for funds flow. In both statements it is noted that cash or funds have been spent in the period on fixed assets, which are ignored thereafter. Depreciation is not a fund and not regarded as a fund.

Funds flow takes into account stocks, debtors and creditors. Turnover is sales invoiced. Materials used are those taken from stock, not necessarily paid for.

Cash flow is pure and certain. Funds flow introduces uncertainty and subjectivity. Stocks have to be valued in some way and charged out according to one of several conventions: the result can be far from objective, as explained in trouble spot 6.1 (p. 48). Debtors are not certain to pay: any provision for bad debts destroys the sanctity of the 'fund'. Creditors are often estimates while awaiting definitive invoices or statements.

Funds flow brings us nearer to a result for the period which takes into account the costs that match the revenue. Only depreciation of fixed assets is omitted.

Long-term performance could be computed on a funds flow basis in a similar manner to Statement 15.3 (p. 198) for cash flow, although indexing the figures for inflation would not be as pure as for cash flow. Funds flow, which includes stocks, would have a similar problem with inflation as CCA.

Funds flow may be regarded as a kind of half-way house between historic cost profit and cash flow. It may suffer as an uneasy compromise which has not yet found an established and fully acceptable basis.

ADVANTAGES OF FUNDS FLOW

(1) It is free from the troubles and problems of true and fair depreciation.
(2) A funds flow statement is cheap and easy to prepare.

(3) It has no problem of fixed asset valuation.
(4) Results are not likely to be so erratic in the short-term as cash flow because stocks and work-in-progress are taken into account.

In the long-term
(5) It can show the extent of reliance on outside finance over a period of years in a similar way to cash flow.

DISADVANTAGES OF FUNDS FLOW

(1) It takes no account of the long-lasting use and benefits of capital equipment and buildings (the same as for cash flow).
(2) It has valuation problems with stocks and work-in-progress (and possibly, to a small extent, with debtors).
(3) It has a definition which has evolved over time and is not yet fully established.
(4) Funds flow is not so familiar and acceptable as cash flow or profit.

In the long-term
(5) It becomes tempting to introduce valuation of capital expenditure (the same as for cash flow).
(6) Indexing the figures for inflation is difficult because of the presence of stocks in the measurement medium.

WHERE FUNDS FLOW IS GOOD

In the short-term funds flow can be a more useful measure than cash flow. Credit transactions, stocks and seasonal variations are all catered for. In times of inflation, however, stocks become a problem, requiring a CCA kind of approach if inflation becomes moderate to high.

If few fixed assets, but large amounts of working capital, are employed in a business, funds flow could be a useful measure. The absence of depreciation (as in cash flow) may not seriously affect the overall result. But where capital expenditure is large and erratic, the funds flow statement could be most misleading as a performance indicator.

The key measure is the operating funds flow before interest. With care and discretion it could be as useful a measure as operating cash flow or operating profit.

Cash flow is more direct, clear and definite than funds flow. Funds flow uses not simple cash but a new currency of working-capital-plus-cash which is difficult to translate. Generally, increased working capital is thought to be bad, but it is only bad if it is not being used. Increased cash is equally bad if it is simply left lying in the bank.

In common with all the measures and bases of accounting, funds flow is useful only where it is understood. The 'working capital fund' is frequently confused with 'working capital control'. As a performance measure, the bigger the fund the better.

It may be, however, that excessive stocks have been purchased or debts have not been collected promptly, or even creditors have been paid too early, all leading to increases in the elements of working capital. This must mean that net liquid funds have been reduced or not increased as much as they should have done if these elements had been properly controlled. The total fund depends on the 'sources' less the 'applications'. The amounts of individual items in the fund depend on 'working capital control'.

CONCLUSION

Funds flow does not have a history of performance measurement. 'Funds' are not well defined, but recently they have come to mean 'net current assets' or 'working capital'. Using the size of this fund as a measure provides a further dimension of performance.

The working capital fund, however, includes stock and work-in-progress, which have valuation problems. In high inflation there has to be some adjustment.

Funds flow can be used for the short-term very much as profit. It excludes depreciation though, or any valuation of fixed assets.

The funds flow statement shows how the capital expenditure has been financed, but this is irrelevant to business performance. Nevertheless funds flow must rank as a viable basis for measuring performance. It is probably not fully appreciated because working capital has come to be regarded as something to be minimised whereas the working capital fund (including cash) should be something to be maximised.

STATEMENT 16.1 *Funds flow based accounts as they would be published*

PRINTAPRESS plc

FUNDS FLOW STATEMENT –
more usually known as
GROUP SOURCE AND APPLICATION OF FUNDS

	1983 £'000	1982 £'000
Source of funds		
Profit before taxation	440	320
Adjustment for item not involving the movement of funds: Depreciation	165	130
Funds generated from operations	605	450
Funds from other sources: New share issue	650	—
	1255	450
Application of funds		
Dividends paid	104	87
Taxation paid	124	94
Capital expenditure less disposals	435	352
Repayment of short-term loans	160	—
	823	533
Increase (decrease) in working capital	432	(83)
Comprising:		
Increase in stocks	67	80
Increase in debtors	334	250
(Increase) in creditors	(280)	(208)
Increase (decrease) in net liquid funds	311	(205)
	432	(83)

PART III: REFERENCES

1. W. J. Baxter, *Accounting values and inflation* (McGraw-Hill, 1975), pp. 51 and 7.
2. Publications of the Accounting Standards Committee of the Consultative Committee of Accountancy Bodies:

SSAP 7	(Provisional) *Accounting for changes in the purchasing power of money*	1974
SSAP 10	*Statements of source and application of funds*	1975
SSAP 16	*Current cost accounting*	1980
SSAP 20	*Foreign currency translation*	1983
ED 24	*Current cost accounting and Guidance Notes on ED 24*	1979
ED 35	*Accounting for the effects of changing prices*	1984
'HYDE'	*Inflation accounting – an interim recommendation by the ASC*	1977

3. *Inflation Accounting: Report of the Inflation Accounting Committee* ('Sandilands Report') Cmnd 6225, (HMSO, 1975) pp. 168, 151, 130 and 237.
4. D. R. Myddelton, *On a cloth untrue: inflation accounting: the way forward* (Woodhead-Faulkner, 1984).
5. *Guidance Manual on Current Cost Accounting* including the Exposure Draft (ED 18) (Tolley and Institute of Chartered Accountants in England & Wales, 1976).
6. Peat Marwick Mitchell & Co., *Reporting under CCA: A Survey of current cost accounting practice* (Tolley, 1982) pp. 108 and 23.
7. T. A. Lee, *Company Financial Reporting: Issues & Analysis* (Nelson, 1976) p. 129.
8. G. H. Lawson, 'Cash Flow: Was Woolworth ailing?,' *The Accountant*, 4 November 1982, p. 613.
9. G. H. Lawson and A. W. Stark, 'Equity Values and Inflation: Dividends and Debt Financing', *Lloyds Bank Review*, January 1981, no. 139, p. 50.
10. R. W. Knox, *Statements of Source & Application of Funds: A Practical Guide to SSAP 10* (Institute of Chartered Accountants in England & Wales, 1977).

Part IV
Performance Ratios

'There is no excellent beauty that hath not some strangeness in the proportion.' — Francis Bacon

'Any observed statistical regularity will tend to collapse once pressure is placed upon it for control purposes.' — Goodhart's Law

17 Ratios in general

NEED FOR COMPARISON

So far in this book we have been concerned with absolute amounts, expressed in £s. The only comparison that can be made is of one period with another. Ordinary accounts do not compare one amount with a related other amount or physical unit. This requires another calculation which results in some form of ratio.

Bare numbers can easily be lost in a desert, without background, colour or environment. Some kind of comparison is needed to show a measure of performance in context. A comparison of profit with capital employed, or some similar base, gives 'profitability'. A comparison of production with resources used gives 'productivity'. There are many other '-ity' words which turn absolute concepts into relative ones. 'Conduction' becomes 'conductivity', 'available' becomes 'availability', 'continuing' becomes 'continuity', and 'relative' becomes 'relativity': all implying 'how much?' in relation to some other measure.

The other 'measure' is often time, for example per hour, per day, per year. Absolute amounts become relative when they are expressed in time periods. Annual accounts obtain their only comparison when expressed as profit per year. Time is one measure which is totally reliable and absolutely certain.

The most familiar example of a ratio based on time is speed – or velocity – expressed as miles per hour. The length of journey, measured in miles, is of little interest on its own. When compared with the hours taken there is a sense of achievement – a measure in ratio form that can be compared with other speeds of other cars on other journeys.

But there is a difference between speeds on long journeys and on short journeys, and in different conditions of traffic, whether in cities or on motorways. This difficulty applies to all ratios. They answer the question 'how much in relation to . . .?' but they tell you nothing about the scale, the significance or the causes.

ABSOLUTE VERSUS COMPARATIVE

An absolute number, for example, turnover, shows the size of the business, the significance of the business compared with others and the scale of its operations. A business with £10 million of turnover probably works in very different circumstances from one with £10 000.

A business can basically have one of two major objectives:

either (1) to maximise profit
    or (2) to maximise profitability, e.g. return on capital employed

One measure is absolute; the other is comparative. In most businesses both objectives apply, but with varying emphasis.

The gross margin percentage, for example, is regarded as paramount in many businesses (see Chapter 6, p. 44). A small rise of 0.2 per cent may be regarded as a great achievement. Other businesses may care little about margins, perhaps because they are fairly fixed, and they therefore concentrate on expanding turnover, the absolute amount.

Accountants tend to be cynical about ratios. There is only one (earnings per share) that must be shown in published annual accounts. For accountants a ratio is too simple. It disguises the absolute significance of the numerator and denominator, the original numbers being easily lost.

FORMS OF RATIO

Business and accounting ratios are expressed in different forms, which tend to be the most easy to grasp, without any particular logic. The main forms are:

(1) Simple proportion, e.g. cash to credit sales, 1:2.5.
(2) Times covered or turned over, e.g. times dividend covered by profit, 2.1; times stock turned over, 5.2 per year.
(3) Per unit, e.g. sales per employee, £9224; profit per ton, £2.35.
(4) Days taken, e.g. days of credit given to debtors, 51; days of sales in stock, 32.

(5) Percentage, e.g. return on capital employed, 8.4 per cent; gross margin 27.6 per cent.

All of the above could, of course, be expressed as a percentage, but the 'per unit' form of ratio in particular, if converted to a percentage, would be intelligible to very few.

CAVEATS ON RATIOS

Every ratio, to be reliable, must have a numerator and denominator which are logically related. Examples of cases where this rule is sometimes breached are:

(1) Expenditure on an 'accruals' basis should not be compared with revenue on a cash flow basis (and vice versa).
(2) Sales should not be related to production or output without taking into account stock.
(3) Output at cost should not be compared with sales at selling price.
(4) Interest should be included only when the capital, loan or balances related to that interest are also included.
(5) Operating profit should be related to operating assets, excluding such items as investments or goodwill.

Inflation demands further caveats. Money amounts compared with other money amounts of the same currency should be inflation-proof, and this is an important advantage of such ratios. But money amounts compared with physical units must be adjusted for inflation when the ratios themselves are compared between periods.

Where there are long time lags, involving especially depreciation of old assets, money to money may not be the whole cure for inflation: a depreciation or other special adjustment is then needed.

The use of averages gives another cause for vigilance. If the periodic measures that are examined in Part II (i.e. turnover, profits, value added and so on) are compared with one 'snapshot' reading of items such as fixed assets, debtors, stocks, loans or net current assets, then like is not being compared with like.

If the period of the measure is one year, the correct comparison is with the fixed assets (or whatever) averaged over the year. If the period is one month, then an average over the month is needed.

Usually an average of the beginning and the end of the period is taken. This may be fine for a month, but for a year two readings may be quite inadequate, and may mask substantial fluctuations during the year. For seasonal businesses averages of working capital, for example, can be very misleading if the year-end balance sheets coincide either with the high season or the low season.

MEASUREMENT BY RATIO

As a performance measure ratios should generally be regarded as a first shot. They are by definition simplified, a combination of ingredients which can go wrong in the cooking.

They are not very good at the extremes, when one of the numbers is very small or very large compared with the other, and a ratio of infinity or zero may result.

They are not very good with minus quantities such as losses or credits when the recipe expects debits.

They are not very good when too much emphasis is placed on the ratio number. A target expressed as a ratio can make it open to manipulation. While one figure alone (the primary measure) may not be immune to some fiddling with the trouble spots in Part II, two figures combined may more than double the chances of erroneous or doubtful results.

Research has found that 'popularity reduces a ratio's usefulness'.[1] Once a ratio becomes popular, people begin to know how to use it to produce the 'best' result.[2]

Ratios rarely seem to produce a feeling of what is the right answer. There may be 'rules of thumb', for instance, on margins, but there is always a niggling feeling about the volume.

Businesses are frequently compared by massive lists of ratios (so easily produced by computers) which do not provide any explanations for the huge variations in the figures. Ratios may show better in some companies than others, but one does not know whether they are due to good management, accounting policies, or a rather unusual structure of operations or finance.

Ratios are best used as a comparator, for results at a glance, as one might use summary chapters of a book. No action, no decision, no blame nor acclaim should be made without going to the original figures of numerator and denominator.

18 Return on capital employed

INTRODUCTION

Return on capital employed (ROCE) is regarded by most businesses (excepting very small ones) as their key measure of total performance. It puts together profit and capital. More capital should give a capability to earn more profit. The ROCE ratio shows profitability: how profit produced stands up to the capital being used to generate it.

A whole chapter is devoted to ROCE because of its leading position in the catalogue of business performance measures. It is frequently used as a major target. Robert Heller says, 'Strong profitability [measured by ROCE] is the ultimate management objective'.[3]

The use of ROCE as a sole objective, however, is dangerous. In both the numerator and denominator of the ratio there is a myriad of trouble spots. And there are very many different ways of expressing the ratio.

ROCE itself is not useful unless compared with some other number. It can be compared with other businesses or with previous periods, but neither are satisfactory. No two businesses are exactly alike and previous periods do not show what the ratio *ought* to be.

ROCE has become more fashionable in recent years following the revival of the stock market as a means of raising capital. The cost of capital to a company depends partly on how it has used its existing capital, which ROCE partly answers. When businesses are financed largely by loans or fixed interest stocks, or bonds, ROCE is not so important. Equity financing brings it out into the limelight.

When ROCE is applied to large groups of companies, the ups and downs of the many anomalies are more likely to cancel out. In smaller companies or divisions there may be substantial distortions resulting from all the loose components of ROCE.

In a classic article written in 1969 by Dearden, he said, 'I believe that it is most important to get away from blindly using the ROI [i.e. ROCE] system and to develop procedures that best satisfy the requirements of each individual company . . . ROI is now obsolete'.[4] In the UK, at least, no such obsolescence is yet apparent.

TYPES AND DEFINITIONS

ROCE is basically of two types:

(1) Equity based, where:
- the denominator is shareholders' funds, i.e. share capital, reserves and retained profit, sometimes known as the 'equity interest';
- the numerator is profit after interest, and before tax (usually).

(2) Entity based, where:
- the denominator is shareholders' funds plus long-term loans and (often) plus short-term loans and overdrafts;
- the numerator is profit before interest, i.e. operating profit (usually).

Each of the denominators can be expressed in terms of assets rather than funds, thus:

(1) Equity based denominator: fixed and current assets, less all loans and liabilities of any kind.

(2) Entity based denominator: fixed and current assets less current liabilities only, or interest-bearing liabilities only (to match with profit *before* interest).

The two basic types of ROCE differ in their purpose and rationale, as follows:

(1) The equity based ROCE:
- focuses on shareholder's interest
- provides a clue to the equity value
- is associated with earnings per share (see Chapter 20, p. 247)
- is primarily an external measure
- can be compared by shareholders with returns on other investments

- is normally expressed in terms of capital and reserves rather than in terms of assets

(2)   The entity based ROCE:
   - focuses on the business as a whole
   - is of interest to management rather than shareholders
   - is used mostly as an internal measure
   - can be compared with other businesses, only under certain rather rare conditions
   - is mostly expressed in terms of net assets rather than in terms of capital and reserves plus loans

The above summary does not necessarily follow the practice, especially of external agencies, which show astonishing variations in their definitions of ROCE. Four examples are given below of the definitions used by publishers of lists of company ROCEs:

- *The Times 1000*: net profit *before* interest and tax as a percentage of total tangible assets less current liabilities, excluding bank loans and overdrafts.
- *Jordans Quoted Industrial and Top 2000 Private Companies*: profit before tax and *after* interest as a percentage of share capital plus reserves, provisions, long-term loans, less intangibles.
- *ICC Business Ratio Reports*: profit *after* interest and before tax as a percentage of shareholders' funds plus long-term loans.
- *Management Today's British Business Profitability League*: net profit after tax as a percentage of share capital plus net reserves, intangibles and deferred liabilities.

The above examples are difficult to classify. *The Times 1000* is clearly entity based, although its purpose seems mainly to give information to investors and their advisers. *Management Today* is an extreme equity form, using profit after tax. *Jordans* and *ICC* are hybrids, with interest taken out of the numerator but loans put into the denominator.

Return on capital employed (ROCE) has two other names:

- Return on investment (ROI)
- Return on assets (ROA)

Neither have a clear definition.

ROI usually implies an equity-based ROCE, following the concept of *invested capital* as the denominator of the ratio. It is used mainly in USA.

ROA is usually (but not always) taken to mean a return on total assets with no deduction for any loans or liabilities of any kind. This is the extreme form of an entity-based ROCE. How the assets are financed is of no consequence. ROA is concerned only with how the assets are used.

The numerator for pure ROA must clearly be operating profit, i.e. profit before interest. The financial arrangements are effectively left out. If creditors can be stretched or cheap finance can be obtained from the bank, this will be good but will be reflected lower down the profit and loss account and will not form part of the operating ROA.

Unilever, interestingly, uses a terminology all of its own in the UK. It calculates a *'yield' on capital employed* which is defined as 'profit after taxation but before loan interest as percentage of capital employed'.

NET PRESENT VALUE AND RATE OF RETURN

ROCE must not be confused with net present value (NPV) and internal rate of return (IRR). Both of these measures arise from a different concept of accounting based on pure cash flow, in which there are no assets, no liabilities, no balance sheet and no profit or loss. The cash flows are discounted according to the year when they arise to take account of the time value of money.

Both are used primarily in capital investment appraisal before the event and there are very rarely any accounts after the event that show the actual result in terms of NPV or IRR. Neither are used as a measure of performance.

The main reason for the lack of NPV accounts is the dominance of ROCE based on traditional accounts. Discounted cash flow (DCF) appraisals are invariably *ad hoc* statements with some data taken from the ordinary accounting system. But the ordinary system as a whole is so radically different in most cases from DCF that it cannot be used to produce the actual figures for a particular capital investment, except in a very simple case.

In appraising an investment an internal rate of return (IRR) is usually calculated. Unfortunately ROCE is not compatible with IRR, and it is only by sheer coincidence that the two will match. The main differences are:

(1) IRR applies to a particular capital investment. ROCE applies only to a company or division; the change in ROCE as a result of the investment cannot be easily calculated.
(2) IRR is based on cash flow. ROCE is based on the accruals concept.
(3) IRR does not use depreciation anywhere. ROCE does not necessarily require it in fixed assets, but it is essential in arriving at the profit numerator.
(4) IRR is produced in isolation. ROCE is inevitably involved in valuation of assets acquired in previous years.
(5) IRR has simple obvious rules. ROCE has a variety of bases on which it can be calculated.

ROCE is sometimes known as the accounting rate of return (ARR) in contrast to IRR, which has nothing to do with ordinary accounts.

FORMULA FOR ROCE

No ideal formula for ROCE can be prescribed. Businesses vary considerably in the kind of assets and liabilities appearing in their balance sheets. For some, a bank overdraft may be simply short-term negative cash; for others, it may be in effect a long-term loan.

In any comparative league, lines have to be drawn and arbitrary classifications made to suit the average business. Inevitably, for some businesses, the formula does not fit.

We have seen in Part II that different levels of profit are needed for different purposes in different businesses. And even then, at any particular level, for the same purpose and using the same basis of accounting, the profits of one business may not be comparable with another due to the different treatment of the trouble spots. The numerator of the ROCE is not likely to be very reliable.

The denominator of the ROCE is the assets of the business, less loans and liabilities according to type. It is known for short as the *asset base* (or 'investment base' in USA, or sometimes 'capital base'), which can have as many variations and problems as the profit numerator.

The next six sections of this chapter are devoted to the problems of the asset base.

BASIS OF ACCOUNTING

Historic cost, current cost or a mixture of the two can be used for the asset base.

The pros and cons of historic cost and current cost are recited in Chapters 13 and 14. The main conclusion is that, in times of low inflation, it would be generally sufficient to adjust the historic cost depreciation of older assets and ignore the other 'current cost' adjustments. If there are two similar assets, one new, and another (say) 15 years old, and the new one doing the same work is valued in the balance sheet at three times the old one, the asset base is scarcely a true one. If no adjustment is made, when the old asset is replaced, there will be a large increase in the asset base, leading to a big drop in ROCE.

In times of inflation (or past inflation) current cost certainly provides a more logical asset base than historic cost. In times of high inflation stocks are most logically valued at replacement cost, but the difference is not likely to be material for the asset base with only low or moderate inflation.

FIXED ASSETS GROSS OR NET OF DEPRECIATION

The statutory balance sheet (with notes to the balance sheet) shows fixed assets at cost (historic or current) less accumulated depreciation. The net figure (or book value) is most commonly used for the ROCE asset base.

There are, however, some telling arguments for using the gross cost without deduction of depreciation. The arguments are rather different for historic than for current cost.

(1) The *gross historic cost* in times of inflation is likely to be more realistic than the net.
For example:

Two similar machines: 15 year life

(1)	Bought 1974:	gross historic cost	100
		accumulated depreciation to 1984	73
		net book value	27

(2)   Bought 1983:   gross historic cost   300
                     accumulated depreciation to 1984   13
                                                                 ———
                     net book value   287
                                                                 ═══

The gross historic cost appears to better reflect the true position in the absence of current cost. The new asset is valued at three times the old one on a gross basis but at over ten times the old one on a net basis. In a very rough and ready way in this example inflation has been accounted for.

Many businesses have assets which are fully written off (see depreciation trouble spot 7.1, p. 68). On a net basis these are omitted from the asset base altogether. On a gross basis the original cost is maintained until the asset is scrapped.

(2)   The *gross current cost* is a more reasonable and useful valuation than the net. The accumulated depreciation deducted, in the absence of backlog depreciation (see Chapter 14, p. 176), is a meaningless figure as the depreciation is never adjusted for past inflation.

The gross replacement cost puts all fixed assets on a comparable basis, although the 'cost' itself may be somewhat hazy. If the assets are machines which have become very much improved over the years, there is a danger of the replacement cost of the old machine being greater than the replacement cost of the new, more efficient, machine. (This is particularly the case when the replacement costs are calculated by the use of price indices: the problem of the 'modern equivalent asset' (see Chapter 14, p. 179).

In both cases the gross cost is most suitable when old and new assets are equally well maintained and have similar capacity. If the assets are vehicles, for example, retained for (say) four years, and fully maintained, gross costs are ideal.

If there is heavy new investment and net-of-depreciation costs are used for the asset base, the new investment (put into the balance sheet initially as the gross cost) will cause a large increase in the asset base, which will suddenly reduce the ROCE. A simple example may illustrate the point:

The business makes a profit of £10 000 each year.

		Net basis £000	Gross basis £000
1983: Gross cost of fixed assets		200	200
Less: Accumulated depreciation		160	
Net cost = asset base		40	200

ROCE: net: 10 ÷ 40 = 25%
ROCE: gross: 10 ÷ 200 = 5%

		Net basis £000	Gross basis £000
1984: Gross cost of old assets		200	200
Less: Accumulated depreciation		170	
Net cost		30	
Gross cost of new assets	300		300
Less Depreciation (this year only)	15		
Net cost		285	
Total asset base		315	500

ROCE: net: 10 ÷ 315 = 3.2%
ROCE: gross: 10 ÷ 500 = 2%

Comparing the gross and net asset bases, the ROCEs are:

	Gross basis	Net basis
1983	5%	25%
1984	2%	3%

The example is extreme, but the phenomenon is correct and applies both to historic and current cost bases. The lesser distortion of ROCE caused by the use of gross cost when there is substantial new investment is a big plus-point for the gross cost approach.

Using gross fixed asset costs also avoids any assumption of asset life. It is needed for depreciation, but not for the asset base of ROCE. However, the ROCE based on gross cost is regarded by many as a bastard. The scale of the numbers resulting is quite different from the true (net basis) ROCE. It is a different measure to which people must have time to adjust. It would need probably two or three years before users of the measure would fully be able to understand it and interpret it.

For external ROCE, gross cost is scarcely practicable at all because the asset base figures always tie up with the published balance sheet, which shows net costs.

For divisional ROCE, some companies use gross replacement cost. A change from historic to replacement cost requires anyway a new understanding and familiarity, so gross cost is no worse, and probably easier, to absorb than net cost. Very few companies, it seems, use gross historic cost.

INCLUSION OF CASH IN THE ASSET BASE

If cash balances are included in the asset base, the ROCE will be lower than if they are not.

As we saw in Chapter 16 (p. 203), cash can be regarded as working capital where it is needed for use in the business through seasonal fluctuations, exceptionally large orders or the erratic nature of sales or stocks. A mountain of cash, however, which is never likely to be used in the business, is scarcely capital employed.

The difficulty arises also with bank overdrafts. If an entity-based ROCE is required, bank overdrafts to cover seasonal and exceptional situations should be deducted from the asset base, but not overdrafts that are more or less permanent loans.

Where ROCE is equity-based, cash and overdrafts are usually included in the asset base. Interest received or paid is included in a profit after interest, which forms the numerator.

'INTANGIBLES'

Intangible assets are fixed assets, such as goodwill, patents, licences and know-how, which are not represented by any concrete object. Generally these assets, in published ROCEs, are omitted from the asset base, because the capitalisation of intangible assets is largely decided by the company. This discretion produces large intangible assets in some companies while in others similar 'assets' are entirely written off. The treatment of goodwill, often a substantial item, is the worst offender against consistency and propriety (see trouble spot 11.2, p. 147).

Capitalisation of the interest on large capital projects is another example of a discretionary intangible asset (see trouble spot 9.2, p. 108). Again, in published ROCEs, it will probably be ignored.

There are also many intangible assets that are never capitalised. They are listed in trouble spot 7.2, Revenue investment (p. 75), sometimes known as 'quasi-assets'. They cannot be regarded as fixed assets because they cannot be verified and it is not at all certain that they will eventually yield future benefits.

For ROCE based on published accounts the only practical, though unsatisfactory, rule is to omit intangibles altogether. For divisional ROCE, all intangibles, or certain intangibles which are closely specified, can be capitalised and included. (Depreciation to match should be charged against profit.)

ASSETS AT LOWER THAN COST

Where the market value of an asset is lower than the cost, the cost has to be *written down* in the balance sheet to the lower market value figure. This applies most usually to stocks and work-in-progress, rarely to fixed assets at historic cost, but sometimes to fixed assets at current cost (if the rules are properly obeyed).

This 'writing down' of the assets causes the asset base to be reduced and can cause the ROCE to be higher than it would have been without the 'write-down'. Take the following example, where the value of fixed assets are drastically reduced and the loss of value is taken as an extraordinary item:

	Before *write-down*	*After* *write-down*
Operating assets:		
Fixed assets	200	142
Working capital	50	50
	250	192
Operating profit	25	25
ROCE	10%	13%

In the case of a write-down of stocks, however, the reduction would normally be reflected in the operating profit, in which case the ROCE would never be larger as a result.

LEASED ASSETS

A purchased asset is included in the balance sheet and forms part of the asset base. Depreciation is charged to the profit and loss account.

A leased asset is provided on rental. Normally there would be no asset in the balance sheet and rentals would be charged in full to the profit and loss account.

A business with all purchased assets would thus show a low ROCE while a similar business with all leased assets would show a high ROCE.

This distortion will be to some extent corrected by SSAP 21, *Accounting for Leases and Hire Purchase Contracts*, when it comes fully into force in 1987.[5] Assets leased under 'finance leases' (where the lessee has full control of the asset as if he were the owner) will be capitalised and shown as an asset in the balance sheet. A liability will be shown for the lease payments. Interest and depreciation will be charged to the profit and loss account; all as if the assets were in fact owned.

Operating leases, where the lessee does not have full control (e.g. when maintenance is undertaken by the lessor), will remain as before. To provide full comparability of ROCE between businesses with purchased assets and businesses with operating leased assets, a similar adjustment has to be made. This is possible for divisional ROCE, but for published ROCE the anomaly of the long-term operating lease will remain.

PUBLISHED AND DIVISIONAL ROCE

There are many differences between ROCE derived from the data in published accounts and the ROCE used internally as a measure of divisional performance. The differences are so marked that the two ROCEs are almost different animals:

(1)   Published ROCE is constrained by the profit and loss account and balance sheet as presented. Divisional ROCE components can be prescribed by management with a choice of asset base.

(2)   For published ROCE comparison is difficult, because few businesses are the same and accounting policies can also differ. Internally,

if standard accounting definitions, policies and financial structures are enforced, divisional ROCEs should be fairly comparable, leaving only any differences in the types of business as requiring some subjective judgement.

(3) The sheer size of the monetary amounts providing the numerator and denominator of published ROCE tends to produce fewer overall anomalies than may be apparent in divisional ROCEs, where the amounts are smaller.

(4) The trap of failure to consider the absolute figures is more serious in divisional ROCE than in published ROCE (although still important). A simple example reinforces the point:

	Division A	Division B
	£	£
Operating assets	1000	6000
Operating profit	250	1200
ROCE	25%	20%

(5) Published ROCE concerns primarily shareholders and other outside interests. Divisional ROCE is concerned mainly with the objectives and motivation of managers.

(6) Published ROCE tends generally to be equity-based. Divisional ROCE is usually entity-based, using a ratio which is dependent of how the business is financed.

(7) Divisional performance can usually be better measured by a finance charge levied on the business than by ROCE. Published accounts have no such option (see Chapter 9, p. 99).

ALTERNATIVE TO DIVISIONAL ROCE

It is always possible in fairly independent businesses to make a charge in the profit and loss account for the use of the capital employed in the business. How the charge might be arrived at is explained briefly in trouble spot 9.1 (p. 104). It is usually based on some estimate of the cost of capital to the company or group owning the business.

Let us extend the example in (4) above.

		Division A		Division B
		£		£
Operating profit		250		1200
Capital charge:				
15% on operating assets:	£1000 =	150	£6000 =	900
Profit after capital charge		100		300
ROCE		25%		20%

The alternative 'profit after capital charge' or 'profit after interest' is known in textbooks as *residual income*. It is widely used in America and generally commended in all the authoritative American books (see Bibliography). Solomons, in his book on *divisional performance measurement* regards 'the excess of net earnings over the cost of capital as the measure of managerial success'.[6] He states categorically that residual income is 'the quantity which a manager should try to maximise'. Other authors have some reservations, but, on a straight 'do you agree?', the answers would be an almost unanimous 'yes'.

In the UK, however , the residual income approach is very much in the minority. In one survey only one-third of companies used residual income as a means of accounting for capital employed, and two-thirds of these used ROCE as well as residual income.[7] In visits made as a result of the survey, some reasons emerged for the lack of use of residual income.

(1) The cost of capital was difficult to estimate and not generally understood (see trouble spot 9.1, p. 105).
(2) Most boards of directors have a company objective expressed in terms of ROCE and they therefore wish to see divisional performance in the same terms.
(3) ROCE is familiar, and figures for several years are usually available.
(4) Residual income appears to demand independent divisions, whereas ROCE apparently (and mistakenly) is believed to apply in any situation.

The asset base problem is exactly the same for residual income as for ROCE. The fundamental difference is the way in which the result is expressed: an absolute amount against a ratio.

The cost-of-capital trouble may be exaggerated. It does not need to be precise. In some companies very arbitrary rates are used with good effect. Few divisional managers would wish to be involved in the financial theories of the cost of capital. A reasonable rate that is accepted may work better than one that would be continually changing with the market.

A main advantage of the residual income approach to those using it is that it encourages economy in the use of capital. Any management action that reduces or increases the asset base is connected immediately with the capital charge. Residual income fosters directly the truism that capital costs money.

LABOUR AND CAPITAL INTENSIVE

Some businesses, by their very nature, need a lot of labour. Others need a lot of capital in the form of buildings, plant, ships, vehicles, stocks and so on.

In general, service industries such as retailing, publishing, cleaning and advertising employ small amounts of capital, but have a large payroll of staff and workers. The asset base then tends to be small in relation to profits, producing a high ROCE.

In manufacturing industries, people employed are being reduced in numbers while automation and mechanisation continue to raise the amount of capital. The most capital-intensive industries such as oil, mining, cement and brewing tend generally to appear low down the ROCE league table.

Fair comparison between businesses would require that their capital intensiveness be taken into account. But that is extremely difficult, especially with the problems of the asset base that have been described earlier.

Only in businesses in similar industries is a fair comparison really possible. Even then, no businesses in the same industry are likely to be exactly similar. One business, for example, may have a greater service element than another.

If, of course, ROCE became the sole objective, there would be a tendency for companies gradually to become service businesses, where ROCE is higher. The ratios would be good but the absolute amounts of profit, which make up the country's gross national product, would be lower.

The same misapprehension may apply to divisional ROCE. Often there is one 'star' division with ROCE much higher than the rest. The temptation then may be to attempt to expand this division at the expense of the others. There may, however, be particular reasons why the star division, ROCE-wise, is so successful and the conditions, such as a particular niche in the market, cannot be repeated, or at least not without further capital expenditure. If the star division is small and it were possible to expand, the group could end up, as we have seen with a higher ROCE overall but lower total profits.

NEW AND OLD BUSINESSES

For new businesses it is generally acknowledged that ROCE is a poor measure. Capital investment always has a time lag before the resulting profits appear. The lag is rarely less than six months and may be five years or more.

If a company uses ROCE (as apparently 80 per cent of public companies do), it is calculated for new and old businesses alike. A mental qualification is usually made about the ROCE number, but the danger then is that the qualification will continue for longer than is justified.

Old businesses, given they are alike otherwise, tend to have a lower asset base than new businesses, because many fixed assets are likely to have low book values or be completely written off (unless gross replacement cost is used). The old business thus has a higher ROCE, but probably lower efficiency than the new business.

A similar situation arises with major capital projects. Many take several years to complete. In the meantime, the asset base is piling up but there is no revenue arising. ROCE deteriorates unless some adjustment is made. Some companies do not include uncompleted capital projects in their divisional ROCE, but in published ROCEs they are usually included.

MERITS OF ROCE

(1) It provides a measure of profit that is related to the capital that, at least partly, produces it.

(2) It is familiar and has usually the backing of several previous years' figures.

(3) It is protected from inflation, provided that some adjustment is made for the values of old and new assets.

(4) It can compare the performance of similar businesses of different sizes.

(5) It is useful for preliminary diagnosis that prompts further analysis.

(6) When equity based, it ties up with the financial measures of earnings per share and price/earnings ratio.

PITFALLS IN ROCE

(1) It is specific to a type of business and can only be compared with businesses of a similar structure.

(2) It is unsuitable for short-term measurement and requires several periods to form a fair view of a business performance.

(3) It is not suitable where there are substantial changes in activity, organisation, trade or markets.

(4) It is misleading when applied to a new business or major capital investment on which the profits will be spread over future years.

(5) It has awkward problems of definition, especially with the asset base.

(6) It requires an adjustment for leased assets.

(7) It needs caution with old assets, which are usually undervalued, leading to an excessive ROCE.

(8)   It requires special treatment for assets fully written off.

(9)   It is based on profits, with all the appropriate trouble spots in Part II.

(10) It can be misused as an objective by ruling out proposed capital investment with an ROCE below the one presently earned.

(11) Its familiarity, although helpful, can breed contempt – and a tendency to manipulation.

CONCLUSION

ROCE is a good measure which may have unfortunately gone wrong through over-indulgence.

It has many drawbacks which have been swept aside in a search for a universal measure that can be displayed in a league table. Most accountants disown it because of the flimsy base, especially the asset base, on which it stands.

It is a ratio which, on its own, is no way to run a business. It is good for diagnostics, but no use in the decision on how to cure.

The size of any problem does not show. A different ROCE is needed for different purposes in different businesses. The detail is important. ROCE is like a barometer which shows a basic atmospheric pressure in pounds per square inch; but it does not show the weather conditions or how to deal with them.

Because ROCE has the image of a catch-all, it is expressed in many different ways to suit the particular audience. The equity-based version now seems to dominate, due probably to the increasing move towards equity finance and the search for ever more information on company performance that can show light on the movements of the stock market ratios.

But rule by ratios could be disastrous. If one chases the highest ROCE, any investment yielding lower than the current ROCE is rejected, regardless of the extra amount of profit that might result. If all managements religiously followed the ROCE line, their businesses would be earning higher ROCE but at a lower level of total profit.

The more comprehensive measures tend to go unused because they do not fit the syndrome of published accounts → key ratio → stock market performance. Gross replacement cost of fixed assets (or even gross historic cost) is better for the asset base than cost after deducting depreciation, but it does not run on that particular track. Residual income is better than ROCE, because it shows an amount that can be used directly in decision-making, but again it does not fit the conditions.

Sophisticated users of suitable business performance measures should beware of ROCE, as it has developed in its multifarious guises, like the plague.

19   Other operating ratios

INTRODUCTION

Return on capital employed (ROCE) is a composite measure of performance embracing many facets of business. Standing alone it must be used with great care.

ROCE can be broken down into many component measures which may explain in more detail why the ROCE has gone down or gone up. An examination of these subsidiary measures may also reveal compensating changes in two important factors that otherwise might be overlooked.

Chart 19.1 shows what is known as the *pyramid of ratios*. It applies only to entity-based ROCE and is most useful in self-contained business or divisions. Hence the primary ROCE ratio is operating profit/operating capital. Loans and overdrafts are not deducted from the asset base. The pyramid can stand firm only when the means of financing the capital are totally excluded.

A commentary on each of the ratios shown in the pyramid follows. These are the ratios which can best be used as supporting performance measures. They divide fundamentally into profit and cost ratios and asset turnover ratios.

There are many other ratios which use the components of ROCE at a secondary or tertiary level, depending for their usefulness on the type of business. The ratios become more specific to a business and to its systems and organisation as they go lower down the pyramid. The purpose of most of these lower ratios is to identify problems, errors or inefficiencies which may need management attention. They have little purpose as measures of performance.

OPERATING PROFIT/OPERATING CAPITAL

This is the basic ROCE measure which directs all the lower level ratios.

CHART 19.1

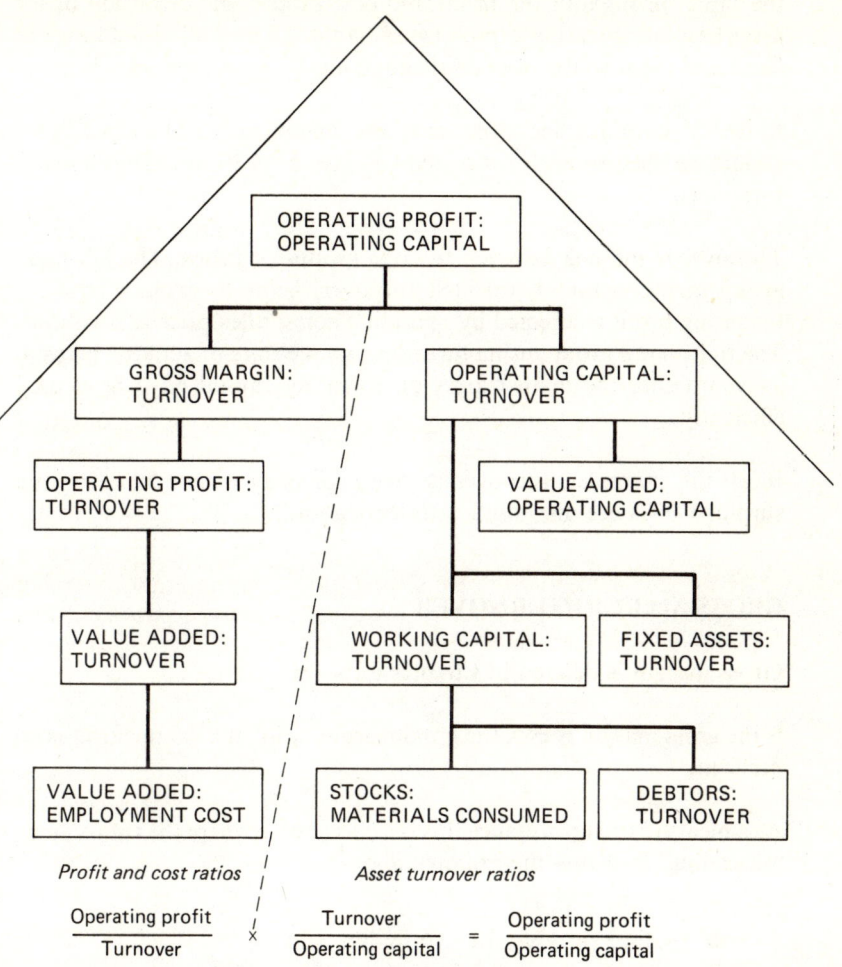

The definition of operating profit (see Chapter 8, p. 81) should remain the same throughout the profit and cost ratios. The definition of the asset base of operating capital (see Chapter 18, p. 218) should also be fixed and consistently applied throughout.

Many of the ratios use turnover as the denominator. The same figure should be used in each ratio (see Chapter 5, p. 29, for definitions of turnover).

Turnover is the link between the two groups of ratios. The left-hand group in the pyramid, through turnover, helps to explain how the operating profit is affected by operating costs, sales price and volume. The right-hand group, using turnover as a measure of activity, helps to show whether the main classes of operating capital have been used efficiently.

In all the examples, turnover is taken for convenience as £100, and surplus £'000s are dispensed with throughout.

GROSS MARGIN/TURNOVER

Gross margin is defined in Chapter 6 (p. 43).

If the gross margin is £40, the gross margin ratio on £100 turnover is 40 per cent.

As a measure of performance this is a classic case where the ratio can be misleading. Pursuing the example above:

(1) Suppose that an increase in selling price would:
  ● reduce turnover by £10 to £90, and
  ● increase gross margin *ratio* by 2% to 42%.
  It would then reduce the gross margin *amount* by £2 to £38 (i.e. 42% of £90)

(2) Suppose that a reduction in selling price would:
  ● increase turnover by £23 to £123, and
  ● reduce gross margin *ratio* by 5% to 35%.
  It would then increase the gross margin *amount* by £3 to £43 (i.e. 35% of £123)

In these cases a higher gross margin ratio does not lead to a higher gross margin amount nor a lower ratio to a lower amount. The ratio can therefore be defective as a measure of performance over different periods in the same business.

For similar businesses, but of different size, the ratio is a good comparative performance measure. But rarely are businesses sufficiently similar to stand up to a true comparison. In retailing, where the gross margin ratio is used almost universally, shops and stores selling the same kind of goods may be far from similar. One store may price low (with low gross margin ratio) to obtain high turnover in a basic harsh environment; another may price high (with high gross margin ratio) accepting lower turnover in a more congenial environment for the customers.

Another point of increasing difference in retailing (over time and between businesses) is the use of own labels instead of branded products. Stores selling a high proportion of own labels would expect to operate on a lower gross margin ratio than those selling only branded products with lower administrative and selling expenses to compensate; subject, of course, to the buying power of the retailer compared with the selling power of the manufacturer.

OPERATING PROFIT/TURNOVER

Operating profit is defined in Chapter 8 (p. 81).

If operating profit is £15, the operating ratio on £100 turnover is 15 per cent. The same caveat applies to this ratio as to the gross margin ratio; 14 per cent on a high turnover could be better than 16 per cent on a low turnover.

The ratio can be expressed also as turnover/operating cost. In many businesses (especially non-profit-making organisations and financial institutions where a profit is not recognised) this *expense ratio* is an important measure of performance. In the example, the expense ratio is 85 per cent; in a charity it is likely to be around 15 per cent and in a life insurance business 30 per cent.

Comparisons between businesses may be more feasible for the operating ratio than for the gross margin ratio. The definition of gross margin is largely a matter of convenience whereas operating profit generally covers all revenues and costs except interest, taxation and extraordinary items. The operating ratio is not upset by the definitions which have to be adopted for gross margin. It does not have to compensate subjectively for extra cost or extra revenue above the gross margin line by lower or higher cost below the line.

The operating ratio does, however, include fixed costs in the operating cost. This means, especially in capital-intensive businesses, that the ratio is sensitive to capacity utilisation. In a recession the gross margin ratio (depending on the definition) could be fairly stable, but the cost of unutilised capacity may reduce the operating ratio considerably. In these circumstances the ratio as a measure of performance needs interpretation by comparison with the actual amounts before and during the recession.

VALUE ADDED/TURNOVER

The definition of value added is given in Chapter 7 (p. 59). The value added ratio is illustrated in the specimen value added statement 13.2 (p. 171).

If turnover is £100 and bought-in materials, services and depreciation are £62, the value added ratio is 38 per cent. The ratio has the same snags as the gross margin ratio in that the value added ratio may rise while the added value amount falls, and vice versa.

Otherwise, when the ratio increases, and provided the structure and nature of the business is not changed, it can be said that the performance of the business has improved, taking the remuneration of employees not as a cost but as actors in the performance. It is a good ratio for overall performance measurement to which everyone in the business can relate.

VALUE ADDED/EMPLOYMENT COST

This ratio is usually expressed as the amount of value added per £ of employment cost.

If turnover is £100, value added is £38, and employment cost is £32, value added is £1.19 per £ of employment cost. £1.25 per £ of employment cost is a better performance; it can be achieved by a value added of £40 produced for the same employment cost or the same value added produced at an employment cost of £30.40.

Value added is defined in Chapter 7 (p. 59). Employment cost is defined as wages or salary plus all related costs, such as national insurance and pensions contributions and 'fringe benefits'.

The ratio is good as a measure of the performance of employees in that it takes into account their full cost compared with their net output. As a measure of the productivity of employees where physical output cannot be used satisfactorily (and this applies to most businesses) this ratio is probably the best available and seems, with experience, to produce results in line with the observed situation.

The ratio, however, is not immune from anomalies caused by changes in turnover, and hence value added, that are not connected with employee performance. Examples are changes in selling price or discounts. On the other hand, it may be argued that if the products sold are not competitive and prices have to be reduced, the employees have to take the rap; if the product is in high demand and prices can be increased, the employees are in luck. But bad and good luck are part of performance.

OPERATING CAPITAL/TURNOVER

This ratio is usually expressed as the number of times that operating capital is turned over in a year, or more precisely: turnover as a multiple of operating capital.

If operating capital is £67 and turnover is £100, then the operating capital is turned over 1½ times. The higher the number of times the more efficiently is the capital being used. A ratio of 2 times, for example, could be achieved by reducing operating capital to £50 with the same turnover, or increasing the turnover to £133 with the same operating capital.

Operating capital is defined as fixed assets and net current assets, excluding intangibles, investments and surplus cash not held for purposes of the business (see Chapter 18, p. 218). More usually it is called 'operating assets' as there are few liabilities to be deducted. Creditors and short-term liabilities are usually deducted from the assets, however.

In the 'Weinstock yardsticks of efficiency' (1968), quoted by Westwick,[8] the ratio is regarded as a measure of the productivity of capital, but this depends on:

- sales turnover being a good measure of the productive activity of the business
- the operating assets being valued in a consistent way in the same currency as the turnover
- production output itself, regardless of cost, being a meaningful element of business performance

Turnover is rarely synonymous with production. Most businesses keep stocks of finished products and many have work-in-progress. This can be corrected by using the *sales value of production*, whereby all the elements of production are valued at cost for the accounts but at an imputed selling price for this particular ratio.

The valuation of operating assets raises the problem of defining consistently the asset base, adjusted to current cost, where necessary, to compare equitably with turnover. This is discussed fully in Chapter 18 (p. 218).

The production output is good for the basis of a productivity measure of particular machines or processes (see Chapter 21, p. 252), but it is not directly related to business performance, which requires a net result arising from that output. Factories that continue to produce output or sales turnover at very high cost may make a very good showing on this ratio, but with disastrous consequences if no profit is made from the operation.

It must be said, however, that no ratio of this kind should stand alone and any use of the ratio in decision-making should be checked against the profit and cost ratios.

VALUE ADDED/OPERATING CAPITAL

Half-way between operating profit/operating capital and turnover/ operating capital is value added/operating capital. This ratio is usually expressed not in terms of 'times turned over', but, like ROCE, as a percentage.

If operating capital is £67 and value added is £38, the value added/

capital ratio is 57 per cent. Performance would be improved to 60 per cent if value added increased to £40 or operating capital reduced to £63.

The ratio is not widely used, but it does express the 'productivity of capital' better than the turnover-based ratio. Costs of materials are taken into account but the costs of employees are not.

The value added approach has considerable advantages in attempts to separate the productivity of capital from the productivity of labour (or employees). Value added/operating assets represents capital productivity and value added/employment cost represents employee productivity. Of course, one ratio is still affected by the other; capital cannot be operated without employers and employees cannot work without capital. But value added is still better than turnover or profit as the basis of the analysis.

FIXED ASSETS/TURNOVER

This ratio takes us to the third level of analysis in the pyramid, attempting to show which kind of assets are being used efficiently and which are not.

If fixed assets are £25, and turnover £100, then fixed assets are turned over four times.

The serious weakness of the ratio is the valuation of the asset base, discussed at length in Chapter 18. The value of fixed assets can vary widely according to depreciation policy (trouble spot 7.1, p. 65) use of current or historic cost (p. 220) and gross or net of depreciation (p. 219).

Where fixed assets are small in relation to total assets the ratio is likely to be erratic and almost useless. Replacement of the one major fixed asset could well change the ratio from four times to 0.5 times or less.

Where fixed assets are large, as in capital-intensive businesses, the ratio can be more useful provided there is a consistent and relevant accounting policy and there are no sudden changes in the type of assets in use. The ratio is likely to be of limited use in comparison between businesses because of the lack of standards and the varied composition of the asset base.

WORKING CAPITAL/TURNOVER

Working capital is defined in Chapter 16 (p. 204).

If working capital is £41 and turnover £100, working capital is turned over 2.4 times.

This is an important and very useful ratio with few snags. Like is usually compared with like, as the assets are measured broadly (at least with low inflation) in the same currency as the turnover. The only scope for discretion is in the valuation of stocks, and in the definition of surplus cash (or net liquid funds) which should not form part of working capital for this purpose.

As a performance measure the ratio gives rather equivocal signals, according to whether a short-term or long-term view is taken.

If working capital is increased to £45, the turnover of the capital is reduced from 2.4 to 2.2 times. In the short-term overall business performance is worse because working capital has to stay longer in the business, which thereby incurs a higher cost of finance, either as interest paid or interest forgone. This does not show up in the operating ratios, but it will show in the profit after interest. There is also a higher risk of loss of value in stocks and debtors.

On the other hand, the extra working capital can be regarded as an investment which will lead to benefits in the long run. Stocks may be increased to give better service to the customers or debtors increased to attract sales by easier credit terms. Working capital levels may be regarded as a strategy to boost turnover in the same way as advertising.

Given some kind of separation and control of the strategic aspects, the working capital ratio is a notable performance measure. Working capital can be easy to waste and the ratio can show whether the waste is being reduced or increased.

The ratio is frequently used as an investment guideline, especially in small businesses considering expansion. If sales increase by 23 per cent to £123 in our example, then working capital must increase from £41 to £50 if the same level of service is to apply.

In using the ratio for establishing the working capital required for expansion, working capital is generally expressed as a percentage of turnover, in the example: 41 per cent.

STOCKS/MATERIALS CONSUMED (OR TURNOVER)

Stocks comprise materials, work-in-progress and finished goods (see trouble spot 6.1, p. 48).

If stocks are £20 and materials consumed are £80, stocks of materials are turned over 4 times. This number is often called the *stock-turn*.

So that like is compared with like, stocks and the goods or materials taken from stock should be valued on the same basis. Stocks of materials at cost should be compared with materials consumed at cost. In retailing businesses, and for finished goods, stocks may be valued at selling price and compared with turnover. Work-in-progress at cost should be compared with cost of sales, or, if the sales value is available, it can be compared with turnover.

The ratio can be badly upset by stocks written-down under the accounting rule of 'net realisable value or cost whichever is the lower'. If stocks are written down in the example from £20 to £16 at the year-end, and the average stock value is reckoned as £18, the stock-turn is increased from 4 times to $4\frac{1}{2}$ times, which would normally be a sign of greater efficiency in the use of stock. In fact, there has been no change in the efficiency. Indeed, it could be argued that the loss of value through holding obsolete stock is itself a sign of inefficiency.

If the stock-turn falls to 3 times, that would normally be bad. There would be a greater risk of obsolescence of the stock and a greater cost of holding stock which is apparently not required. However, the reduction in stock-turn may have been deliberate. Perhaps there were too many stock-outs when stock-turn was 4 times and customers were being turned away. Or a new product was being launched and substantial stocks were needed in anticipation of heavy demand.

Stock levels in most large businesses are fixed by *economic order quantity* or similar models. The level of service or delivery thought to be necessary is built into the model (e.g. the number of stock-outs that can be tolerated) and, when strategic decisions (if any) are taken into account, the stock-turn should come out as planned. But the plan may easily be upset by changes in costs and failures to achieve sales forecasts.

The actual stock-turn numbers provide a measure of performance in an important area which can be very prone to inefficiency.

DEBTORS/TURNOVER

Debtors are amounts owed to the business, usually by customers (known in the USA as 'accounts receivable').

If turnover is £100 and the average amount of debtors is £13, the debtors turnover ratio is 7.7 times.

It is more usual, however, to express the ratio as the average number of days credit taken. In this case, the days outstanding on average are $365 \div 7.7 = 47$ days.

If the average days credit can be reduced to 40 days, average debtors will be reduced by £2 to £11. This will save interest on the £2, which will be reflected in the profit after interest. With a shorter period of outstanding debtors there should also be a lesser risk of loss from bad debts.

The ratio is a useful measure of performance in collecting money, which is of considerable importance in times of high interest rates.

20 Earnings per share

INTRODUCTION

To whom is the performance of a business most important? The answer could be the managers, the employees, the lenders or the owners. So far we have rather neglected the owners of the business, i.e. the shareholders.

Shareholders may take a different view of performance from the other interested parties. They own the equity of their company and they are interested therefore in the equity view.

Business performance, as we have seen, is based largely on the entity view, which produces the same result irrespective of the way that the business is financed. Indeed, most large companies comprise many businesses, which may be very different in the measures that can be applied, and therefore difficult to add up. At the consolidation stage the equity view is inevitable. It is the shareholders who are most interested in the ultimate aggregated result of the group.

The equity-based ratios can apply to single business companies which are largely financed by equity capital. There are several large almost single business companies, such as Marks & Spencer and Sainsbury, as well as many small and medium-sized companies in the same category. The business entity view is refocused only slightly in this case to obtain the equity view.

The equity view adds a further dimension. It is seen on a background of the stock market, where the company is quoted on the Stock Exchange. The share price provides another kind of measure of performance, which may be useful, although far from complete. Profit and share price combined in the price/earnings ratio give another perspective on performance, related more, however, to the predicted future than to the actual past.

243

Earnings per share is a measurement of performance tailor-made for the shareholder. It is an important extra measure of business performance for the single business company.

DEFINITION

Earnings per share (Eps) is the only ratio which must be shown in published accounts. The definition is laid down in an accounting standard (SSAP 3).[5]

Eps is normally expressed in terms of pence per share. If profit after taxation is £84 000 and there are 700 000 shares in issue,

$$\text{Eps is} \qquad \frac{£84\,000}{700\,000} \quad = \quad \text{12p per share}$$

The profit after taxation is defined in detail as 'after deducting minority interests and preference dividends, but before taking into account extraordinary items'. It applies only to consolidated accounts of a group and not to individual companies within a group.

The number of shares is the weighted average of equity shares ranking for dividend over the period covered by the profit. If there are convertible loans or shares that will rank for dividend in the future, these should be added to the equity shares in issue if the resulting Eps would thereby be lower. This is known as *dilution* of the basic earnings.

SSAP 3 recommends that, where the dilution is material, the fully diluted Eps should be disclosed in addition to the basic Eps.

TAX AND DISTRIBUTION BASIS

Profit after taxation suffers from all the trouble spots listed in Chapter 10 (p. 116). Trouble spot 10.1 (p. 117) deals with deferred tax, and trouble spot 10.2 with dividends, surplus ACT and losses brought forward. Surplus ACT (p. 129) is particularly irritating for Eps.

If a company has large losses for tax purposes, it pays no mainstream corporation tax. If the losses have arisen largely from capital allowances, it is probable that the company will be showing a profit in its accounts and paying a dividend. Payment of the dividend will require a payment of ACT. If no dividend were paid, there would be no tax to pay.

ACT in these circumstances is not a tax on profit but a tax on dividend, and the higher the dividend, the higher the ACT. The earnings part of Eps becomes dependent on the dividend paid, when its very rationale is to show the earnings attributable to the shareholders irrespective of dividend.

The normal basis of earnings for Eps is known as the *net basis*, which uses the profit after taxation with all its problems, as described in Chapter 10. Where ACT paid is really a tax on dividends, it is still regarded, for profit after taxation, as a tax on profit.

To counteract this error, SSAP 3 allows a *nil distribution basis*, which produces a profit after tax on the assumption that no dividend is paid and therefore no ACT would be paid. 'Where there is material difference between Eps calculated on the net basis', it says, 'it is most desirable that the latter is also shown'.[5]

The other alternative is the *full distribution basis*, which asumes that the whole pretax profits will be distributed as dividend and full ACT paid on the accounting profit. This method is favoured particularly by investment analysts and is used for earnings calculations by the Extel Statistical Service, where it is called *maximum distribution basis*.[9]

The radical changes in corporation tax announced in the 1984 Budget will gradually eliminate in most cases the anomalies of ACT as a pure dividend tax (see trouble spot 10.2, p. 131). In the meantime Eps will continue to be unsatisfactory in the treatment of taxation.

The net basis, sometimes referred to by analysts as the *company accounts basis*, is factual in that the figures all derive from the audited profit and loss account, including the deferred tax charges demanded by accounting standards. These may be far from realistic but they are at least uniform in company accounts.

The nil distribution basis and the full distribution basis are both hypothetical, showing what Eps would be under certain standard conditions. Both have an attraction. The nil distribution basis simply eliminates ACT as a tax on profit when it is appearing as a tax on dividend: primarily an accountant's historic view. The full distribution basis assumes that all equity profits will eventually be paid out to shareholders: primarily a long-term investor's future-oriented view.

The Extel Card,[9] which is the leading quick reference on company performance, uses two different methods of calculating 'earnings'. For 'earnings yield' the maximum (or full) distribution method is used, but for its own brand of Eps, known as the *net (actual) basis*, the standard SSAP 3 method is used *except* that *all* ACT not set off against mainstream corporation tax is regarded as 'irrecoverable', that is, no surplus ACT is carried forward (see trouble spot 10.2, p. 129) and the full ACT is deduced in arriving at net profit after tax. As only one year's surplus ACT can be carried forward in accounts, the difference between the 'company accounts' Eps and the 'net (actual) basis' is normally quite small. When surplus ACT is being carried forward the Extel 'net (actual) basis' shows a lower Eps than the standard net basis.

The Extel earnings ratio is expressed, not per share, but as a percentage of the amount of share capital so that a calculation is needed to compare with the standard Eps.

For the price/earnings ratio (see p. 250) Extel uses the 'net (actual) earnings'.

EXTRAORDINARY ITEMS

The problems of extraordinary items are discussed fully in trouble spot 11.1 (p. 142). Eps excludes extraordinary items on the grounds that it seeks to reflect the trend of normal earnings.

In the long-term, however, extraordinary items should be included. If they represent losses, they are losses of the shareholders' equity funds which must eventually affect their dividend. It would seem logical, if a full distribution basis is used, that extraordinary items should not be excluded from the profit to be hypothetically distributed.

One solution (adopted in USA and by at least one company in the UK) is to compute two Eps figures: one showing the result of normal activities and the other showing the result of total activities including extraordinary items. The figure to use can then be chosen according to the purpose of the analysis.

VERSIONS OF Eps

There could be 32 different versions of Eps, each of which could be reasonable for a certain purpose. They are permutations on:

(1) Number of shares:
    (a) Not diluted
    (b) Fully diluted
(2) Distribution basis:
    (a) Net (company accounts)
    (b) Nil
    (c) Full (or maximum)
    (d) Extel 'net (actual)'
(3) Extraordinary items in earnings:
    (a) Excluded
    (b) Included
(4) Basis of accounting
    (a) Historic cost
    (b) Current cost

A few companies show in their accounts an Eps using profit *before* taxation, in addition to the mandatory Eps using profit after taxation. The profit before taxation avoids all the tax trouble spots and the difficult choice of a fair distribution basis.

RELATIONSHIP WITH ROCE

The pure equity-based ROCE, as defined for the *Management Today* Profitability League,[10] has similar properties to Eps. The level of profit used is almost the same. Both use profit after taxation, excluding extraordinary items. The Profitability League does not deduct preference dividends from profits to obtain profit for ordinary shareholders, while standard Eps does in order to obtain a true equity view. However, preference dividends are very small compared with ordinary dividends in most companies.

The main difference between the ROCE for equity and Eps is in the denominator. ROCE requires an asset base of fixed assets and net current assets minus all loans. This is equivalent to share capital and reserves. Eps is based on share capital only.

A ratio of profit to share capital is exactly the same in effect as Eps. 'Per share' is used in order to tie up with the Stock Exchange prices, which are generally expressed per share. (A few older companies have stocks instead of shares, and for these Eps can be expressed only as earnings per £ of stock.)

Companies vary enormously, for no obvious reasons, in the nominal value of an ordinary share. £1 shares are very common but so are shares of 10p. Eps therefore is in no way comparable between companies.

Even if the Eps of company A (with shares of £1) were multiplied by 10 to compare with company B (with shares of 10p), the figures are still not likely to be comparable. The reason is that, unlike ROCE, Eps is based on share capital only.

The division of capital employed between share capital and reserves (i.e. retained profits in most cases) is purely arbitrary. Reserves can be capitalised (i.e. changed into share capital) almost at will.

ROCE includes reserves, but the reserves are the counterpart of the shaky asset base which is discussed at length in Chapter 18 (p. 214). Share capital, although arbitrary, needs no assumptions, estimates or subjective judgements.

Because of the simplicity of its denominator, Eps is very popular as a company performance measure. It is probably more widely quoted among shareholders and investors than any other single measure.

However, when looked at more closely, it is only a dubious profit after taxation compared with a solid, rarely changed, legal number, which adds little to the comparative qualities of the ratio. Eps is highly specific to the company and can be truly compared only with the Eps of the same company in previous years.

Being a money amount compared with a numeral, Eps is vulnerable to inflation (even when current cost earnings are used), whereas ROCE is a money-to-money ratio which is inflation proof subject to care with fixed assets and stocks (and probably completely inflation proof when current costs are used).

The difference between ROCE and Eps is determined by the amount of reserves or retained profits per share. It is indicated by another ratio: total shareholders' funds (i.e. capital and reserves) per share, sometimes called equity assets per share (EAps).

Equity ROCE is $\dfrac{\text{Eps}}{\text{EAps}} \times 100$

Equity ROCE always moves in the same way as Eps. An increase in one is an increase in the other, likewise with a decrease. If reserves are increasing in relation to share capital, as is usually the case, Eps will rise faster than ROCE, but the direction is not affected. To achieve a better Eps requires a better ROCE. As Eps becomes the leading company performance measure, so equity ROCE becomes a leading measure in support. Where equity ROCE is not practicable at the business level, then entity ROCE is used, which unless there are large changes in loans, would follow the same trend.

The drawbacks of Eps are many and this is inevitable with simple ratios that attempt to be comprehensive.

DRAWBACKS OF Eps

(1) It suffers from all the troubles of profit after taxation as a measurement.
(2) It has the extremely arbitrary base of numbers of shares in issue.
(3) It is not comparable between companies even when nominal share values are standardised.
(4) It involves a most confusing choice of distribution bases in order to deal with the problems of taxation dependent on dividends.
(5) It needs interpretation as regards extraordinary items.
(6) It has problems of 'dilution' when equity rights are not reflected in the current share capital.
(7) It requires adjustment for inflation, whether based on historic or current cost.
(8) It is not useful when there is a loss and earnings are negative.

PRICE/EARNINGS RATIO

Eps links up with the price/earnings (P/E) ratio.

The P/E ratio of a company share is:

$$\frac{\text{Market price per share}}{\text{Earnings per share}}$$

The numbers of shares in issue cancel out as price of one share is compared with the earnings of one share. In effect, the ratio is the number of years needed to cover a purchase of the shares by earnings.

For example, if the market price is 108p and the earnings per share (last year) are 12p, the P/E ratio is $108 \div 12 = 9$, i.e. the share price is 9 years' purchase of the annual earnings.

P/E ratios may vary between about 5 and 20 in what would appear from the accounts to be similar companies. If the earnings per £1 share of two companies are the same, the difference in P/E ratio is due only to the market price, which in turn must be due to the market's view of future prospects, assuming that the earnings figures are trusted and reserves as a proportion of share capital are the same.

The P/E ratio adds a dimension to the company performance measurement. Profit is compared not with capital or with previous profit but with a stock market evaluation of the company's prospects. A view of prospects is not performance; the prospects may never be achieved. But a company with a P/E of 20 feels good, and confidence before the performance sustains the actual performance.

That said, the market price is no more than an indicator of performance; it is not a measurement. Market price is affected by so many other factors, such as general economic conditions, financial strength of the company and prospects of take-over, that business performance may be only a small element in the stock market's judgement of the company.

CONCLUSION

Earnings compared with the stock market price are the end of the line;

the ultimate performance measurement. With the 'privatised company' it becomes increasingly important.

This ultimate measurement is built up from many subsidiary measurements at the business level. Where the business and the company are the same, the Eps and P/E ratio shed extra light on the business performance. Where the company has many diverse businesses, Eps and P/E are needed for shareholders and the stock market, but they cannot easily be transferred downwards to the business level.

Eps is very specific to the company. Comparisons one year with another, adjusted for inflation, give a simple answer to the shareholder's question: is the company doing better or not? The drawbacks can be minimised if the same basis for Eps is used each year with an alternative treatment of extraordinary items when a long-term view is required.

The trend of Eps is the most important to shareholders and small anomalies in the figures are not going to be material to them. The Eps numbers are to be regarded as for shareholder use only, not applicable to any *other* company or business.

21 Productivity ratios

INTRODUCTION

Operating profit is probably the leading measure of performance for most businesses. It is the prime element of the most important financial ratios. These ratios can be split down into subsidiary ratios as is shown in Chapter 19 (p. 232). But there is still one element missing that has a significant effect on profit; and that is the efficiency of production.

The significance varies from one business to another. In some businesses it may be the success of marketing that has most effect on profit; in others it may be the attractiveness of design, the quality of research, or the expertise of the staff, or the stability of industrial relations. Each business management may have their own idea on what factors have the most influence on their ultimate goal, assumed to be some form of profit. The importance of each of these factors may change from year to year. They need to be identified and measured, if possible, so that the ultimate profit when it is computed does not come as too much of a surprise.

Production efficiency is not confined to manufacturing businesses, although the importance in manufacturing is obvious. Services are in a sense 'produced' by applying 'labour' and 'capital' to make a 'product' that is sold to a customer. Businesses providing a service suffer a fall in profits, other things being equal, if their service becomes inefficient in the same way a manufacturer suffers from production inefficiency.

The measurement of production efficiency is productivity and it is to this that we now turn.

DEFINITION: VOLUME-TO-VOLUME RATIOS

The economist's definition of productivity is 'a measure of the quantity of output of goods and services that can be produced for a given input in factors of production'.[11] The *Oxford Dictionary* says, 'capacity to produce; . . . production per unit of effort'.

True productivity is essentially a volume-to-volume ratio. No money amounts are involved. Production is measured as a volume or quantity such as:

- tons of coal
- litres of paint
- number of cans
- square metres of cloth
- kilos of biscuits
- passenger miles

Factors of production are also expressed as a quantity and can be divided, for example, into labour, capital and energy:

- number of employees involved ⎫
- number of man/hours worked   ⎭ labour
- number of machines available ⎫
- shelf space available in store ⎭ capital
- units of electricity used   ⎫
- therms of gas used   ⎭ energy

The volumes of output listed above can each be compared with labour input, capital input and energy input. The resulting productivity ratios could be, for instance:

'Labour' productivity:
- tons of coal per employee
- litres of paint per man/hour

'Capital' productivity:
- square metres of cloth per number of looms
- passenger miles per number of seat-miles available

'Energy' productivity:
- number of cans per unit of electricity
- kilos of biscuits per therm of gas

These productivity ratios by themselves do not support directly any of the profit-type measures, as is shown in the following very over-simplified and somewhat unrealistic illustration:

A biscuit factory has 200 employees and 5 ovens, produces 4000 kilos of biscuits per week and consumes 6000 therms of gas.

It calculates productivity ratios as follows:

Labour: kilos per employee: 20 (4000 ÷ 200)
Capital: kilos per oven: 800 (4000 ÷ 5)
Energy: therms of gas per kilo: 1.5 (6000 ÷ 4000)

There is suddenly a fall in demand for biscuits, reducing output per week to 3500 kilos. 5 ovens are still required. The number of employees is reduced by 35 to 165 (taking advantage of making redundant the least efficient employees). Gas consumption is reduced by half of the 12½ per cent fall in output.

The productivity ratios are then:

Labour: kilos per employee: 21 (3500 ÷ 165)
Capital: kilos per oven: 700 (3500 ÷ 5)
Energy: therms of gas per kilo: 1.61 (5625 ÷ 3500)

Labour productivity has improved but capital and energy productivity have worsened. The effect on profit may be surmised, but cannot be computed without information on costs.

Productivity is popularly perceived as productivity of labour. This is because 'labour' seems nowadays to be more controllable. The labour force, in the 1970s regarded almost as fixed, can now be changed more easily both downwards by redundancy and upwards by recruiting new staff.

Capital, in the shape of fixed assets, seems to be more fixed than ever. In larger, more automated, factory units there is little flexibility for contracting or expanding the capacity. Productivity of capital becomes a matter of capacity utilisation.

Energy consumption may have a strong fixed element in that a certain minimum amount is needed to operate the plant at all. Energy efficiency is a science of its own, which is not usually recognised as productivity, but which deserves in nearly all industries the same kind of attention.

SPECIFIC PRODUCTIVITY RATIOS

Productivity is a technical measure requiring experts to specify units of output and sometimes also units of labour or capital. The ratios often involve technical terms which would not be useful in this book.

However, some further examples of true volume-to-volume productivity ratios may show the wide range covered in a variety of industries, service and manufacturing, which can help to support and explain the main measures of business performance.

Hotels

Capacity utilisation:	Rooms occupied/rooms available, per cent
	Beds occupied/beds available, per cent
Labour productivity:	Rooms occupied per employee
	Beds occupied per employee

Restaurants

Capacity utilisation:	Meals served/seating capacity, per cent
Labour productivity:	Meals served per employee

Passenger transport (e.g. railways, airlines)

Capacity utilisation:	Passenger-miles carried/seat-miles available, per cent
Labour productivity:	Passenger-miles carried per employee
	Seat-miles available per employee

Bed linen manufacture

Capacity utilisation:	Maximum output of unit/output produced, per cent
Labour productivity:	Duvets produced per man-hour spent

Selling

Capacity utilisation:	Cars available/cars on the road, per cent
Labour productivity:	Number of calls per salesman-day

DRAWBACKS OF VOLUME-TO-VOLUME RATIOS

(1) They demand a measurement of physical output which is often difficult to count, estimate or assess.
(2) They assume that factors of production are homogeneous, but usually there are many grades of employee or types of machine.
(3) They do not support directly any profit-type measure of performance.
(4) They take no account of the value of the output in the market.
(5) They take no account of the costs of the factors of production.
(6) They are restricted to businesses whose products, processes or services are sufficiently standard to be correctly counted as single units.

MONEY-TO-VOLUME RATIOS

Volumes of production can be computed without difficulty in extractive industries such as oil and coal, in manufacturing of one dominant product such as a litre of paint or a metre of thread, or in standard services such as freight and passenger transport.

In many industries there is such a large variety of products that their output cannot be counted without some kind of weighting or standardisation. The difficulty is usually that the only basis for weighting the various products is either cost or selling price. The difficulty is not so great, however, where there is one generic product, but with many types and sizes, and the production mix does not change very much.

At RHP, which manufactures bearings with a catalogue of thousands of types, sizes and prices, a single measure is used to reduce all these types to a common factor known as *constat* (short for 'constant unit measure'). The current year standard cost is used as the basis of the weighting. Each year the mix of catalogue products sold is checked for significant changes.

If the mix radically changes and new weightings are introduced, the comparison of periods before and after the change is spoiled. If the changes occur frequently the reduction of the variety to standard units is probably not worth the benefits to be obtained from a volume rather than a monetary number.

The main money measures available are turnover, cost of sales, sales value of production, and value added:

(1) *Turnover* is the worst because it does not measure production at all unless all output is sold immediately it is produced; normally there are stocks and work-in-progress which lie between production and turnover. Also, output is valued at selling price, which has nothing to do with true productivity.

(2) *Cost of sales*, like turnover, does not take into account production in stocks or work-in-progress. Costs may rise and fall for reasons such as changing material price which have no connection with the volume of production.

(3) *Sales value of production* is better than turnover in that it counts production for stock into the output. But it has the same flaw when used as a productivity measure in assuming a value based on selling price.

(4) *Value added* is the most remote from any concept of volume of output. However, it eliminates some of the anomalies arising in sales value or cost by subtracting one from the other. It is generally more stable over short periods than any of the other three.

The volume or quantity with which these monetary values are compared may be, for example:

(1) For labour productivity:
  ● total number of employees
  ● number of operating employees
  ● number of hours worked
  ● number of hours in attendance
(2) For capacity utilisation:
  ● rooms available (hotels)
  ● sq.ft. of shelf space (supermarkets)
  ● seat-miles available (passenger transport)
  ● cu.ft-miles available (freight transport)

Generally they are expressed in terms of £ per unit, for example, value added per employee, turnover per room available (hotel). A ratio used in selling performance is sales per call.

The usefulness of the money '£ per unit' measurements depends largely on the homogeneity of the unit. In the capacity measures in example (2) each unit is likely to be similar to any other, although hotel rooms may vary in size and position, and airlines and railways have first and second class seats. Some sales calls may be difficult and distant; others may be easy and near.

The '£ per unit' for labour productivity will produce useful results only if:

  ● all employees are of similar status with similar remuneration, *or*
  ● the composition of the work-force does not change significantly between periods.

In most businesses today, with widening differentials and diminishing employment of lower-paid unskilled people, the employee can no longer be regarded as a standard unit.

Total hours worked in a period are better than number of employees where substantial overtime (or short-time) is worked, or where there are part-time workers. But this still does not deal with the many different classes, types and grades of employees, that are all counted alike.

A further difficulty arises for money-to-volume ratios when there is inflation. All the quasi-output figures such as turnover and value added increase with inflation, producing lower ratios against quantity. These can be adjusted by a price index, but then there is a problem of which index to use.

DRAWBACKS OF MONEY-TO-VOLUME RATIOS

(1) They introduce value of output in the market-place which is not logically associated with production.
(2) They require standard units for the 'volume' part of the ratio.
(3) For labour productivity they assume that employees are all of the same type, class or grade.
(4) They are vulnerable to inflation.
(5) They have a logical weakness as measures of performance in that they can rarely match the monetary values in the same terms as the quantity of 'labour' or 'capacity'.

MONEY-TO-MONEY RATIOS

As money-to-volume ratios have so many drawbacks, the next possibility for productivity measurement is money-to-money ratios without the often troublesome measuring of volume or quantity.

The money-to-money ratios which tend to be regarded as productivity measurements are:

(1) For labour 'productivity'
   ● turnover/total employment cost
   ● value added/total employment cost*
(2) For capital 'productivity':
   ● turnover/fixed assets*
   ● value added/fixed assets.

The reader of each chapter of this book in sequence will have noticed that the ratios marked * also appear in Chapter 19: Other operating ratios. The reason is that none of the money-to-money ratios above are truly productivity ratios, hence the inverted commas for 'productivity'.

However, as a direct lead-in to overall business performance the ratios are very useful. Where volumes cannot be counted they produce a more logical result than the money-to-volume ratios.

For labour 'productivity' total employment cost is the best denominator. It is superior to wages or salaries alone for almost any purpose. Value added is probably the best numerator, as we have seen earlier, although where turnover itself is a good measure (see Chapter 5, p. 29) it can be used equally well.

For capital 'productivity' the balance sheet value of fixed assets is an extremely poor denominator as explained at length in Chapter 18 (p. 218). Unless there is an easy definition of capacity in volume terms, there is little possibility of producing a reasonable productivity measure for the use of capital.

CONCLUSION

Productivity measurements tend to focus on 'labour' in times of recession and unemployment because there is more scope for improving the ratio in the short term.

The only true productivity ratio, measuring the efficiency of production, is a volume-to-volume ratio, where the volume of production is compared with the quantity of effort of time spent by the employees. Such a ratio is feasible only when the volume of production can be counted without complicated, often self-defeating, weighted averages and employee time can properly take into account part-time, overtime, shift work and contracted staff.

Failing any such measure, the monetary value of output has to be used and compared with the cost of employees. Money-to-volume ratios are difficult to match logically, and it may often be the case that where there is no standard unit of output there is no standard employee.

The money-to-money ratios are more logical and can be linked easily into the pyramid of ratios of Chapter 19. But they are only quasi-productivity ratios – not the real thing.

The best of these is generally value added/employment cost.

22   Strategic ratios

INTRODUCTION

At this point we enter a new area of performance measurement, opened up to cater for the cultivation of decisions on business policy which take an increasingly long time to appear as a financial harvest. The current annual profit-based measurements become unable to reflect any measure of how the objectives of these longer-term decisions are progressing. The decisions are often part of a strategic plan, and the objectives are strategic objectives.

The profit and loss account can only show, on the basis of defined periods, what has happened by way of financial transactions of the business, without any external comparison. The strategic objectives inevitably require expenditure which shows little or no revenue for perhaps two or three years ahead. But compared with other businesses, the strategic objectives may have reached a point, which can be measured, and which may show that favourable financial results are very likely to emerge in the future.

Some of these strategic objectives come into the class of 'revenue investment' or 'quasi-assets', which are described in trouble spot 7.2 (p. 75). The bulk of expenditure in advancing the strategic objectives cannot by law be capitalised in published accounts and in divisional accounts it is not practicable to follow a different course. But a management which relies only on the periodical profit or value added without reference to the progress of the planned strategy may be using only half measures of performance.

If exclusive attention is paid to the conventional measurements, strategic plans might never be implemented. But if the profit and loss account is ignored, there could be no credible measure remaining to monitor the performance of the business as a whole.

The way out of this dilemma is to provide strategic measurements as well as current profit and productivity measurements. The strategic plan should indicate strategic objectives, which should determine the strategic measurements.

One objective may be to increase market share, in which case it should be possible to measure the market share of the business from time to time. A very fashionable objective is quality improvement from which a reputation for quality and reliability is obtained.

Speed of delivery, the level of service, and the extent of outstanding orders can each be expressed as strategic ratios when the objective is to gain a reputation for good service.

Where an important strategy is being pursued, the profit measure should be accompanied by a measurement of the progress of the strategy. A strategy for increasing market share, for example, may involve very heavy expenditure charged against profit. If possible, this expenditure should be identified and compared with the increase in market share observed, if any.

There are many difficulties in obtaining the data for this kind of measure. Not unlike many other measurements, the feasibility depends on the type of business, the outside information available and the homogeneity of units that have to be counted.

There is some similarity with productivity ratios, which are in a sense a strategic measure when there is an objective to increase efficiency of production. Productivity ratios, however, are indicators of the *current* profit or value added measurement, whereas the strategic ratios in this chapter are indicators of profit or value added to come as a result of pursuing the strategic objective.

MARKET SHARE

There is considerable evidence that an increase in market share leads to an increase in profit.[12] This is particularly the case in manufacturing businesses which become increasingly more capital-intensive. The bigger the market share, the greater is the turnover and hence the better utilisation of capacity. Where fixed costs are high and variable costs low, heavy expenditure on increasing market share to use idle capacity may be well worth-while.

An effort to increase market share may require months or years of preparation and then probably a gradual effect on turnover as the marketing campaign gets under way. The extra profit takes time to materialise. In the meantime some measure of the actual increase in market share is needed.

Market share is related to a particular defined product or group of products. It is expressed as a percentage of turnover: the turnover of one business compared with the turnover of all businesses selling the product.

Definition of the market can range from very easy to the almost impossible.[13] The motor car market is readily defined by the licensing laws; types of car can be classified by cubic capacity and so on. In contrast the haberdashery market seems impossible to define with masses of variety of pins, needles, buttons, elastic and so on, manufactured and sold by all sorts of different businesses.

Markets are more easily defined when:

● the variety of products is limited
● the product is of a standard type
● the market can be confined to one country
● there is a similar definition overseas when the market covers several countries
● turnover within businesses can be analysed according to the market definition.

If there is a well defined market, the next hurdle is counting the turnover of each business outlet. For new motor cars there is little difficulty because the product is large, each new car has to be registered, and manufacture is limited to a very few companies which control the selling of cars through appointed dealerships.

In the second-hand car market the situation is quite different. There are many dealers of all kinds selling many makes of car and other vehicles.

True turnover is difficult to establish because of part-exchange deals. Also there are many private sales. In this case the market is 'fragmented', with many businesses having a very small share.

Calculations of market share are more practicable when:

- the market is large (but not scattered)
- there are comparatively few outlets
- the selling businesses keep good records (even better if required to do so by law)
- the system for collecting the data is organised and monitored by a reputable trade association
- the market is not fragmented
- the market share figures are well used

It is quite possible in certain cases for the business to keep its own market share records. For example, at major docks there are many businesses providing dock services. One business may be aware of the same service carried out for other ships in the docks and can make a good estimate of their turnover. The advantage of a do-it-yourself approach of this kind is that market share figures can be produced monthly as an almost immediate performance measure.

There are many other ways of collecting market data. If figures of a total market are available, then market share can easily be calculated for one's own business by comparing own turnover with the total of the market. *Business Monitor* shows total market sales quarterly by (1) UK manufacturers and (2) imports, in great detail, measured in £s and in quantities (such as number of units, tonnes or sq. metres).[14]

To obtain the market shares of competitors is more difficult, but there are many sources available, some more comprehensive than others. Examples are:

(1) Figures collected and published by trade associations, e.g. Society of Motor Manufacturers and Traders for cars.
(2) Published company accounts showing turnover by business sector (but these may not be in sufficient detail to identify a particular market).
(3) For single business companies, the issues periodically of turnover (and much other accounting data) by industry sector (used for inter-firm comparison), e.g.
    - ICC Business Ratio Reports
    - a Jordan Survey.
(4) Special reports on specific markets in great detail with market forecasts and some data on market shares, e.g.
    - Key-note reports – an industry sector overview

- Research report – market position series (Centre of Business Research, Manchester Business School).

(5) Consumer surveys commissioned by the company where insufficient data can be obtained from published sources.

Market share as a measurement has the unique property of providing a ratio with which turnover itself, the prime measurement, can be compared.

If the total market is declining, market share indicates that any decline in turnover is not necessarily the fault of the business management. But it may mean that any objective to increase turnover was unwise.

If, in an expanding market, the turnover of the business increases but its market share falls, it may mean that the increase in turnover was inadequate compared with what competitors have done. But there may, on the other hand, be a good reason why the turnover of one business should not rise (or fall) in proportion to all the others.

Market share is a ratio and the amount of turnover must not be forgotten. But if its basis is sound, it may provide better comparative information than return on capital employed (ROCE), which is wrecked by a storm of accounting troubles.

Like ROCE, however, market share can become too popular and may lead to expansion of market share almost at any price. Profitability and cash flow may be thrown out of the window in a scramble for market share that becomes more and more difficult to attain.

QUALITY

Good quality is an objective sought by many businesses. Some seek quality almost for its own sake, as is the case in many Japanese companies. Others regard better quality as a strategy. By improving quality, the business may obtain a good reputation on a strong base of loyal customers which leads ultimately to increased profits.

Measurement of progress towards improved quality is patchy. There are no standard ratios, such as market share or any of the ratios in earlier chapters. Each business must decide for itself how quality can be measured. Many do not measure it at all, although they aspire to it, and very few know the cost of improving and maintaining quality.

Quality, by its very nature, is not amenable to quantitative appraisal. Quality has no set definition. It is a degree of excellence, but there is no standard degree. Different businesses have different standards of good quality depending partly on their markets, their history and their general philosophy. Very few businesses aim for 100 per cent excellence, although there are some, such as aircraft and some computer manufacturers where 100 per cent reliability is required.

However, it is possible in many businesses to measure improvement or deterioration in quality. There are two levels where this can be done:

(1) *Internally*. Goods can be inspected or tested before dispatch and items not passing a specified quality standard rejected. Records are kept of the rejects, which can be classified according to the cause of rejection. The cost of the rejects is probably accounted for in the costing system anyway, but not regarded as a negative quality measure.

   The importance of measuring the internally rejected items is not so much saving the cost of scrap (and all its troublesome implications for the production process) as saving the quality standard of the business in the outside world. If 10 per cent of items are rejected internally as below standard, the chances are that at least 10 per cent of those, that is 1 per cent of the total sales, will also be defective. If the business is endeavouring to make or maintain a reputation of high quality, one in a hundred failures could be a severe blow to the strategy.

(2) *Externally*. Failures outside the business are more difficult to locate and account for. Very much depends on the market, the customers, the importance of quality, the image of the company and the after-sales contacts by salesmen and engineers with customers. The measurements that can be used are naturally specific to the industry and often to the business. A few examples are given below:

   ● numbers of guarantee claims as percentage of appliances, motor cars, home equipment, etc. sold (this requires a good,

preferably computerised, system that correctly matches sales with claims)
- numbers of customer complaints as percentage of turnover or number of products sold, distinguishing between trivial and serious complaints (possibly by a points rating system)
- numbers of items returned as unsatisfactory as percentage of items sold
- numbers of bad reports (or value of sales featured in bad reports) compared with all reports by after-sales representatives
- reviews in magazines such as *Which?* or *What Car?*

Such measurements are an antidote to productivity ratios, which rarely take account of quality as perceived by the customer. Internal failures are usually deducted from output figures but external failures may not be deducted at all. Many of the failures in quality may appear long after the period of production, for which productivity figures have been completed.

Wherever possible, where quality matters, productivity measurement should be tempered by a quality measurement. It is all too easy to improve productivity at the expense of quality.

LEVEL OF SERVICE

In service business quality is exemplified by level of service. The best service is generally regarded as one that is prompt and correct.

These criteria can be measured by numbers and extent of delays and the number of errors or mistakes in carrying out the service.

Examples of levels of service are:
- average length of check-out queues in supermarkets
- percentage of first class letters not delivered the day after posting
- percentage of parcels (carried by quick delivery transport companies) not delivered within 24 hours
- average time taken to issue an insurance policy after receipt of proposal
- average time taken by telephone operators to answer a call

- numbers of trains late by (say) more than 5, 10 and 20 minutes compared with number of trains run
- average length of time to obtain cash from bank cash dispenser (including queue time)

To some customers accuracy of service is more important than speed. Examples are:

- numbers of reported errors on bank statements as percentage of total entries
- numbers of wrong or rejected orders in restaurant as percentage of meals served
- numbers of overbooked seats on airlines as percentage of passengers carried
- numbers of customers of package holidays re-allocated hotels as percentage of total holidays sold.

As with quality in manufacturing, it is easy to improve the service productivity ratios by increasing the delays or allowing more mistakes in the operation of the service.

DELIVERY AND ORDERS OUTSTANDING

Speed of delivery of contracts or products made to order is another aspect of quality. Some businesses regard delivery on time as a strategic objective. If a business becomes known for prompt delivery it may obtain contracts on that account even though the price is higher than competitors.

In these circumstances close monitoring of delivery performance is needed. Failure may cost the business dear in the long-run.

Some businesses may propound a strategy of quick delivery, within a certain short period, say, three days or 24 hours. Again the failures need to be counted as a vital measurement of what is probably its most serious aspect of performance.

When delivery time is important, figures should be produced of all orders behind schedule. Outstanding orders should be reported regularly.

A large number of orders outstanding may signify either a booming business or poor service on delivery. The true situation can be shown by keeping full accounts of orders received, cancelled and carried out (to become turnover), at least every month, or every week for standard items in stock. In many businesses, where cancellation of orders is rare, orders can be regarded as advance turnover and can almost be included as one of the performance measures in Part II.

Performance in delivery, however, may be just as important as performance in obtaining the orders. The two should be examined together. Good accounting for orders along with sales, with regular statements, should enable this to be done.

Examples of the ratios that may be used are:

- average time from receipt of order to delivery (probably stratified according to amount of order, and divided between 'normal' and 'special' orders)
- average delay and delivery after promised delivery date (possibly stratified as above, or weighted according to size of order)
- orders outstanding as a percentage of orders received
- orders outstanding as a percentage of turnover

TRAINING AND EDUCATION

There are not many businesses today where a well-trained, well-educated staff is not essential to deal with new, more sophisticated and more complex markets, products, equipment, processes and procedures. Expenditure on 'investment' in staff training is charged in the profit and loss account, but the benefits do not appear until later.

The benefits indeed, like product quality, are extremely difficult to measure. Improving the 'quality' of staff can similarly be regarded as a strategic objective, that should sustain or increase profit in the future.

Some measurement of the progress made in training and education is possible, and there are some ratios that can be used:

- average number of hours per person spent on training as a percentage of total hours
- numbers of course days attended per employee
- training costs as percentage of profit, value added or total employment cost

GROWTH

In the 1960s and early 1970s growth was regarded as the key strategy. Growth meant growth of profit primarily, with growth of turnover as a supporting objective.

Growth is measured simply as the percentage increase of this year over last year.

There are three problems with measures of growth:

(1) *Inflation*. Even if inflation is low, any monetary measure of growth, to make sense, must be corrected for inflation. If the money amounts show a growth of 10 per cent, it matters very much whether the inflationary element of that growth is 5 per cent or 6 per cent. An index has to be used which can *correctly* reduce the money growth to real growth.

   If the amount concerned is turnover, a suitable index can probably be found, but, if the amount is profit, a whole set of new problems arise, which are not solved by the use of current cost (see Chapter 14, p. 180). No single index applied to all the elements of profit is likely to show a fair inflation-adjusted number.

(2) *Business acquisition*. It is possible to obtain 'growth' by acquiring a similar business and adding it to the one already owned. Arguments rage as to whether this is real growth or not. Certainly organic growth is a different kind of growth than growth by acquisition.

   Organic growth is the result of investment in assets of the existing business gradually developed to produce larger profit. Growth by acquisition buys the extra profit in one lump at a much higher price. Or there may be an exchange of shares which produces a merger of two businesses; neither business should then claim that the merger with the other was the growth of itself.

(3) *Losses*. If a business makes a loss, no measure of growth is possible until a profit is made in two consecutive years. If, however, a business avoids a loss by a very small profit, the subsequent year with a reasonable profit can show an enormous rate of growth. For example (omitting the £'000s):

1980 profit is £200; 1982 profit is £120.

If 1981 makes a loss of £10,
  no growth rate for 1981 or 1982 can be calculated.

If 1981 makes a profit of £10,
  growth rates are: 1981 − 95%;
                    1982 + 110%.

Real growth is difficult to identify and difficult to measure. By itself it is a poor strategic objective. It is based entirely on the profit and loss account, which is very weak as a supplier of information on the progress towards the achievement of strategic plans.

CONCLUSION

All the strategic ratios in this chapter, except growth, provide previews of future profit and loss accounts. They are up to the minute signals of how the key strategies decided for the business are behaving.

Some are extremely difficult to measure but there may well be more measurements available than those initially apparent. If you cannot measure, you cannot control. Any strategy which is not measurable at all can only be viable with a culture and dedication that will pursue it through thick and thin.

Strategic measures, however, are more interesting, more challenging and more vital to most managers than the historic, more out-of-date, periodic profits produced by accountants with their conventions and standards. The measures are therefore more acceptable, more likely to be taken seriously and more debatable on a level that all those involved can understand.

The strategic ratios are mainly volume-to-volume. They do not derive from normal accounting systems. Historic productivity ratios are good but they convey little about the long-term acceptability of the product or service. Strategic ratios, looking to the future, add a living head-piece to the idol of bald production efficiency.

PART IV: REFERENCES

1. J. Robertson, 'Research directions in financial ratio analysis', *Management Accounting*, September 1984, pp. 30–31.
2. W. H. Beaver, 'Alternative accounting measures as predictors of failure', *Accounting Review* (USA), January 1965, pp. 113–122.
3. R. Heller, 'British Business Profitability League 1983', *Management Today*, October 1983, p. 58.
4. J. Dearden, 'The Case against ROI Control', *Harvard Business Review*, May–June 1969, p. 135.
5. Publications of the Accounting Standards Committee of the Consultative Committee of Accountancy Bodies:
   SSAP 3   *Earnings per share*   1974
   SSAP 21 *Accounting for leases and hire purchase contracts*   1984
6. D. Solomons, *Divisional Performance: measurement and control*, (Markus Weiner Publishing (New York), 1965) p. 63.
7. See reference 1, Part II (p. 151).
8. C. A. Westwick, *How to use Management Ratios* (Gower, 1973), p. 56.
9. *Extel Cards – a Users Guide* (Extel Statistical Services, 1982).
10. British Business Profitability League, *Management Today*, published annually in October.
11. 'What "productivity" means', *Economic Progress Report*, no. 141, January 1982, The Treasury HMSO.
12. J. K. Newton, 'Market Share – Key to Higher Profitability?' *Long-Range Planning*, vol. 16, no. 1, February 1983, pp. 37–41.
13. A. R. Oxenfeldt, 'How to Use Market-Share Measurement', *Harvard Business Review*, vol. 37, no. 1, January–February 1959, p. 61.
14. *Business Monitor*, Business Statistics Office/HMSO, published quarterly.

Part V

Business Types and Styles

'One of the most essential ingredients in a successful organisation is motivation.'—Sir Owen Green, Chief executive, BTR

Give me men about me who,
Aren't afraid to join the few
Who choose to take the other view,
That business needs its vision, too!

The profit and the bottom line
Are not, to such a man, divine;
But just the elemental need
From which some mission can proceed.

Returns on assets, he'd contend,
Are just the means and not the end;
The bricks, the shovel or cement,
But not the finished monument.

And what the monument becomes,
A palace, or the worst of slums,
Is ultimately fashioned by
Some vision in the builder's eye.

And so it is that some explore
The question – what is business for?
There are a few who do not seem
Afraid of vision, or to dream!

Bertie Ramsbottom in the *Financial Times*

23 Businesses, industries and organisations

INTRODUCTION: WHICH MEASUREMENT FOR WHOM?

The catalogue of measurements is now complete. There are merits and pitfalls, and advantages and disadvantages in each, but there is no prescribed best buy. Before answering the Which? one needs to know: For whom? What sort of business is to be performance-measured? And what is the main purpose of the measuring?

This chapter attempts to group businesses together and highlight the measurements that would be the 'best buys' for the particular business.

Any grouping is bound to be very vague in its boundaries. Businesses are all different and any classification must leave a lot of blurred edges. Many businesses are in more than one of the categories.

The measurements used by a business could easily be 50 or more. Most of these would be applicable only to a specific aspect or department of the business. The number of measurements that are likely to be generally used would be no more than five or six. In this chapter the measurements that are chosen under each category heading are limited to four – the four measurements that are judged to be the most suitable for the type of business. The judgement is that of the author. There is plenty of room for other opinions.

Any choice of measurements is not the ideal combination, but is tinged with what is usual and acceptable. Value added, for example, is not so widely used and it would not be acceptable if most of the measurements chosen were value added based. The philosophy and style of the business management may have a strong influence on the measurements used (see Chapter 24, p. 292). I have tried to ignore any special influence of this kind and to avoid my own particular policies and preferences.

BUSINESS OBJECTIVES

It may be argued that no performance measurement can be deemed suitable without considering the clear objectives of the business.

For most businesses the maximisation of profit after taxation is the prime objective. But this 'bottom line' can be heavily polluted by the impure taxation charge (trouble spots 10.1, 10.2 and 10.3, pp. 111–37) so that in practice profit before taxation becomes a more credible objective.

Taxation is also regarded by many as a distribution of profit, and likewise interest. In some businesses, such as nationalised corporations and family companies, interest is paid to the owners or to people associated with the owners. This knocks out interest as a true element of performance measurement.

Non-profit making institutions such as professional bodies and societies have generally an objective to minimise the annual subscription while providing services that meet the demands of members.

Charities engaged in fund-raising may have an objective to maximise the net amount available for the benefactors. They have turnover in the form of subscriptions and donations and sometimes sales. Turnover alone is a reliable measure for them, assuming that the marginal expense is not more than the extra turnover.

All these organisations are businesses. The difference between them is in their objectives. By and large the objectives correspond with the consitution and status of the business, but there are many variations. In this chapter the objectives are assumed to be those normally pursued by the particular kind of business.

LONG-TERM AND SHORT-TERM

Long-term objectives may require measurements which are different from short-term. To some extent the need for long-term measurements goes with the type of business, for example, construction business with long-term contracts and hence long-term objectives. In other cases a long-range outlook may be more specific to the style and perceptions of the business.

However, the main reasons for the long-term view are probably the inadequacy of the short-term view provided by conventional accounts. Ways to remedy these defects in accounts are discussed in trouble spot 7.2 (Revenue investment, p. 75), and some practical suggestions are made in Chapter 22 (Strategic ratios, p. 260). The usefulness of accounts can be improved and subsidiary measurements can be added, and this could be sufficient for many businesses. For others the long-term measurement will still be needed.

The revenue investment syndrome covers very many aspects of business today. R & D is justified as necessary to keep pace with the competition in the future, not for short-term profit. Advertising expenditure is regarded similarly. Training and development of staff is another area.

Expenditure may be saved by cutting out the 'revenue investment'. Often we hear, in a deriding tone, 'It's a short-term view'. The dilemma runs all through the subject of performance measurement. We know that in so many businesses the short-term view is not good enough but we still go on taking it for gospel.

No type of business is immune. Even charities have the same problem with advertising campaigns, quality improvement and reputation building. Heavy expenditure on fund raising campaigns may increase funds but may damage the image of the charity as an efficient organisation passing on a high proportion of money received to its established cause.

The main problem is probably with new businesses, new products, new projects, new systems, new processes, new factories, new locations. All of them involve a period of learning and experience gathering for the people concerned. The cost of this is in the nature of a capital investment or a quasi-asset. The cost is not easy to compute in our present accounting systems, but there has been research in the subject with learning curves and experience curves as essential tools. (In the USA there is evidence that costs in new manufacturing projects decline by 20 to 30 per cent each time accumulated experience doubles.)

Efforts should be made to quantify roughly what the learning and experience costs are. The short-term measurements can then become more useful and reduce the need for waiting for the long-term.

Few businesses can manage without some measurement of performance at least quarterly. This chapter concentrates on these short-term measures. Long-term measures are interesting and informative, but they do not have the freshness and urgency of the short-term measurements which, for better or for worse, we must use.

CATEGORIES OF BUSINESS

The categories of business for this 'Which measurement?' exercise are as follows:

For each category of business four problem areas are listed. These are considered to be those most likely to spoil in some way the truth and fairness of the particular measurements recommended for the business category.

The third section in each category is headed 'Remedies to try'. These are suggestions that might alleviate the 'particular problems arising'. Rarely would they solve the problem completely and sometimes they may be quite impracticable.

All the measurements are referenced to the chapters where they are described and reviewed. The problems and remedies are almost all a subject of comment elsewhere in the book and they too are referenced accordingly.

The items in the three short lists are necessarily brief and general.

SINGLE BUSINESS PUBLIC COMPANIES

	Chapter or trouble spot	Page
Measurements to use		
Operating profit	8	81
Profit after taxation	10	111
Operating cash flow	15	190
Earnings per share (Eps)	20	243
Particular problems arising		
Current cost adjustments	14	172
Fair tax charge after 1984 Budget	10.1–10.2	117
Extraordinary items	11.1	142
Consistent basis for Eps	20	243
Remedies to try		
Include CCA depreciation where material in main accounts	14	175
Show tax charges also on payable-for-year basis	10.1	127
Disclose losses carried forward in note to accounts	10.2	129
Show Eps on more than one basis	20	247

SINGLE BUSINESS PRIVATE COMPANIES

	Chapter or trouble spot	Page
Measurements to use		
Gross margin	6	43
Operating profit	8	81
Profit after interest	9	99
Productivity or strategic ratio	21–22	252
Particular problems arising		
Stability of gross margin cost structure	6	43
Fair remuneration of controlling directors	8	81
Adjusting profit for inflation	14	172
Obtaining data for strategic ratios	22	260
Remedies to try		
Consider gross margin and operating profit together	6	45
Regard controlling directors' remuneration as distribution of profit	—	—
Use current cost depreciation on older assets that will be replaced	14	175
Set up systems for measuring market share/quality/productivity	22	260

BUSINESS DIVISIONS OF COMPANIES

	Chapter or trouble spot	*Page*
Measurements to use		
Turnover	5	29
Gross margin	6	43
Operating profit	8	81
Profit after interest	9	99
Particular problems arising		
Lack of independence from Head Office control	8.2	92
Transfer pricing	5.1	34
Allocation of pensions and other central costs	8.1 – 8.2	87
Interest or capital charge	9.1	104
Remedies to try		
Use market prices on transfers between divisions	5.1	34
Make specific charges for services rather than allocations	8.2	96
Ensure any residual arbitrary allocations fully understood and acceptable	8.2	97
Charge interest on capital on a realistic basis, even if arbitrary	9.1	104

SMALL BUSINESSES

	Chapter or trouble spot	Page
Measurements to use		
Turnover	5	29
Gross margin	6	43
Operating cash flow	15	188
Profit after interest	9	99
Particular problems arising		
Adequate records of stock and work-in-progress	6.1	48
Depreciation on assets fully written off	7.1	65
Fair remuneration of controlling directors/owner manager	8	81
Realistic charge for expenses and own time	—	—
Remedies to try		
Instal microcomputerised stock control system	—	—
Provide for extra depreciation if assets are to be replaced	14	175
Regard artificial remuneration as distribution of profit	—	—
Keep proper records and charge time at fair rates	—	—

NEW BUSINESSES

	Chapter or trouble spot	Page
Measurements to use		
Turnover	5	29
Operating cash flow	15	188
Productivity ratios	21	252
Strategic ratios	22	260
Particular problems arising		
Heavy initial expenditure with delayed return	7.2	75
Lack of comparison with previous periods	—	—
Allowance for learning and gaining experience	—	—
Lack of established systems	—	—
Remedies to try		
Account for major initial expense separately	7.2	75
Calculate appropriate productivity and strategic ratios very frequently	—	—
Use learning curves to estimate costs of learning and experience	—	—
Monitor system faults and learn from them	—	—

OLD BUSINESSES

	Chapter or trouble spot	Page
Measurements to use		
Value added	7	59
Operating profit	8	81
Operating cash flow	15	188
Return on capital employed	18	214
Particular problems arising		
Depreciation on assets fully written off	7.1	65
Write-down of obsolete stocks	6.1	48
Effect of past inflation on real capital maintenance	14	172
Integrity of asset base for ROCE	18	214
Remedies to try		
Make charge for use of assets fully written off	7.1	65
Show any write-down of stocks in accounts	6.1	53
Use current costs for old assets devalued by inflation	14	175
Use gross replacement cost for modified ROCE	18	214

SALES-ORIENTED BUSINESSES

	Chapter or trouble spot	Page
Measurements to use		
Turnover	5	29
Gross margin	6	43
Operating profit	8	81
Market share strategic ratio	22	260
Particular problems arising		
Trade-off between margins and turnover	19	232
Calculation of market share	22	260
Effectiveness of advertising	7.2	75
Orders received v. turnover as prime measure	22	260
Remedies to try		
Analyse margins and turnover for each product	—	—
Scour market research reports etc. for market data	22	261
Gather detailed data on responses to advertising and analyse	—	—
Use orders received, checked against subsequent turnover	22	261

PRODUCTION-ORIENTED BUSINESSES

	Chapter or trouble spot	Page
Measurements to use		
Value added	7	59
Operating profit	8	81
Productivity ratios	21	252
Quality strategic ratio	22	260
Particular problems arising		
Stability of inside/outside work for value added	7	59
Physical amount of production in multi-product factory	21	252
Accounting for work-in-progress	6.1	48
Ascertainment of cost of quality	22	260
Remedies to try		
Compute effect on value added of change in work pattern	—	—
Use 'constats' or current sales value of production	21	256
Value work-in-progress at cost of materials and employment cost only	6.1	56
Set up system for controlling and costing quality	22	264

CAPITAL-INTENSIVE BUSINESSES

	Chapter or trouble spot	Page
Measurements to use		
Value added	7	59
Operating profit	8	81
Operating cash flow	15	188
Return on capital employed (ROCE)	18	214
Particular problems arising		
Stability of inside/outside work for value added	7	59
Asset base for ROCE	18	214
Fixing realistic asset lives for depreciation	7.1	65
Accounting for inflation on fixed assets	14	172
Remedies to try		
Compute effect on value added of change in work pattern	—	—
Use gross current cost for ROCE asset base	18	219
Extend or reduce asset lives in line with economic conditions	7.1	68
Use current cost for depreciation of old assets	14	172

LABOUR-INTENSIVE BUSINESSES

	Chapter or trouble spot	Page
Measurements to use		
Gross margin	6	43
Operating profit	8	81
Operating funds flow	16	200
Labour productivity ratios	21	252
Particular problems arising		
Stability of gross margin cost structure	6	43
Definition of working capital for funds flow	16	200
Basis of amount of labour for productivity	21	252
Calculating current employment costs (including pension cost)	8.1	87
Remedies to try		
Change definition if gross margin becomes unreliable	6	45
Include all 'liquid funds' in working capital	16	200
Use employment cost rather than head-count	21	257
Set up system to compute full employment cost of each employee	—	—

CO-OPERATIVES AND CO-PARTNERSHIPS

	Chapter or trouble spot	*Page*
Measurements to use		
Turnover	5	29
Value added	7	59
Operating cash flow	15	188
Productivity ratios	21	252
Particular problems arising		
Stability of outside/inside work for value added	7	59
Selection of useful productivity ratios	21	252
Formulation of relevant strategic ratios	22	260
Regular fair remuneration for employees	—	—
Remedies to try		
Compute effect on value added of change in work pattern	—	—
Use asset turnover ratios	19	232
Choose one key strategic ratio only, e.g. quality	22	260
Regard regular wages or salary as on account of value added share	—	—

NATIONALISED BUSINESSES

	Chapter or trouble spot	Page
Measurements to use		
Operating profit	8	81
Operating cash flow	15	188
Operating ratios	19	232
Productivity ratios	21	252
Particular problems arising		
Unfair profit or loss due to controlled pricing	—	—
Basis of depreciation	7.1	65
Estimation of asset lives	7.1	65
Treatment of grants and subsidies	—	—
Remedies to try		
Isolate any 'tax element' in turnover	—	—
Use current cost for old assets that will be replaced	14	175
Extend or reduce asset lives in line with economic conditions	7.1	68
Show grants and subsidies below the operating profit line	—	—

CHARITIES AND NON-PROFIT-MAKING BUSINESSES

	Chapter or trouble spot	Page
Measurements to use		
Turnover	5	29
Operating profit (surplus)	8	81
Operating cash flow	15	188
Operating (turnover/expense) ratios	19	232
Particular problems arising		
Definition of turnover	5	29
Accounting for subscriptions	—	—
Depreciation of property and equipment	7.1	65
Use of expense ratio	—	—
Remedies to try		
Treat all legacies, donations, etc. on cash flow basis	—	—
Accrue subscriptions in advance or overdue	—	—
Value property and depreciate, even when donated	7.1	65
Fix expense ratio objective to suit business philosophy	—	—

24 Motivation, philosophy and accounting

MULTIPLE MEASUREMENTS

Apart from the type of business, there are many other factors which cause the use of so many measurements. They arise from the individual business objectives. My own summary of how measurements mesh in with objectives is as follows:

(1) Businesses have more than one objective. Each objective needs at least one measurement.
(2) The objectives can be classified as short-term (one year or less) and long-term (two years or more).
(3) The short-term objectives are monitored by short-term measures, such as turnover, operating profit and operating cash flow.
(4) Each objective may be associated with several measurements, partly because the overall objective cannot be measured in the short-term on one scale alone and has to be measured on various dimensions in order to make up the overall measurement (just as height, length and width are needed to obtain volume).
(5) The measurement of long-term objectives can easily be neglected in favour of the short-term.
(6) Long-term objectives cannot be balanced with short-term on any scientific basis but can be partially accounted for in the short-term by extra measurements (see Chapter 22, p. 260).
(7) Long-term objectives may be converted into short-term by the device of 'quasi-assets' (see Revenue investment, trouble spot 7.2, p. 75), but this involves a fundamental change in accounting, which cuts across long-standing rules and conventions.
(8) Long-term objectives can be regarded as an act of faith, a feature of the style of the business management, to which certain resources are dedicated without question.

(9) Short-term performance measurement remains the most crucial and most urgent.

(10) Long-term objectives do not motivate without some extra-measurement driving force. Short-term objectives and measurement have all the running because they can motivate people with quick feedback.

Many endeavours have the same problem of short-term and long-term objectives. An analogy may be made in the field of the training and development of musicians, dancers and other artists.

The short-term objective is to pass examinations and gain qualifications. The long-term objective may be to become an innovative new style performer. The short-term objective is split into (a) technical and merit and (b) artistic impression, because an overall measurement is too difficult and it helps in asessment if the two dimensions are used and combined later. The short-term objective conflicts with the long-term, and, if the short-term is pursued exclusively, the long-term ultimately will be more difficult to achieve.

The position, then, is that multi-objectives and multi-measurements are necessary for three reasons:

(1) To analyse, explain and clarify a basically single objective by the use of subsidiary or related objectives which can be measured with less trouble.

(2) To prevent long-term objectives being squeezed out by the more popular short-term objectives.

(3) To provide at least one simple measurement which rates high in motivation of people.

MOTIVATION AND ACCEPTABILITY

Motivation requires a measurement. There are many other factors in motivation of people on which there is an extensive literature. Feedback, however, is one of the most important.

Long-term objectives with long-term feedback on the whole do not motivate. If there is no feedback some other method, such as dedication, persuasion or even fear, has to be used to support the objective. Short-term objectives have the edge all the time if fair and relevant measurements are regularly available.

The best measurements are broadly those which are the most suited to the particular type of business and to the culture within the business and the style of its management.

In choosing the measurements for various types of business in Chapter 23 only the industry, structure, ownership, size and age of the business are considered. The measurements suggested are restricted to four per business, not solely to make the pages all of the same size, but also to reflect a general feeling that too many measurements become confusing, and damage, rather than enhance, motivation. One single measurement is best for motivation, but, as we have seen, it is neither feasible nor wise to reduce the various goals of a business down to one.

A compromise is necessary between the power of motivation and the true, fair and relevant measurement. More than five different measurements may be too difficult to take in and weigh up between them. Four measurements can probably be absorbed and reviewed intelligently without too much trouble. (Composite measurements have been tried in a few companies with prescribed weightings, but rarely do they seem successful, largely due to the changing importance of particular objectives.)

However, the number of measurements to be presented to any one person is itself a matter of history and style:

(1) The more familiar with the measurements are the users of them, the more easily can they be comprehended and acted on.
(2) The better versed are the users in the accounting process and the data behind the measurements, the more easily can the numbers and their implications be understood.
(3) The more closely are the measurements related to one another, with minor variations between them, the less likely is there to be any confusion.
(4) The more are the numbers explained and discussed the more readily are the users able to interpret and appreciate the measurements produced.

New measurements are to be avoided. If there are already five measures, a sixth is very likely to be ignored, especially if it is difficult to grasp and directly contradicts an existing measure (for example, CCA profit). Motivation decreases in proportion to the increase in the number of measurements.

Value added is difficult to adopt as a key measurement because it is still novel. ROCE continues in spite of its many defects because it is well known.

If they are to motivate, performance measurements have to be:

- prompt
- simple
- familiar
- understood
- acceptable.

What is acceptable as the best measure usually becomes the best measure, like it or not.

INCENTIVES

There has been a large increase recently in incentive schemes to improve performance. These can be based on turnover, gross margin, value added, operating profit or profit after interest.

Once a particular measurement becomes the basis of a bonus, it is automatically promoted to the most important. The other measurements are easily downgraded to interesting information. This effect can be counteracted by the use of more than one measure, suitably weighted, but composite measures for incentives seem to be rare (although not as rare as general composite measures).

Generous bonus schemes seem to be super-motivators in today's climate, and are partly responsible for the increases in profits, on which bonuses for senior executives are mostly based. However, there is a fear that the pursuit of one objective may lead to the abandonment of others, in which are included the long-term objectives and the safety measures such as cash flow.

Reliance on one objective for bonus and motivation puts a heavy burden on the reliability of the measurement used. The trouble spots in the measurement may tend to be cured temporarily in favour of increased profit. But such a cure may become rather like a drug, which is liable to misuse. It could lead eventually to the abandonment (or 'consolidation') of the incentive scheme, and perhaps a difficult return to cultivating long-term objectives when much of the seed has been lost.

The lower down the level of profit used as an incentive the more trouble spots there are, as is shown in Part II (see Chart 3.1 on p. 14 for the 'levels' of profit). To avoid distorting the measurement by abuse of the trouble spots, the higher levels, such as turnover, gross margin and value added, should be used. By themselves these should be good motivators, but they suffer from not being the single measurement of a single objective. Value added, for instance, is an excellent basis for local incentive schemes, but no ordinary business would wish to use value added as its only measure of performance without paying some attention at least to operating profit.

ORIENTATION AND PHILOSOPHY

There are three basic viewpoints of business performance. They can be:

(1) Community oriented, in which case value added is favoured.
(2) Entity oriented, in which case operating profit (before interest and before taxation) is used.
(3) Equity oriented, in which case profit after interest and/or profit after taxation is used.

The orientation depends partly on the physical nature and legal status of the business, which was the basis of the selection of measurements for businesses in Chapter 23 (p. 275). In Part II, where each measurement is reviewed separately, it is suggested that certain measurements may suit a certain kind of 'philosophy'.

'Philosophy' is perhaps a dangerous word to use, but it is intended here as a system of principles for the operation and control of the business, a way of looking at things. The philosophy influences the choice and priority of objectives.

Really, of course, it is not the philosophy of the business but the philosophy of the management that we are talking about. Only people have philosophies. However, a business, or more strictly a firm, can have a culture which is inherited from the past and has become so deep-rooted that it is almost a collective philosophy. These are the kind of companies that have had a very strong, extremely respected founder, that have never acquired or merged with any other company, that have been able through training and low staff-turnover to adopt the same principles in successive generations and that have gathered an enviable reputation in a certain field. (Examples are IBM, Marks & Spencer, Pilkingtons and Sainsbury.) A philosophy of the company then becomes recognisable.

The literature of management would prefer 'culture' to 'philosophy'. The culture of an organisation may determine the character of its staff, the autonomy of its managers, the attitude to its customers and suppliers, the systems which it instals, the methods of arriving at decisions, the importance of quality and reliability and, above all, the objectives which are set for the organisation. Cultures which are long ingrained are difficult to change. People joining the organisation who do not like the culture become unhappy and unwelcome within it. Then they probably leave, and the basic culture remains with little change.

In many other businesses there are not such settled philosophies of how and for what aims the business should be carried on. New directors and managers may be appointed from other cultures and the philosophy of the business may change. New managements may wish to adopt, for instance, more short-term and less long-term objectives, to put more emphasis on operating profit as a management goal, to make divisional managers more independent, to favour productivity rather than quality, and so on. All these will involve different emphasis on the measurements to be used.

Or it may be that newcomers to the management or board wish to adopt measurements which from their previous experience had proved very useful. If a new management knows of a measurement that they understand very well, it may probably be good that it be adopted, provided that it is really relevant to the objectives of the business. But there remains the caveat of new measurements, mentioned earlier.

Accountants too have some role in choosing the measurements that can be used. What they read in books and magazines, what they learn on courses and from outside experience may prompt them to put up proposals for new measurements. Sometimes the time for some innovation in measurement may be right; at other times it may not.

Changes in measurement to improve comprehension are good, but not if they become divorced from objectives. Generally, if an objective is not changed, a measurement should not change.

Objectives are often changed as a result of a change in power. This applies not only to the power of executives, but to the power also of lenders, shareholders, employees, customers and suppliers. Where there is a large overdraft, the bank may have considerable power to alter the objectives towards cash flow and away from any long-term objectives. Shareholders, particularly as institutional investors, may be demanding higher dividends and thereby concentrating the objective on profit after taxation. Employee unrest may focus the attention on costs, productivity and margins.

Successful businesses are unlikely to be involved in power struggles. Their objectives and style will not be influenced by the unrest of any group of stakeholders. Such businesses probably work on a high degree of consensus in an atmosphere of congeniality and co-operation. They have a kind of social conscience that shuns any favours for particular groups and is continuously aware of its relations with employees and those who finance or trade with it. For its objectives to be altered by the pressure of any group on its particular philosophy would be almost unthinkable.

ACCOUNTING LIAISON

Measurements depend largely on accounts and accountants. Nothing can be measured unless there is a system for it. Adoption of the right measurement depends on intelligent liaison between the business accountants and the users.

In many businesses there is a large gap between accountants and other related areas of the business such as strategic planning, engineering, marketing and personnel. Both sides of the gap find it difficult to bridge. The accounting function does not easily communicate with others and the others are repulsed by the apparently technical nature of accounting which seems to them to be increasingly riddled by unintelligible concepts and jargon.

Inappropriate measurements which do not fit objectives are the result of this poor liaison. General management should know more about the measurements that can be used and accountants should know more about the business and its objectives. In the best companies this liaison is probably achieved and the measurements used are properly dictated by the business objectives.

If there is no understanding between accountants who produce the measurements and the managers who use them, there could be objectives which cannot be measured and measurements which have no objectives. Either way people could end up not knowing where they are going.

25   Limitations to measurement

SUBJECTIVITY

People tend to think that accountancy is much more precise than it actually is. Only pure cash flow is free from estimating, projecting, valuing, assuming and forecasting. The normal profit and loss account is far from precise. The profit shown at the bottom line could be very different on equally valid assumptions, estimates and valuations. But the assumptions, once adopted, have a terrible tendency to be taken as reality and people using the accounts forget their doubtful foundations.

The trouble spots of Part II all arise in areas where a judgement is needed. There is no hard fact. Not all apply to every business, but for published and divisional accounts there are 10 which do apply. And the trouble spots which are listed are not necessarily complete. In particular businesses there are further small trouble spots that may be encountered.

Subjectivity itself is not bad, provided that people know it exists and they do not put more weight on the performance measurement than the load of inference and decision can bear. It helps if the subjectivity is systematic. There should be points of reference or guidelines to ensure that the judgement is always the same way in identical cases.

Accounting standards have assisted in reducing the areas of unsystematic discretion, but they are by no means comprehensive. The missing spots in the standards tend to become trouble spots in the measurements.

In divisional accounts no standards need apply, although in practice they usually do apply with probably more rigour than is appropriate. Divisional accounts have special problems of transfer pricing, cost allocation and interest on capital, which are left largely to float because there are no relevant standards.

Standards, in my view, should not be promulgated for internal management accounts. The emphasis in the accounts on particular features is a matter for the management of the business. But there could be more research and discussion on the problems, which could reduce the subjectivity. At present the differences between companies in their divisional accounts are far larger than are justified by the differences in philosophy, style, size, age and type of business.

RISK

Some businesses are more risky than others. And within a business a project or strategy may be launched which is more risky than anything attempted before. A higher return is expected for the risky project than for the normal, more usual project.

The measurements used in risky situations are basically the same as those in more predictable situations, but there are two factors which cause difficulty:

(1) The results of risky businesses, by definition, fluctuate. One period may show a very large profit and the next a loss. The fluctuations may be ironed out in the long-term by averaging, but a short-term measurement is hedged by the query: 'Is it typical?'

(2) Instability of revenues and costs makes it more difficult to estimate asset lives, stock valuation, tax liability and other features of the trouble spots. A stable environment makes all measurement easier and more credible. In a speculative business, adjustment to the measurements is a real problem, the prime example being inflation adjustments when prices are going both up and down (Chapter 14, p. 183).

In spite of these difficulties, is it not possible to take risk into account in the result? After all there are plenty of other subjective features in accounts.

The answer of the financial theorist could be *beta*, which is a measure of risk based on the fluctuation of stock market prices of shares in the business. The higher the fluctuations in the share price (in relation to the normal fluctuations) the higher is the beta and hence the higher is the risk in that particular business.

Beta is used primarily for the analysis of investment portfolios and for the estimation of risk premium on capital investment projects (i.e. an extra return that should be expected on account of the extra risk). It has not been used in practice (as far as I know) to estimate the risk premium embedded in an actual performance measurement. The reason is probably that beta is just too unreliable in a world where economic conditions and risk in different industries are changing all the time. There is always a temptation to modify the beta in the light of recent events or future forecasts.

In any case, beta applies only to the equity measurements, which are the 'bottom line' of profit after taxation or all-inclusive profit (Chapters 10 and 11) and earnings per share (Chapter 20). An entity view of risk in a business is not possible because the risk applying to the loan-financed part of the business is borne outside.

In a single business, what theorists may consider as risk, the practical business man considers as luck. For statisticians and portfolio analysts bad luck and good luck can be 'diversified away' – in the end it all cancels out. But for short-term performance measurement the 'luck of the draw' remains as part of the performance.

It is expected that everything cannot be planned and there are many large transactions that balance on a knife edge; which way it falls may depend on the weather, the delay at an airport, an accident, a traffic jam, someone falling sick, a slip of the tongue or a 'typo' in a letter.

Performance measurement cannot be formally adjusted for risk. It can only be borne in the mind of the users.

TYRANNY OF THE YEARLY ACCOUNT

Divisional accounts are tied too tightly to the annual published accounts. They follow the same pattern because they have to be consolidated or reconciled with the annual accounts of the group. Divisional measurement must therefore be based on the year, and so must every other set of accounts mentioned in this book. Even operating ratios and productivity ratios are likely to be calculated on an annual basis. There are usually, of course, monthly statements but the thrust is annual, with a *year* to date column and a new start with a new *year*.

Any change in accounting, review of policy, revaluation of stock, write-down of assets, calculation of tax liability and deferred tax, adjustment of depreciation – all are left until the end of the year. Interim accounts have not, therefore, the same quality as the annual accounts, which are the aristocrats among the plebeian monthly (unaudited) statements.

The year is the basic time scale for measurement. Every business must respect it and it becomes the normal time horizon of the short-term. Periods of less than a year are interim or very short-term. Periods over a year begin to be long-term.

The best measurement is on the time horizon most suited to the business. For seasonal businesses, it should be the season. For contracting businesses, it should be the length of a contract. For complex manufacturing businesses, it should be the natural length of the production cycle. (The only instance I have seen where the accounts are drawn up for a three-year period is marine insurance, where claims are not known until some years after the event.)

Measurement of performance is constrained by the annual straitjacket; not for every business, but for many businesses the annual diktat makes the subjectivity greater than it need be.

UNMEASURABLE FACETS

Accountancy has the monopoly of performance measures. There are other facets of performance that could possibly be measured by other means. They are touched on in Chapter 22 on strategic ratios. Such measurements, however, are not common and those that are most used do have an accounting flavour.

If excellence is the chief objective and annual profit is subsidiary, a new set of measurements is needed. There are the strategic measures of quality, level of service and speed of delivery. There is the amount of creativity, innovation and ingenuity of design. There is reliability,

immediate attention on breakdown and compensation for any incon-
venience caused. There is the quality of leadership, flair and charisma of
leading executives. There is the whole atmosphere of willingness,
eagerness to get on, and wanting to help. There is the loyalty of staff, the
feeling of contentedness and the reputation which comes from continuous effort.

More of these things can be measured than one might think. Some
companies (IBM is a prime example) carry out regular surveys on such
topics. They act as kinds of pre-performance measurements. If the bases
of committed personnel, customer loyalty and technical quality are all
up to standard, then the performance in the profit and loss account is
almost bound also to be up to standard in the long run.

Subjectivity of estimates of the future is reduced because the whole
structure is more stable and reliable. The risks of failure are reduced
because the ground work is so solid.

Such objectives are long-term objectives, of course – and probably very
long. It may take twenty years to build up a knowledgeable, loyal and
reliable staff in a highly technical business. The companies which have
approached their business in this way have undoubtedly been the most
successful, by any standard, over a very long period.

The limitations to measurement in this area are probably not so tight as
they seem, provided there is the dedicated objective that requires such a
measurement.

USE OF PERFORMANCE MEASUREMENT

At the end of all this, one might ask: 'What is it all for?' The
measurements we have discussed have only been recitals of the past –
and the past is dead and gone. However, it does have a predictive value
for the future, as well as a motivational value, and, if that were not so, it
would be not much more use than a history book.

The trouble is that the performance measures described in Part II are
often assigned more of a predictive value than they deserve. There are
two particular cases when this happens:

(1) Divisions and businesses with a good performance record often tend to be favoured for capital investment projects even though the NPV or IRR (see Chapter 18, p. 217) is lower than for other projects in divisions with an inferior performance record. There is a kind of inbuilt assumption that a good performance measure (computed possibly with much subjectivity behind it) is going to continue good, and a not so good performance is going to continue not so good.

(2) A division or business with a poor performance may be starved of resources because of the low profits which it has had. It may be that such a state will continue and there is no option but to close it or sell it. But before that decision is taken the NPV must be computed for the proposed disinvestment in exactly the same way as for the new investment.

Measurements of performance do not tell you what to do next. This is still not recognised in many quarters. The profit and loss figures are historic, even when based on current cost. Any decision on the future must consider the likely figures for the future, analysed on a cash flow basis, using only the revenues and costs relevant to the decision.

Cash flow measures nearly always take second place to the historic cost profits, as we see in Part IV and Chapter 15 (p. 191). Cash flow has no provision for depreciation. The cash for the fixed asset being depreciated was spent some time ago and finished with. The asset is known as a *sunk cost* which is nothing to do with the decisions for the future. More relevant in divestment situations, such as closure or selling the business, is the value of the business and its assets.

VALUE AND PERFORMANCE

In this book we have considered peformance as something accomplished over a short period (one year or less). In Chapter 4 (p. 22) we argued that changes in market valuation of assets in that period were not part of performance.

For the long term we may still talk of performance, but it is different. Short-term performance cannot just be extended or aggregated to produce long-term performance. It needs inclusion of extraordinary items, conversion to real terms on account of inflation and probably a valuation of assets or of the business as a whole at the beginning and at the end. Unless radical changes are considered, or something like a prospectus is in view, a long-term performance is not so often needed. Stable businesses may never need to consider the value of their assets (except for purposes of depreciation on property or a charge for its use).

Performance measurement records the recent past. It provides information for the future but not about the future. It shows the result of having gone in one direction. It can suggest that it may be better to try another direction, but it will not show where that other direction may lead. That is a separate exercise.

Performance measurement has severe limitations as a guide to policy. It does not take into account risk or changes in asset values. It needs more than one measure to be taken and it may still not catch all the aspects of business objectives in its net. It has a lot of trouble spots. But no business can be managed without it. The key is to understand it and accept it.

Abbreviations

ACT	Advance Corporation Tax
ASC	Accounting Standards Committee
CCA	Current Cost Accounting
COCOA	Continuous Contemporary Accounting
CPP	Current Purchasing Power (or Constant Purchasing Power)
EAps	Equity Assets per share
ED	Exposure Draft
Eps	Earnings per share
FIFO	First In First Out
FYA	First Year Allowance
IRR	Internal Rate of Return
LIFO	Last In First Out
MWCA	Monetary Working Capital Adjustment
P/E	Price/Earnings
R & D	Research and Development
ROA	Return on Assets
ROCE	Return on Capital Employed
ROI	Return on Investment
SSAP	Statement of Standard Accounting Practice
VAT	Value Added Tax

List of Measurements Used

(Excluding industry-specific measurements)

Chapter	Terms used in book	Alternative terms
5	Turnover	Sales
6	Gross margin	Gross profit; Contribution
7	Value added	
8	Operating profit	Profit before interest and tax; Trading profit
9	Profit after interest	Profit before tax
10	Profit after taxation	After-tax profit; Profit on ordinary activities after tax
11	All-inclusive profit	Profit after extraordinary items; Profit for the financial year; Attributable profit; Profit available for appropriation
14	Current cost operating profit Current cost profit after interest Current cost profit after taxation	
15	Operating cash flow Net cash flow	
16	Operating funds flow	
18	Return on capital employed	Return on investment; Return on assets; Operating profit/operating capital
19	Gross margin/turnover Operating profit/turnover Value added/turnover Value added/employment cost Operating capital/turnover Value added/operating capital Working capital/turnover Fixed assets/turnover Stocks/materials consumed Debtors/turnover	Gross profit/sales Trading profit/sales Value added/sales Value added/payroll cost Capital employed/sales Value added/capital employed Net current assets/sales Fixed assets/sales Stocks/sales Debtors/sales

List of Measurements Used (cont.)

Chapter	Terms used in book	Alternative terms
20	Earnings per share Price/earnings ratio	Profit per share
21	Productivity ratios	Efficiency ratios
22	Market share Quality ratios Level of service ratios Delivery time ratios Growth ratios	

Bibliography

Income and value

Boulding, K. 'Economics and Accounting: the Uncongenial Twins', in W. T. Baxter and S. Davidson (eds), *Studies in Accounting Theory* (Sweet & Maxwell, 1974).

Lee, T. A. *Income and Value Measurement* (Nelson, 1974) chs 3 and 4.

Lee, T. A. *Company Financial Reporting: Issues & Analysis* (Nelson, 1976) ch. 6.

Macdonald, G. *Profit Measurement: Alternatives to Historical Cost*, (Accountancy Age Books, 1974).

Transfer pricing

Horngren, C. T. *Cost Accounting: a Managerial Emphasis* (Prentice-Hall (USA), 1982) ch. 19.

Kaplan, R. S. *Advanced Management Accounting* (Prentice-Hall (USA), 1982) ch. 14.

Solomons, D. *Divisional Performance: measurement and control* (Markus Wiener (USA), 1965) ch. 6.

Stocks and work-in-progress

Gemmel, J. H. F. (ed.) *How to Value Stock* (Institute of Chartered Accountants in England and Wales, 1983).

Horngren, C. T. *Cost Accounting: a Managerial Emphasis* (Prentice-Hall (USA), 1982) ch. 22.

Value added

Cox, B. *Value Added: an appreciation for the accountant concerned with industry* (ICMA/Heinemann, 1979).

Gray, S. J. and Maunders, K. J. *Value Added: Uses and Measurement* (Association of Certified Accountants, 1980).

Morley, M. *The Value Added Statement* (Gee & Co. for the Institute of Chartered Accountants of Scotland, 1978).

Whiting, E. 'Value Added Statements and their Application', in J. P. Carty (ed.), *Practical Financial Management* (Gee & Co. in association with the Institute of Chartered Accountants in England and Wales, 1983).
Wood, E. G. *Added Value – the Key to Prosperity* (Business Books, 1978).

Cost of capital

Levy, H. and Sarnat, M. *Capital Investment and Financial Decisions* (Prentice-Hall International, 1978) ch. 16.
Schall, L. D. and Haley, C. W. *Introduction to Financial Management* (McGraw-Hill (USA), 1983) ch. 7.
Weston, J. F. and Brigham, E. F. (1979) *Managerial Finance* (British edn) (Holt Rinehart and Winston, 1979) ch. 19.

Interest capitalised

Philip, T. 'Interest cost – How a standard for capitalisation would be applied', *Accountancy*, June 1984, p. 128.

Taxation

Devereux, M. P. and Mayer, C. P. *Corporation Tax: The Impact of the 1984 Budget* (Institute for Fiscal Studies, 1984).
Saunders, G. and Noakes, P. *Tolley's Corporation Tax 1984/85* (Tolley, 1984).
Westwick, C. A. 'Deferred tax: how much to provide now', *Accountancy*, December 1984, p. 156.

Current cost accounting

Baxter, W. T. *Accounting values and inflation* (McGraw-Hill, 1975).
Baxter, W. T. *Inflation Accounting* (Philip Allan, 1984).
Carsberg, B. and Page, M. (eds) *Current Cost Accounting: The Benefits and The Costs* (Institute of Chartered Accountants in England and Wales, 1984).
Clayton, P. and Blake, J. *Inflation Accounting* (Longman, 1984).
Peat Marwick Mitchell & Co. *Reporting under CCA: A survey of current cost accounting practice* (Tolley, 1982).
Walton, P. 'The Carsberg CCA research report: summary', *Accountancy*, December, 1983.
Inflation Accounting, Report of the Inflation Accounting Committee ('Sandilands Report') Cmnd 6225 (HMSO, 1975).

Cash flow

Lee, T. A. *Cash flow accounting* (Van Nostrand Reinhold, 1984).

Divisional performance and residual income

Anthony, R. N. and Dearden, J. *Management Control Systems: Text and Cases* (Irwin (USA), 1976) ch. 8.
Anthony, R. N. and Welsch, G. A. *Fundamentals of Management Accounting* (Irwin (USA), 1981) ch. 11.
Bierman, H. Jr. and Dyckman, T. R. *Managerial Cost Accounting*, (Macmillan/ Collier, 1976) ch. 17.
Garrison, R. H. *Managerial Accounting* (Business Publications (USA), 1982) ch. 11.
Horngren, C. T. *Cost Accounting: a Managerial Emphasis* (Prentice-Hall (USA), 1982) ch. 20.
Kaplan, R. S. *Advanced Management Accounting* (Prentice-Hall (USA), 1982) ch. 15.
Sizer, J. *An Insight into Management Accounting* (Penguin, 1979) ch. 6.
Solomons, D. *Divisional Performance: measurement and control* (Markus Wiener (USA), 1965) ch. V.

Quality

Deming, W. E. *Quality, Productivity and Competitive Position* (Massachusetts Institute of Technology, 1982).
Feigenbaum, A. V. *Total Quality Control* (McGraw-Hill (USA), 1983) Part Two.

Philosophy and motivation

Goldsmith, W. and Clutterbuck, D. *The Winning Streak* (Weidenfeld & Nicolson, 1984).
Kaplan, R. S. 'Measuring Manufacturing Performance: A New Challenge for Management Accounting Research', *The Accounting Review* (USA), vol. LVIII, no. 4, October 1983, pp. 686–705.
Peters, T. J. and Waterman, R. H. *In Search of Excellence: Lessons from America's Best-Run Companies* (Harper & Row (USA), 1982).
Vroom, V. H. and Deci, E. L. (eds) *Management and Motivation* (Penguin, 1970).

Index